CATSKILL PEAK
E▲X▲P▲E▲R▲I▲E▲N▲C▲E▲S

MOUNTAINEERING TALES OF ENDURANCE, SURVIVAL, EXPLORATION & ADVENTURE FROM THE CATSKILL 3500 CLUB

Edited by

Carol Stone White

Published by
Black Dome Press Corp.
1011 Route 296, Hensonville, New York 12439
www.blackdomepress.com   Tel: (518) 734–6357

First Edition Paperback 2008
Copyright © 2008 by Carol Stone White

ISBN-13: 978-1-883789-59-6
ISBN-10: 1-883789-59-1

   Library of Congress Cataloging-in-Publication Data

Catskill peak experiences : mountaineering tales of endurance, survival, exploration & adventure from the Catskill 3500 club / edited by Carol Stone White. — 1st ed. paperback 2008.
   p. cm.
 ISBN 978-1-883789-59-6 (trade paper)
1. Mountaineering—Anecdotes. 2. Mountaineering—New York (State)—Catskill Mountains. 3. Hiking—New York (State)—Catskill Mountains. 4. Wilderness survival—New York (State)—Catskill Mountains. 5. Catskill 3500 Club. I. White, Carol, 1940-

 GV200.C39 2008
 796.52'20974738—dc22
                              2008006364

Front cover photograph: *Sunset over Black Dome Valley,* by Vincent Bilotta
Back cover photograph: *Gilboa Falls,* by Larry Gambon
Catskill Park map: 2004, New York State Department of Environmental Conservation
Design: Toelke Associates
Printed in the USA

10 9 8 7 6 5 4 3 2 1

CAUTION

Outdoor recreational activities are by their very nature potentially hazardous and contain risk. All participants in such activities must assume the responsibility for their own actions and safety. No book can replace good judgment. The outdoors is forever changing. The authors, editor and publisher cannot be held responsible for inaccuracies, errors, or omissions, or for any changes in the details of this publication, or for the consequences of any reliance on the information contained herein, or for the safety of people in the outdoors

This book is dedicated to the many organizations and individuals who have adopted a trail, lean-to, or wilderness area and devoted countless volunteer hours to our Catskill and Adirondack Forest Preserve. We also thank the generous supporters of organizations dedicated to the preservation and acquisition of public lands.

Rip Van Winkle Hikers club volunteers maintaining the trail on Thomas Cole Mountain, a section of the Black Dome Range Trail. Photograph by Susan Lehrer.

CONTENTS

The Catskill Park

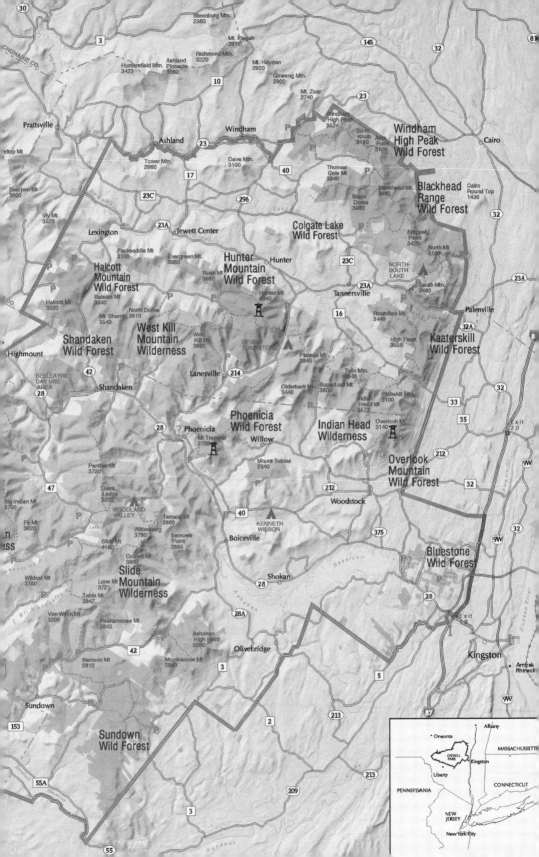

GEOGRAPHICAL INDEX TO THE STORIES

BY STORY NUMBER

THE 35 CATSKILL MOUNTAIN PEAKS OVER 3,500 FEET:

MOUNTAIN	ELEVATION IN FEET
Slide^	4,180
Hunter	4,040
Black Dome	3,980
Thomas Cole	3,940
Blackhead^	3,940
West Kill	3,880
Graham	3,868
Doubletop*	3,860
Cornell	3,860
Table	3,847
Peekamoose	3,843
Plateau	3,840
Sugarloaf	3,800
Wittenberg	3,780
Southwest Hunter*	3,740
Lone*	3,721
Balsam Lake	3,720
Panther^	3,720
Big Indian*	3,700
Friday*	3,694
Rusk*	3,680
Kaaterskill High Peak	3,655
Twin	3,640
Balsam Cap*	3,623
Fir*	3,620
North Dome*	3,610
Eagle	3,600
Balsam^	3,600
Bearpen	3,600
Indian Head	3,573
Sherrill*	3,540
Vly*	3,529
Windham High Peak	3,524
Halcott*	3,520
Rocky*	3,508

* Summits with canisters

^ Required winter peaks—must be climbed between December 21 and March 21.

FOREWORD

New York State's Catskill Mountain region, an area of broad peaks and deep, cool valleys, played a pivotal role in the wilderness movement in this nation's history and provided a rich contrast to the nation's growing industrial cities. These very mountains provided both the setting and the inspiration for the Hudson River School of painters, who changed the public's view of wilderness from one of fear of the dark, daunting and alien landscape to one of appreciation for an area of great natural beauty, a sanctuary in which one can find respite from the demands of civilization.

Yet it would be many years after painters like Cole and Durand brought such attention to the region in the early 1800s that the mountains were fully explored. It was not until 1872 that Princeton Geologist Arnold Guyot determined Slide Mountain to be the highest summit in the Catskills, and his 1879 map of the Catskill Mountains was the first published map of the region. Considering that the first ascent of Mount Washington in the nearby White Mountains of New Hampshire occurred in 1663, and Mount Marcy, the highest peak in New York, was first climbed in 1837, the Catskills have provided and will continue to provide, as evidenced in the stories that White has assembled in *Catskill Peak Experiences*, a rare opportunity to explore the uncharted, to experience a true wilderness adventure, and to challenge one's abilities.

Reading *Catskill Peak Experiences* has brought back fine memories for me of the value of gaining more than an appreciation—indeed a real love for the mountains—by exploring their numerous summits. I can think of no better way to learn about and understand a region than to discover it on foot, to navigate by map and compass, to experience its many moods and seasons with no more than the provisions that can be carried on one's back.

But there are many reasons beyond pleasant reminiscing that the seasoned Catskill climber will enjoy this book. Perhaps its greatest value will be to those new to the region, and especially those new to backcountry hiking. Nearly all of the stories resonate with lessons learned, be they the bluntly worded warnings concluding many stories, or the subtle messages conveyed in others that illustrate such things as the importance of being considerate of everyone in your group—even if it's your husband or wife! Indeed, there is much to be gained by the novice, from the reminder to consistently check your compass when hiking off trail to the necessity of carrying plenty of water. Even the veteran hiker will benefit by learning from others' mistakes, which the authors, in hindsight, freely admit. Perhaps those of us less willing to admit to such mistakes will learn a bit of humility as well.

And while those who frequent the Catskill high peaks may more readily find the humor in many of these stories, all will take delight in reading of such wild-land experiences. Of particular note are the unexpected adventures brought on by changing or unplanned-for weather, unexpected conditions, mistakes in judgment or an injury. These unanticipated circumstances provide opportunities for personal growth, for challenges that the individual would not likely have been willing to take on otherwise. They force one to take innovative approaches to solving problems, to take a different route than may have been planned, clearly building character, self-confidence and, when hiking with others, a bond that builds lifetime friendships.

The individual stories in *Catskill Peak Experiences* may appeal most to those in pursuit of, or those who have already ascended, the 35 peaks above 3,500 feet in elevation in the Catskills. But collectively these stories provide a broader understanding of the region and serve to increase public awareness of the Catskill Forest Preserve, that historic piece of legislation adopted by the State Legislature in 1885 and later incorporated into the State Constitution, thus providing lasting protection to the region, which states in relevant part:

> "the lands of the state, now owned or hereafter acquired, constituting the forest preserve ... shall be forever kept as wild forest lands. They shall not be leased, sold or exchanged, or be taken by any corporation public or private, nor shall the timber thereon be sold, removed or destroyed."

Reading these stories will instill an appreciation for the many values this tremendous wilderness resource provides.

William J. Rudge
Natural Resources Supervisor, Region 3
New York State Department of Environmental Conservation
February 2008

ACKNOWLEDGMENTS

I wish to thank C. William Spangenberger, founding member and first president of the Catskill 3500 Club, and Franklin B. Clark, long-time editor of the *Catskill Canister,* who shared valuable information about the establishment of the club and some of its early leaders.

I am indebted to many gifted writers whose tales of adventure and love of the Catskills will tempt readers to explore our beautiful wild lands and discover an exciting new life. I also thank the other former editors of the *Catskill Canister*, Douglas H. Robins and Darielle Graham, and current editor Martin Cohen for their role in preserving a treasure trove of hiking literature. Wanda Davenport is the inspiration behind chronicling the history of this unique club. Thanks to Andrea Masters of the Adirondack Mountain Club for permission to reprint four stories from *Adirondac* magazine.

I would like to express my deep appreciation to photographer Larry Gambon, who generously shared his collection of beautiful photos of the Catskill Forest Preserve—which could fill another book. I am grateful as well to Vincent Bilotta for providing a stunning photograph to grace the book's cover. Thank you, also, to Andrew Moroz, Tom and Laurie Rankin, Paul Misko, Scott Lane, Ken Metzner, Mark Schaefer, Susan Lehrer, Tom Farre, Ted Shemella, Susan Puretz, Ken Krabbenhoft, Lisa Weismiller, and Wanda Davenport for supplying additional photographs.

Great thanks to William J. Rudge for devoting valuable time to reading *Catskill Peak Experiences* and sharing an insightful foreword to this anthology. Bill's personal knowledge of the Catskill Forest Preserve, combined with his long professional work to preserve its natural resources, makes his commentary especially important. I am honored that he is part of this work. I also thank accomplished conservationists and outdoor enthusiasts Joe Gardner and Skip Doyle for reviewing the manuscript and contributing useful and lyrical commentary about the book's warnings and delights for explorers of our wild land.

I appreciate the diligence of proofreaders Matina Billias and Christl Riedman, and I thank Ted Ripley-Duggan for his cheerful willingness to answer questions as we edited the work. It has been a pleasure to work with Deborah Allen, owner and publisher of Black Dome Press, and Steve Hoare, editor, for their ready assistance and excellent communication skills.

Most of all, I am grateful for my husband Dave's great good humor, many kindnesses and patient encouragement on the trails to keep me stretching the boundaries of what I think possible, with rich rewards. Discovering new paths on this journey of life with Dave has been a true peak experience.

INTRODUCTION

If you're lucky, you've heard about hiking clubs and high peaks and have gotten involved in the great life of mountain hiking. Climbers of the 46 Adirondack High Peaks or of the 115 New York-New England 4,000-footers learn that two 4,000-footers are in the Catskills: Slide and Hunter mountains. We bought the comprehensive guidebook, *Catskill Trails* published by the Adirondack Mountain Club (ADK), and a set of five maps of the Catskill Forest Preserve published by the New York-New Jersey Trail Conference. The book and the maps are available from either www.adk.org or www.nynjtc.org (membership discounts available.) We were soon hooked by the scenic mountain climbing in the Catskills and learned that there is a hiking club, the Catskill 3500 Club, whose members climb all 35 of the Catskills' highest peaks, those over 3,500 feet.

In climbing all of an area's high peaks, you are treated to many attractive areas not seen by the average hiker. For all this work, you receive a certificate of accomplishment, a patch for your backpack, and a feeling of well-being second only to that felt in the mountains. In these adventure stories, written mostly by members of the Catskill 3500 Club, you are struck by how people relish their misadventures and keep coming back for more, how they can't get enough of climbing mountains, exploring the wilderness, and experiencing the special happiness that the mountaintop bestows, how lifelong friendships are formed, new love is found, and longtime relationships are invigorated, and how "cares drop off like autumn leaves," as explorer John Muir wrote.

John Burroughs, a Catskills native of Roxbury and a largely self-taught naturalist, put it best: "Nature we have always with us, an inexhaustible storehouse of that which moves the heart, appeals to the mind, and fires the imagination—health to the body, a stimulus to the intellect, and a joy to the soul." "The longer I live," Burroughs wrote, "the more I am impressed with the beauty and wonder of the world."

FOREVER WILD
THE CATSKILL FOREST PRESERVE

In September 1609, Hendrick Hudson watched the sun fall behind the mountains as he stood aboard the *Half Moon* on his explorations of the great river soon to be named after him. He must have imagined what delights and dangers the vast wilderness might offer to future explorers. The Native Americans hunted and farmed mostly in the Hudson Valley, avoiding the dark, hemlock-covered mountains on the Great Wall of Manitou, as they called it. Early settlers also feared the area, as reflected in the names they bestowed on the cliffs and crags, like Devil's Kitchen and Devil's Tombstone. Even the Catskill Forest Preserve's most famous trail is called the Devil's Path.

Washington Irving described the Catskill Mountains in his saga of Rip Van Winkle:

> Whoever has made a voyage up the Hudson must remember the Kaatskill mountains. They are a dismembered branch of the great Appalachian family, and are seen away to the west of the river, swelling up to a noble height, and lording it over the surrounding country. Every change of season, every change of weather, indeed, every hour of the day, produces some change in the magical hues and shapes of these mountains, and they are regarded by all the good wives, far and near, as perfect barometers. When the weather is fair and settled, they are clothed in blue and purple, and print their bold outlines on the clear evening sky, but, sometimes, when the rest of the landscape is cloudless, they will gather a hood of gray vapors about their summits, which, in the last rays of the setting sun, will glow and light up like a crown of glory.

Rip Van Winkle, we are told, slept away twenty years behind Rip's Rock above what is now the Sleepy Hollow Trail, a former carriage route that snaked up the escarpment to the famous Catskill Mountain House, built in 1824. Steamboats and then railroads brought the famous and wealthy from polluted urban areas to the pristine forests, mountains, and waterfalls atop the Great Wall of Manitou, where fabulous hotels were built nearly on the edges of cliffs. Night boats beamed great spotlights on the thirteen gleaming white Corinthian columns that adorned the front of the Catskill Mountain House.

In 1882 a three-foot-wide, narrow-gauge railroad was constructed through Stony Clove from Phoenicia to Hunter; from there, the "Huckleberry Line" continued to the Haines Falls hotels. It earned its nickname because it moved so slowly that a passenger could jump off, pick huckleberries, then climb back on. Stony Clove, before railroad tracks and a road were blasted through it, wasn't regarded as the picturesque scene it is today, the site of the Devil's Tombstone Public Campground. A walk north up NY 214 from the campground, past Notch Lake, gives a slight sense of the wild territory it must have been—a very narrow notch between the rocky cliffs of 4,040-foot Hunter Mountain and 3,840-foot Plateau Mountain. One writer lamented "In single file did we pass through it … this loneliest and most awful corner of the world." The characteristic mountain fog must have enveloped the tangled narrow pass. Today these steep notches, created when erosion gouged out the ancient Catskill Delta, challenge and delight our hikers. The Catskill Delta was created when a tectonic collision created the New England Mountains and caused the uprising of the delta from a former sea, created by even more ancient collisions that formed the Appalachian and Taconic mountains.

Thomas Cole and other artists of the Hudson River School of landscape painting produced monumental works in the "Land of Falling Waters," trying to capture this rugged and scenic land. John Burroughs wrote so lyrically about the mountains, streams, and living things that special editions of his thirty books became required reading in schools and colleges across the United States. He was befriended by great men like Henry Ford, Thomas Edison, Theodore Roosevelt, and John Muir, but he never forgot his Catskills roots: "I have shared the common lot and it is good enough for me. The most precious things are near at hand, without money and without price. Each of you has the whole wealth of the universe at your very door." Burroughs believed that the everyday miracle of nature and its solitude brings out our interior spirituality, and that regular retreat to the natural world will be the catalyst for moving back to simplicity and reverence. He offered an unforgettable image: "One cannot but reflect what a sucked orange the earth will be in a few more centuries. Our civilization is terribly expensive to all its natural resources. One hundred years of modern life doubtless exhausts its stores more than a millennium of the life of antiquity."

After decades of deforestation, in 1885 New York became the only state where the citizenry gave constitutional protection to public land, deeming that it shall "be forever kept as wild forest lands." Article XIV of the New York State Constitution mandated that the newly-created Forest Preserve lands in the Catskills and Adirondacks "shall not be leased, sold, or exchanged, or be taken by any corporation, public or private, nor shall the timber thereon be sold, removed, or destroyed." The forests are growing back, and our grandchildren will again marvel at stands of old-growth hemlock. Hiking clubs, dedicated to the protection of our public lands, help keep these wondrous places nearly as wild and pristine as they were in 1609. Four hundred years later, the explorers in this book find inspiration, adventure, and re-creation in New York's Forest Preserve, established by those far-sighted lovers of nature who created this magnificent heritage for all the generations to come.

THE BIRTH OF A HIKING CLUB: THE CATSKILL 3500 CLUB

Bill and Kay Spangenberger had been hiking the same Catskill Mountains repeatedly and thought it would be fun to try something new. In 1949 an idea came to them: let's climb all the mountains in the Catskills that are 3,500 feet or higher. In the next three years they climbed them all and shared their idea of establishing a Catskill hiking club with others, but they were unable to motivate any real interest. The subject remained dormant for another decade. They hiked in New Hampshire's White Mountains and in the Adirondacks, and knew about the Adirondack Forty-Sixers Club, established in 1948, whose members climb all forty-six Adirondack peaks over 4,000 feet.

"Kay and I are both ninety-nine years old," Bill told my husband David and me during a lively and extensive talk on a beautiful autumn day in 2005. For their seventieth wedding anniversary they were planning a "small gathering." Their 100 years of working and playing hard must be a recipe for health, for both Bill and Kay are in robust health. "One icy day last winter I walked out to get the mail and when I came back in the house, I slipped on a rug and broke my hip!" he told us, somewhat amused.

Born in 1905 in Rondout, New York, Bill Spangenberger worked for the Ulster and Delaware Railroad during high school and spent a summer as station agent at one of the Catskills' great hotels, the Laurel House, near the Catskill Mountain House. He was president of the Cornell Steamboat Company after the death of Edward Coykendall who, with his brother Frederick, had headed the 127-year-old company. Kay Spangenberger was an editor for HarperCollins in New York, after graduating *summa cum laude* from college. "Kay proposed to me three times," Bill joked. He proposed to her in 1934 at North Lake near the Catskill Mountain House when the 750-room hotel was still thriving. Their hiking gear was a pack basket with a knapsack attached to it.

The couple lived in Greenwich Village in New York City, moved to 45 Fifth Avenue, and then to Ardsley-on-Hudson before finally settling in Woodstock, New York. In their mid-nineties they moved to Rhinebeck where they still maintain a beautiful garden. They were always active. Kay swam across the Hudson River from Rhinecliff to Kingston Point. Sometimes they rode their bicycles one hundred miles a day, after which they stripped and threw buckets of water on each other. They played tennis, and he played basketball. Bill credited splitting wood and hiking with keeping him strong enough to play tennis twice a week at age eighty-four. Bill hiked Overlook Mountain near their home hundreds of times. A reporter caught up with him at age eighty-four on the 1,500-foot climb, when the 2.5-mile hike took him just 58 minutes. "I used to summit in twenty-seven minutes," he said. The couple traveled widely, scaling Uluru (Ayres Rock) in Australia, hiking New Zealand and Scotland, and exploring the American West.

Brad Whiting was chairman of the Mid-Hudson Chapter of the Adirondack Mountain Club (ADK) in 1962. One day, while descending Doubletop Mountain, he said to Bill, "Wouldn't it be interesting to organize a club to hike all of the Catskill peaks 3,500 feet and over?" Spangenberger replied, "An excellent thought, but not a new one!" This was the beginning of what is now the Catskill 3500 Club. Together with the Brad Whitings, the Spangenbergers organized a first meeting at the beautiful Lake Mohonk Mountain House to form a hiking club. Nancy Locke, then a member of the Vassar College Outing Club, and Dan Smiley also attended; founding member Gunter Hauptman of IBM was unable to be there.

Dan Smiley had studied the Bicknell's thrush and its habitat, balsam fir found above 3,500 feet, and had compiled a list of peaks over 3,500 feet. Because there are multiple peaks in close proximity, a definition of what is a separate mountain had to be determined. Borrowing principles established by the Adirondack Forty-Sixers and reducing figures proportionately, the following rule was established: to be considered a separate summit there must be at least a 250-foot drop between peaks or a peak must be at least one-half mile away from others. After studying the United States Geological Survey topographic sheets and county sheets, they determined that thirty-four peaks must be hiked to qualify for membership in the Catskill 3500 Club. (In 1990, Southwest Hunter was added, making thirty-five.)

In addition, Slide, Panther, Blackhead, and Balsam mountains must be climbed when snow conditions prevail between December 21 and March 21. This winter requirement is unique among Northeast hiking clubs and is highly valued because it introduces people to winter mountain hiking. Many people discover to their delight that winter is one of the most beautiful and interesting times to be out in the wild. Peter Fish, charter member and long-time forest ranger in the Adirondack High Peaks, suggested that other winter mountains might have more rewarding views than the designated Balsam and Panther. The Executive Committee took the idea under advisement, but the required peaks have not changed.

In November 1962, the Catskill 3500 Club was born, headed by Bill Spangenberger. Virginia Smiley was put in charge of designing an insignia—an attractive oval in blue and green, outlined in gold, containing the skyline of Twin and Indian Head mountains. Nancy Locke mailed lists of required peaks and membership rules to ADK chapters, college outing clubs and other hiking clubs, and publicized the new group in ADK's magazine, *Adirondac*. To encourage early participation in the club, charter memberships were offered through 1965, and twenty-seven people are charter members. After completing the required peaks, candidates submit a tally sheet to the club's membership chairman (visit www.catskill-3500-club.org). The new member receives a card, letter, and patch and is assigned a hiker number that is printed on a certificate presented at the annual dinner. Unlike the Adirondack 46ers, the Catskill 3500 Club issues a separate number to those members who have climbed the thirty-five mountains in calendar winter, December 21 to March 21.

The required peaks were slightly different from those the Spangenbergers had climbed more than a decade earlier, so the following spring the couple climbed the new qualifying peaks, Sherrill and Friday, after returning from a trip. (The United States Board on Geographic Names was petitioned to make official the names "Friday" and "Sherrill" for these two 3,500-foot peaks added to the required list.) While the Spangenbergers were away, their friends Elinore and Bill Leavitt became the first two charter members, on April 13, 1963. John MacPherson was the last charter member.[1] After serving as treasurer, Elinore Leavitt was the club's membership chairman from 1969 to 1990, with the coveted job of handing proud new climbers a patch and membership scroll, which in the early years was homemade and hand-colored. There was an initial $3.00 membership fee, and active members paid $1.00 in dues annually

Elinore was the associate editor of the *Catskill Canister* through 1987, typing and mimeographing the final copy on an old hand-fed machine owned by Franklin Clark, the publication's long-time editor. Before the days of word processing, each letter and each space on each line had to be counted carefully. Clark says there is one "error" in all those *Canisters:* he had asked Bill Spangenberger to write an article for the spring 1968 issue about the founding of the club, and Elinore changed his word "thought" to the word "idea," to save space! Elinore also helped organize the annual dinners, trail cleanups on her beloved Wittenberg Mountain, and cooked huge meals for the executive committee when they met at the Leavitt camp.

"For many years there was a special hike that was led by my mom," Elinore's and Bill's daughter, Ann Clapper, writes:

> It was a joint hike with the 3500 Club and some ADK chapters on New Year's Eve, and starting after midnight she led the hike down Slide Mountain. We'd start in the early evening on snowshoes with overnight packs, as we had to keep warm at the top; we had down suits and

sleeping bags. We also carried one bottle of champagne along with our midnight lunch. We hiked with carbide lamps, often tricky as a stiff wind would blow out the flame and you had to fuss around to get it started again; the lamps worked with carbide and water, so you had to be sure that your water did not freeze. Memories of the views from the top on a cold winter night, the church bells ringing in the New Year in the valley at midnight ... priceless. Surprisingly, there was always a good turnout of hearty folks.

The club was chartered on January 1, 1966. The Finger Lakes Trail Conference asked for a list of the Catskill peaks over 3,500 feet that the club wished to remain trailless. After careful consideration, it was decided that the club should work to preserve the following peaks in their trailless state: Balsam Cap, Big Indian, Doubletop, Fir, Friday, Halcott, Lone, North Dome, Rocky, Rusk, Sherrill, Vly, and West Kill. The New York State Conservation Department and the New York-New Jersey Trail Conference agreed to cooperate with the club to keep these peaks trailless.

Soon, however, orange paint blazes were reported on Lone Mountain. Elinore Leavitt suggested that the club draw up a creed to encourage good stewardship of the wilderness by aspiring 3500ers. LEAVE NOTHING BUT FOOTPRINTS, REMOVE ALL LITTER FROM TRAILS, ALWAYS TAKE TRASH HOME. CLEAN WOODLANDS ARE YOUR RESPONSIBILITY was written in the second issue of the *Catskill Canister*. Illegal trail-blazing has always been discouraged. The club supports state acquisition of land for public use, and legislation toward this end. From its inception, the motivating force behind the club's activities has been the preservation of the Catskill Forest Preserve in its wilderness state. The Reverend Ray Donahue served as the club's chair of conservation through 1994.

Forty-eight people attended the first annual dinner on March 26, 1966, at the Governor Clinton Hotel in Kingston. Edward West, the New York State Conservation Department's Superintendent of Land Acquisition, spoke about reviving old trails in the 10,000-acre North Lake complex that were so popular during the era of the great hotels: the Catskill Mountain House, Laurel House, and Hotel Kaaterskill. Brad Whiting was elected president of the club, but soon moved west. Bill Hentschel next assumed the presidency and started club-sponsored hikes, beginning with a hike up Panther Mountain in September 1966. Hentschel also promoted winter hiking. Hentschel, a mountaineer throughout New York and New England, organized a group to climb the steep slide on the north face of 4,180-foot Slide Mountain in winter, but an avalanche ended that area as one of the winter requirements! Thus began the Catskill 3500 Club-sponsored outings that encourage winter climbing and introduce thousands of people safely to the wilderness. Walter Gregory was chairman of Winter Weekend through 1988. The club progressively expanded its hiking schedule and now leads hikes every Saturday and Sunday throughout the year, except during big game hunting season.

In 1968 the *Catskill Canister*, the club's official publication, was launched. The *Canister* is a quarterly newsletter and hike schedule that is one source of the stories in this book. The Adirondack Forty-Sixers Club preserved an invaluable treasure trove of hiking literature by asking hikers to write up their adventures and send them to their club historian, Grace Hudowalski. The Catskill 3500 Club has preserved Catskill hiking literature through the *Canister*. All club members received the *Canister*, and nonmembers paid an annual subscription fee of $1.00!

In response to a request from the New York-New Jersey Trail Conference, the club began maintaining a section of the Long Path in the Catskills from County Route 42 over 3,843-foot Peekamoose and 3,847-foot Table mountains to the East Branch of the Neversink River. John MacPherson's high-school outing club, the Red Hook Mountaineers, began Long Path maintenance in the Peekamoose-Table mountain area. In October 1970, Peter Fish proposed rerouting the Long Path up Peekamoose somewhat west of Buttermilk Falls. This was approved by the New York State Conservation Department and accomplished by 1973.

The first Winter Weekend was held in January 1969 in Oliverea, near Big Indian. At the annual meeting that year, membership was sixty-five and dues were increased to $2.00. Elinore Leavitt reported a new type of member coming into the club—#1-D, Smokey Spangenberger, canine. No dues would be extracted from this class of member; however, neither are such members entitled to receive the *Canister*, hold office, or vote. Two years later, three of "man's best friends" had earned the "dog patch." There were four marriages involving members, two of which were performed in the mountains with clergymen club members officiating.

Franklin Clark was one of the earliest members of the 3500 Club and edited the *Catskill Canister* from its first issue in winter 1968 through autumn 1987. Franklin and his wife, Winifred, met on an ADK trip to Norway in 1966 and married in 1969. Winifred was a member of ADK's New York City Chapter. Franklin is the only person to have served as president of the Catskill 3500 Club and as president of ADK. He is an Adirondack 46er, and he reclimbed all qualifying Catskill peaks when he was past age seventy.

He was also a long-time hike leader. Once, Franklin was scheduled to lead a 12.4-mile hike from North Lake over 3,940-foot Blackhead Mountain and down to Big Hollow Road near Maplecrest. The week before the big hike, he sprained his ankle on a descent from Slide Mountain. He remembered what a friend who had grown up in a circus family had once told him: circus performers had to go to work the next day, regardless, so they would put a sprained foot in the hottest water possible—which anesthetized it—and then walk and exercise the foot without a bandage. This did the job!

Bill Leavitt, a truly marathon hiker, was in charge of placing all the original canisters on the trailless peaks. Because he and his daughter Ann affixed the cans—literally coffee cans—to a summit tree in the winter, by summer it was noted the cans were too high for folks to reach. They had been standing on four or five feet of snow! The original canisters consisted of a one-pound coffee tin inside a two-pound coffee tin. Kay Spangenberger, the first woman to climb all the peaks by 1952—unofficially—took charge of painting the two-pound tins orange. Bill Spangenberger described these canisters to the New York State Conservation Department and asked officials to approve placement of canisters on trailless peaks, then including Table and West Kill,[2] and in September 1965, the department approved placement of canisters on the trailless summits. In May 1966, Peter Fish became chairman of the Canister Committee to service the cans and develop a more substantial canister—porcupines were eating the coffee cans! In December 1966, Bill Hentschel was asked to design a new bronze prototype to be put on Doubletop. A year later Pete Fish developed a porcupine-proof, non-condensing can, which was placed first on Rusk.

Bearpen, Graham, and Kaaterskill High Peak have informal paths or old roads to their summits, and therefore have no canisters. Thirteen of the thirty-five Catskill mountains that exceed 3,500 feet still have canisters affixed to a summit tree. Inside these canisters are notebooks for hikers to sign. The logbooks are replaced annually by the canister maintainer, who files a report with the Department of Environmental Conservation documenting the volume of traffic on the peaks in wilderness areas.[3] The books are then forwarded to the 3500 Club's membership chair.

These mountains are truly trailless, many without any beaten path to the summit. "Herd paths" developed in the Adirondack High Peaks after canisters were placed on those trailless summits, starting in 1950 on Emmons Peak in the Seward Range east of Tupper Lake. Twenty-one canisters in the Adirondack High Peaks were removed in 2001. Herd paths may develop on some Catskill high peaks over time, but for now the hiker is offered a genuine wilderness route-finding experience. One club member recently said, "I hope that you never take these canisters down. They really set the 3500 Club apart from the crowd."

Today there are over 1,700 members of the club, many of whom lead hikes on weekends all year round. A weekend outing of winter climbing is offered in late January. The club meets annually in early spring, when new members receive their certificates at a dinner and program. The club is active in conservation and environmental matters. Club members maintain the Long Path over Peekamoose and Table mountains, and participate in Adopt-a-Highway litter patrol on Route 214 in Stony Clove. The club educates its members in outdoor recreational skills through its hikes and periodic workshops, and encourages responsible recreational use of the region's natural resources. Service awards are given to those who participate in activities to benefit the club and the Catskill Forest Preserve.

In *Catskill Peak Experiences,* ardent hikers of the Catskills write in loving and often heart-pounding detail about journeying into an unexpectedly wild world. They attempt to explain why, in spite of myriad challenges, they keep coming back for more. Many write about "being hooked" during a special day in the wilderness or by a region that has charmed people since the early nineteenth century. The Catskills, once the playground of the rich and famous, has been rediscovered in recent decades as still-primeval forest—vast areas of wilderness accessible to all who are willing to explore new territory and seek new adventure on this journey of life.

Many writers in this anthology love to bushwhack the wild and trackless regions. One writes: "I look for secret places. Lovely, hidden spots perhaps known only to me, where I can hang my hammock and relax for an hour or even a day, enjoying a special tranquility while absorbing the sensory gifts the forest offers." Others love a good, rugged day trip followed by a hot shower and fine food. Some writers backpack long trails in the Catskill Forest Preserve, and one sums it up: "Just pick up your things and go. Life won't wait."

Venturing into the wilderness, however, is an endeavor that requires serious preparation. This is a book of true stories, not a guidebook, and these tales have been written by some of the most experienced hikers in the Northeast. Yet they get lost, miscalculate the time required to hike difficult terrain, get injured, go out in dangerous weather, minimize the equipment and sustenance necessary to survive should the unforeseen occur, and as novices they got into trouble by not knowing that the mountains can be treacherous while the valleys are warm and benign, or how fast the weather can change. References listed in this book offer some essential tips.[4] Hiking clubs such as the Catskill 3500 Club, chapters of the Adirondack Mountain Club, Rip Van Winkle Hikers, the Sierra Club, the Appalachian Mountain Club, and the Catskill Mountain Club provide knowledge about hiking and the safety of numbers in group hiking.

The following tips from John Lounsbury's tale, "Lessons Learned in the Wild," provide some general guidelines:

(1) Always set a turnaround time with a safety margin. The safety margin should include allowances for differences in terrain and conditions for the rest of the day, and allowances for the tiring factor.

(2) Refer to your compass continuously. If you take too few readings, very serious complications can arise.

(3) When hiking in unfamiliar terrain, be conservative.

(4) Never start a day in the woods without gear you would need if you had to spend the night.

(5) Don't start a hike without a plan. Don't change the plan without considering contingencies if the unexpected were to arise.

And please remember that clean woodlands are our responsibility. Leave nothing but your footprints.

[1] See following page for a list of charter members.

[2] The Devil's Path was extended in 1973–74 from the Devil's Acre lean-to, to Diamond Notch Falls and over West Kill Mountain.

[3] See "Maintaining the Canisters on the Trailless Peaks."

[4] *Catskill Trails*, 3rd Edition, Vol. 8, Adirondack Mountain Club's Forest Preserve Series, 2005. Comprehensive guide to all trails in the Catskill Forest Preserve. Editors David and Carol White measured all trails with a surveying wheel from 2001 to 2003.

Catskill Day Hikes for All Seasons, by Carol and David White, Adirondack Mountain Club, 2002. Sixty favorite day hikes with extensive information about equipment, clothing, and hiking safety in all seasons.

Set of five Catskill maps, New York-New Jersey Trail Conference.

Guides and maps are available from www.adk.org, 800-395-8080, or www.nynjtc.org, 201-512-9348 (*Catskill Trails*/map combination). Member discounts.

3500 CLUB CHARTER MEMBERS

1		William H. Leavitt
2		Elinore G. Leavitt
3		C. W. Spangenberger
4		Kathleen Spangenberger
5		Betty Hurd
6		Brad Whiting
7		Dorothy Whiting
8		Jerome Hurd
9		Dr. Lee H. Bowker
10		Paul Almer
11		Chris Burchill
12	2	C. Peter Fish
13	21	Ann L.Clapper
14	5	Rudolph Strobel
15		Gertrude Bohm
16	9	William Hentschel
17		Arthur G. Beach
18	8	Walter L. Gregory
19		Carol Schlentner
20		Ted Wolfrum
21		Arthur H. Pass
22		Will D. Merritt, Jr.
23	1	Rev. Ray L. Donahue
24		George Whitbeck
25		Clarence Beehler
26		George Gyukanov
27	3	John C. MacPherson

First column: 3500 Club number
Middle column: winter numbers

Part I:

MARATHON HIKES

I lay down, looked up at the starlit night, and realized how much a night hike has to offer. You see eyes shining in the dark forest and you are never sure what they are. Everything is so quiet—all you hear are owls and occasional coyote yelps howling in the cold crisp night.

Ralph Ryndak

Photograph by Andrew Moroz.

1

DEVIL'S PATH END-TO-END

TWENTY-EIGHT MILES UP SIX PEAKS

Tim Stone, #1116, 401W

In March 1998, after becoming a Catskill 3500 regular and winter member, I started focusing on planning for long-distance hikes. I would group together mountains in close proximity and plan various day hikes with routes that probably most people wouldn't consider. It was always day hiking (versus backpacking), because I knew I could gain the most trail mileage with my lightweight backpack, leaving the sleeping bag and mass quantities of food at home. A long-time dream of mine was to hike the 24.75-mile Devil's Path from end to end in a day. This trail scales five peaks—Indian Head, Twin, Sugarloaf, Plateau, a shoulder of Hunter, and West Kill—with about 9,000 feet of vertical ascent. *Backpacker* magazine in April 2003 rated it "Toughest Day Hike."

I was twenty-four, a mechanical engineering graduate fresh from Clarkson University and working as a gas turbine engineer for General Electric in Schenectady, near the Catskills. In 1998 GE decided to move its headquarters to Atlanta, and I decided to move with it.

To train for the Devil's Path, I originally wanted to do the section from Prediger Road to Devil's Tombstone and then, on a separate day, from the Devil's Tombstone Campground to Spruceton Road. I realized now that if I were ever going to do the hike end-to-end, it had to be without my preparation section hikes. I decided that I would deviate from the trail and include 4,040-foot Hunter Mountain in my trek. (The Devil's Path runs over a shoulder of Hunter, 500 feet below the summit.)

I picked June 13th, a day on the only weekend I had remaining before the move and a day with the most sunlight. I didn't have a good backup weekend if it was storming. Whether it was cloudy or not didn't make a difference, because I wasn't hiking for stopping and smelling the roses or looking at the views. During the drive up the Devil's Kitchen (Platte Clove Road) it began to drizzle, but there was no turning back. If there were thunder and lightning, I probably would have thought twice. At 5:50 AM, armed with my daypack filled with two double-decker peanut butter sandwiches, a bag of gorp (raisins, peanuts, and M&Ms), three liters of water, raingear, a headlamp, and a handheld shortwave radio, I hit the trail just as the sun began to rise.

On the way up to the chin of Indian Head Mountain, the rain had subsided enough so that I thought it might completely clear up, but that was an illusion—the opposite would occur. On the summit of Indian Head, I felt strong and I thought I could feel that way on every summit. The double peaks of Twin were a breeze. Cruising on by the summits, I stopped only in the notches for a minute or two to chomp on gorp and guzzle water. I had to make it to the Spruceton Road terminus by sundown.

In the meantime, behind the scenes, my parents were shuttling my car from Prediger Road to Route 214 at Devil's Tombstone Campground or Spruceton Road. I was to contact my father with a ham radio if I was having trouble or needed to bail out at the halfway point, Route 214. We are both licensed operators. If they didn't hear anything, the plan was to park the car at Spruceton Road.

Sugarloaf was just a hurdle in the path to get to the next notch. With light rain and low clouds, there was no need to go off-trail to the outlooks near the summit. On the ascent up Plateau from Mink Hollow, as the rain fell harder, fatigue began to set in. Nearing the top of Plateau, the worst occurred (or what I thought the worst could be)—lightning! Extremely loud thunder followed immediately after the first flash of lightning. The lightning-thunder series continued to occur frequently as I made my way across the flat summit.

Despite the bright, close-by flashes of lightning (and the fact that I was 3,800 feet up in the air), I knew I had to make radio contact with my father. If not now, it would have to wait a couple of hours until I reached the top of Hunter. I am not proud of this, but I took out the dry radio that was safely sealed in a Ziploc baggy, extended the meter-long metal antenna, adjusted the frequency to what we agreed and gave two quick calls—hunched under my rain jacket. I heard nothing back. I quickly packed the radio away, took a couple bites from my peanut butter sandwich, and continued.

As I made my way over the rock ledge on the western end, my right hamstring cramped up and I could feel the left one tightening. The first time I experienced this, I immediately took my pack off and did a series of stretches to alleviate the pain, which seemed to work. I continued down the steep trail with a flurry of thoughts, trying not to focus on the pain in my right leg. After it was too late, I realized that I had been putting too much force on my left leg because of the discomfort in my right leg. This caused severe pain in my left knee, which I had never experienced before. At Route 214 the thunder and lightning had subsided, but it was steadily raining. With a slight limp and Notch Lake in sight, I was determined to keep going.

I signed in at the trail register before making my long, slow ascent up Hunter. I was exhausted. My hamstrings were okay, but my left knee still had pain, which was bearable on ascents. At the junction of the yellow trail near Devil's Acre lean-to—1.7 miles from the summit—I had a decision to make. Do I risk the hike's success trying to include Hunter's summit, or simply finish the Devil's Path, an acceptable accomplishment. I decided I needed to bag the peak. Halfway up, where it levels off with fir trees on either side, a foot of water covered the entire trail. I tried to step on the sides of the trail, waddling back and forth to avoid stepping directly in the water. The thick fir made it impossible. I had to wade through it, my boots completely underwater.

At the ranger cabin next to the fire tower, I took my longest break of the day. I emptied the water out of my boots and wrung out my socks while I listened to a conversation between two people on the ham radio. I tried to break in, but they had it timed perfectly: when one stopped, the other continued talking. Still not able to patch through to my father, I continued, returning through the trail full of water to the Devil's Path. I stopped at Devil's Acre lean-to only to empty the water out of my boots (again) and pick the M&Ms out of my gorp which, thanks to my exhaustion, seemed to be the only food I could eat without throwing up.

On the Devil's Path, view of Twin Mountain summit (right) and Sugarloaf Mountain (left). Photograph by Larry Gambon.

On the descent into Diamond Notch, the pain in my left knee was strong, but I was (mentally) stronger. There was nothing to do but try to ignore it. The rain had stopped, and it even started to clear up. At Diamond Notch Falls, I had to ascend another Catskill peak, 3,880-foot West Kill Mountain, something that seemed impossible at this point! On reaching Buck Ridge Lookout just below the summit, I switched on the radio. This time I had great reception and the line was clear. I gave a call out to my dad, "NZ2S, NZ2S, this is KB2EET" (our FCC-assigned call signs). He responded! I told him where I was, a place he had been to many times, as he is also a 3500 Club member (#299 and #98, summer/winter respectively). I assured him I was okay, only a bit fatigued and looking out at the glacial cirques. Everything had worked out shuttling the car around; he wished me well.

On the top of West Kill, I looked at my altimeter watch (Avocet Alpine) with which I was tracking the vertical ascent, and it read just over 8,800 ft. On the way to West West Kill, I can only remember that the forest was peaceful and that it took longer than I expected, though I couldn't really recognize the summit (not that I was paying that close attention, as I was approaching complete exhaustion). When I started dropping below 2,500 feet, I knew it wouldn't be long now. My knee was hurting more than ever, but I was so excited I started to run. I probably ran the last half mile, finishing at 7:30 PM. I had done it! Full of emotion, I signed out, taking up much space to write all of my trip statistics and to record one of my long-time dreams—to conquer the Devil's Path in a day! 🏃

2

CAVE DOG IN THE CATSKILL HIGH PEAKS

HIKING BY NIGHT WITH RECORD-BREAKING MOUNTAINEER

by Ralph Ryndak, #1186, #451W

Editors' Note: Ralph has been hiking the Catskills since his youth. He became an invaluable part of Ted "Cave Dog" Keizer's record-breaking hike of all thirty-five Catskill high peaks over 3,500 feet. Cave Dog broke the speed record for hiking these peaks—which had been four days, ten hours, and twenty-four minutes—by almost two days! A fifteen-member support team, the Dog Team, met Cave Dog with meals and equipment along the trails and along the course of his road walking between ascents. Cave Dog slept fifteen- or twenty-minute catnaps for the two days, fifteen hours, and twenty-four minutes it took him to hike 135 miles and 37,000 feet of elevation gain. Ralph Ryndak not only helped Cave Dog plan his route, but hiked two nights with him, carrying food, water, and extra clothing for twelve-hour stretches during two consecutive nights. The best part of the marathon, Cave Dog said, was the wildlife, including four bears.

Night One

After the reconnaissance hike up Fir with Cave Dog, we next got together at our base camp, a lovely place with several homes and two large ponds in Windham. We had set up eight tents around the larger pond for the support team members, and other team members stayed in the guesthouse. Cave Dog and support team members studied the route and estimated where the support stations would be and at what times. The maps were pieced together and a red line marked the 131-mile continuous route. Cave dog would start the challenge on Peekamoose Mountain at 6:00 AM, September 11, 2002.

I didn't sleep much the night before because I was excited, so I drove to the base camp early and tried to rest before hiking with Cave Dog that evening. I lay down on my sleeping bag and rested only briefly before the wind started howling. The tent stakes let loose and actually blew some of the tents into the pond. So much for sleep before the challenge! Support team members and I secured the tents. I called home and found that the winds were so intense that the power had been knocked out. My companion, Maddy, had gotten out the generator.

It was late afternoon now and excitement was building. Terry Finnan, a wonderful gentleman, would drive me to my nocturnal destination with Cave Dog. We headed out to Margaretville for dinner and engaged in hours of conversation about the Catskills and Adirondacks, his home turf. Then it was time to head to Seager, where Cave Dog would be coming off of the Turner Hollow trail end. Cave Dog started sixteen hours earlier on Peekamoose Mountain and had hiked Table, Lone, Rocky, Balsam Cap, Friday, Cornell, Wittenberg, Slide, Panther, Fir, Big Indian, Double Top, Graham and Balsam Lake Mountains. It was now 10:14 PM, and Cave Dog arrived at Seager. Friendly locals gathered around with interest as he came down the mountainside with his headlamp glowing in the clear, crisp evening.

Without skipping a beat, he was fed, given liquids, and I was loaded up with supplies and extra clothing. Off into the chilly night we went. Cave Dog was glad to see me, and I him; we talked about how the challenge had been going and how beautiful the evening was for a great hike. We proceeded at a pace quicker than my usual hiking pace and at 10:43 PM we were at the true summit of Eagle, marked by a cairn about 100 yards off-trail. Amazingly, Cave Dog found his lost car keys on the ground just past the Shandaken lean-to he'd used while scouting out the area! We proceeded rapidly over Haynes Mountain to the junction with the McKenley Hollow trail where Groove Dog (Mike Guerette), a support team member, was ready with food and energy drinks for us. This would be our last support until we reached the base of Belleayre Mountain. We continued over Balsam Mountain and took a break just before the summit of Belleayre; Cave Dog needed a nap!

My job was to wake him in twenty minutes. I lay down, looked up at the starlit night, and realized how much a night hike has to offer. You see eyes shining in the dark forest and you are never sure what they are. Everything is so quiet—all you hear are owls and occasional coyote yelps howling in the cold crisp night. Twenty minutes were up, and Cave Dog jumped to his feet and off we went. We came to the ski center and took a couple of minutes to look up at the stars; a meteor shot by and glowed longer than usual. We were in great spirits, running down the ski slopes like kids having a ball. I was having more fun than I could possibly imagine. Even with little sleep for days, I felt more energy than I had in a long time.

It was now 3:00 AM and we were on what seemed to be an abandoned Route 28, not a car in sight. We soon met up with Slo Dog (Terry Finnan). Cave Dog and I received more nourishment and walked to his next 3,500-foot peak, Halcott Mountain. We left the Birch Creek trailhead at 4:47 AM and bushwhacked up Halcott, arriving at the canister at 5:36 AM. It was a challenge bushwhacking in the dark, making sure a branch did not smack you in the face. Wearing headlamps created shadows, and rocks and roots became hidden in those shadows. We both took an occasional spill. Just prior to reaching the canister, Cave Dog knew from his GPS how far we were from it, and there we were—at the canister just at dawn. We proceeded down to the Elk Creek trailhead, passing abandoned farmland and old foundations in the early gray dawn. Cave Dog and I engaged in conversations about the outdoors and the history of the Catskills.

We were both getting tired. We arrived at the trailhead at 6:55 AM, and Slo Dog was there for support. It was good to see him after the long, intense night. I had never experienced a night like that before, covering so much territory! We made it to the Johnson Hollow trailhead by 9:30 AM and hiked up to the hunters' cabin in the col[1] of Vly and Bearpen. There, I waited for Cave Dog while he climbed Bearpen. When he descended, I gave him food and water and told him that I would meet him later that night for another twelve-hour night hike. We were both pleased on the progress made and parted company in very good spirits.

Night Two

After I left Cave Dog at the Vly-Bearpen col, Slo Dog drove me back to our Windham base camp. I slept for three or four hours before one of the support team woke me up. It was time to go to the Hunter Mountain trailhead at the end of Spruceton Road to rendezvous with Cave Dog for the next leg of the journey. Team members were cooking up a feast for Cave Dog and the rest of us. They fed me well, resupplied me, and off I went to the John Robb lean-to. Cave Dog was in the North Dome–West Kill vicinity. My mission was to hike with him through the night, so we calculated that he would be near the lean-to at nightfall. I took my time going up the trail; I had plenty of time. It was a spectacularly beautiful late afternoon, cool and clear. I arrived at the lean-to at dusk and sat on a rock that afforded a

On the trail. Photograph by Larry Gambon.

wondrous view of the Spruceton Valley, wondering where Cave Dog was on the mountain. Cave Dog was well fed at the trailhead, but I laid out more provisions for him; huge amounts of calories are consumed on such a challenge, and it's hard to eat large amounts at one time. I radioed Cave Dog and was able to pick up from him that he was near the canister on Rusk. It was dark and I should be hiking with him now, but I knew I'd better stay put. I stared up at the countless stars and went in and out of strange dreams. I had no lights on.

All of a sudden I was awakened by the sound of something large coming up the trail in the dark. I thought it was Cave Dog, but why doesn't he have his headlamp on? I turned mine on, and about twenty feet away I saw a black bear. We were both startled to the same degree; he ran into the woods, and I jumped up and turned on both headlamps. My heart was pounding! He must have smelled the food that I had laid out on the rock, and was probably a frequent visitor at the lean-to.

Cave Dog must be off of Rusk by now; he received my transmission and said that he was having trouble staying alert. This happens to him when night falls and lack of sleep and many miles are under his belt. I told him that I would pack up everything because of the bear and head down the trail to meet him. I wouldn't miss him now, because he was on the trail. Once we met up and started talking, he perked up. I told him about the bear encounter. We soon made it back to the lean-to where we had some food and water. He rested for a short time, and then it was off to Hunter Mountain. We made good time to the tower, and Cave Dog made sure that he was at the true summit of the flat peak by standing on a rock. We admired the starlit night sky.

I was told that Groove Dog would be at the Devil's Acre lean-to with more supplies. We radioed ahead to give him an estimated time of arrival. This way, the food would be hot when we arrived. We finally saw lights at the lean-to, and several propane stoves were going. Mike had prepared a feast—porcelain dishes, metal cutlery, and a four- or five-course meal. What a nice surprise! We ate, Cave Dog changed clothes, and off to Southwest Hunter we went. We found the herd path and followed it for about twenty minutes, making sure to protect our eyes while traveling the tree branch-infested path. We were looking for the small gully that heads up to the canister; it's not hard to find in daylight, but at night it was problematic. We hit it right on and in six or seven minutes we were at the canister. We made it back to the Devil's Path, passed the lean-to and thanked Groove Dog for his fine nighttime support. We took our time going down the steep trail to the notch at Route 214.

Cave Dog was getting groggy again, and my job was to keep him alert, so we engaged in conversation. We knew that Deb James (Crazy Dog) would be in the notch for support. One benefit about the Catskills is that there are many easily accessible areas for support. The only missed provision was on Big Indian Mountain.

That caused Cave Dog to experience dehydration, so the team took extra efforts to be sure that would not happen again. Once in the notch, Deb gave out more supplies. Cave Dog needed a rest and got one. After a specified time for a nap, I woke him and we ascended very steep Plateau Mountain. He shot up so fast I had a hard time keeping up. It wasn't long before I noticed the 3,500-foot sign. Even though we had support people with supplies, I always carried two or three quarts of water, food and extra clothes, radios, batteries, headlamps, even a camera in case of a missed support station.

Sunrise was approaching and Rad Dog (P. J. Keizer), Cave Dog's brother, would be on Plateau waiting for us. We later found out that he had injured his knee ascending Plateau at night from Mink Hollow. It had now been close to 100 miles for Cave Dog and thousands of vertical feet; he needed a good rest! Rad Dog told us of his injury, but he was able to bring up a sleeping bag for Cave Dog, who immediately crawled into it. Rad Dog and I watched the sun come up over Kaaterskill High Peak; what a sight to behold! Rad Dog took a picture of me that would be on the front page of the Kingston *Daily Freeman*, along with pictures of Cave Dog and the team. Rad Dog said Cave Dog was getting up, and soon we were off over the top of Plateau and down the Devil's Path, where more support was waiting by the lean-to at the col between Plateau and Sugarloaf.

That team member said that a fairly aggressive bear was very interested in the food supply that she was carrying. She was able to chase it away, but asked if I would walk out with her after the resupply. I had wanted to go at least to Indian Head, but it was daytime and my job was done. I bid Cave Dog good luck, and down the trail I went with D Dog (Anne Eldridge). I had to go home to attend to business, but later that night returned to base camp and found out Cave Dog had completed the challenge in record time. That night we all celebrated.

I had been part of a fine team that worked with great synchronization. It was a learning experience for me, and I went on to join the team in 2003 for the Long Trail challenge that was cut short because of bad weather and trail conditions; it was successful in 2004, when I joined up with the team again for the night hiking support. In 2005 I was in the Adirondacks when Cave Dog completed his fifty-kilometer hikes in all fifty states.[2] 𝕏

---

[1] A gap between peaks in a mountain range, used as a pass.

[2] The Hike Fifty Challenge was a tribute to conservationist Bob Marshall, who had set a goal of hiking thirty-plus-mile day hikes in every state. Marshall completed his treks in over forty states before his untimely death. Cave Dog determined to do a fifty-kilometer hike in all fifty states within seventy-five days, and he completed his goal in the Adirondack High Peaks. He and Ralph recount that truly incredible day and night in the High Peaks in the forthcoming book, *Adirondack Peak Experiences*.

3

BACKPACKING ACROSS THE LONG SIX

A PLACE LIKE NO OTHER

Bleecker Staats, #272
from Autumn 1988 *Catskill Canister*

There is a place in the Catskills like no other that epitomizes "forever wild" and "bushwhack." It is an area of lonely peaks so densely forested that a compass, although necessary, is often difficult to use—a quiet place where only occasional wind and rain in the spruce tops break the summer stillness. At twilight the fluted notes of the hermit thrush are heard from somewhere below. In winter it is a brilliant landscape of white silence where a rime of ice-encrusted branches pointing frosted fingers to the wind's direction stand out against an azure sky. When referring to this place, Peter Fish used the term "the Long Six," meaning an all-day hike to Friday, Balsam Cap, Rocky, Lone, Table, and Peekamoose mountains.

It's been eleven years since we first looked from the deep snow of Slide's summit to the tops of the Long Six. Although I had never hiked the route, I had covered it often in my mind, memorizing almost every contour on the map. I tried to picture the wooded miles and elevations. In retrospect I had no idea of how physically ambitious bushwhacking with a backpack would be. It all seemed like such an exciting adventure. My enthusiasm for the plan sparked the interest of six others, who asked to join us. Matt, Patrick, and Jim had been over these peaks on a day trip with Mr. Fish. To them, the idea of such a backpack was that it would be a snap; but then, one has to remember they were teenagers. They hiked in the day before and camped on Giant Ledge. Jim's eleven-year-old sister, Kathlene, my daughter Amanda, thirteen, and my friends Sid, Hop, and Kath made up our group of nine. The girls looked so small under those packs.

The day of the big trip arrived. In delicious spring air under a clear sky, we ascended Slide and met the boys as planned. After a snack and picture-taking, we descended into the col between Slide and Cornell. I was impressed with how well the little ones handled the descent of Slide's east slope. We ate lunch at the spring in the col and picked a spot off the trail to set up camp. Then we climbed Cornell and walked over Bruin's Causeway to Wittenberg. The view east over the rich greens and blues of the Ashokan landscape was so breathtaking that we hated to leave that breezy spot.

The "teacher-teacher-teacher" song of an ovenbird serenaded us as we ate a relaxed dinner. Later, drifting clouds cast shadows on our moonlit camp. My pack, with all our food, was suspended from a high limb because porcupines were everywhere. Hop and Kath were under a tarp and spent much of the night defending their territory from those spiny creatures. Matt awakened at 2:00 AM with some difficulty breathing. He was alarmed to see a large porcupine curled up on his chest! The sleeping bag protected Matt from the spines; he carefully slid out of the bag before encouraging his "guest" to rest elsewhere. It was not a porcupine, but some other creature, that had climbed up into my pack in the dark and taken a bite out of each package of instant oatmeal. Boiling water kills most bacteria, so we ate it anyway.

We broke camp and began day two. At 10:00 AM we left the trail for the serious bushwhack of the Long Six. Matt and Patrick took the lead down the slope toward the right that heads to Friday. Bushwhacking downhill with a pack is an odd experience. First we would step out into the air, but soon we were hanging from limbs by our pack frames, our feet dangling in air like limp puppets. If we were lucky, we could touch ground and wiggle till both feet were ready to try the next step. I soon learned that bushwhacking the Long Six was seldom in a straight line. On level

View from Wittenberg. Photograph by Carol White.

ground (of which there was very little) we went through heavy spruce—over and under downed trunks with hidden stubs that could get quite personal.

Going uphill was a different challenge. Keeping balance and gaining elevation at the same time seemed impossible. It is remarkable that we reached Friday in two hours. Peering through the weathered trunks, I will never forget the thrill of seeing the orange box for the first time. Worn, scratched, and hungry, we sat among the stubs eating our lunch beneath my very first canister.

We plunged back into the dense forest in a light rain. Soon we came to that "wall" on the south slope of Friday that at first seemed impossible to descend with packs. Using downed trees and roots to check our fall, we were soon at the col between Friday and Balsam Cap. What a great place to camp some day! I was reminded of John Burroughs's account about spending a night with friends there, sitting around a campfire and telling eerie tales of the ghost of a screaming girl who haunts that area at night.

I was convinced I would never go back the way we came; we had probably been through the worst. I was soon to learn differently. The rain let up as we struggled to the top of Balsam Cap and our second canister. Several of us fell while descending the damp slope of Balsam Cap. At the saddle before Rocky, Sid suggested that for safety's sake and the lateness of the hour we should consider spending the night there. I, too, was exhausted and realized my goal to make Lone that day was unrealistic with packs. Pushing and crawling through the dense blowdowns, we reached the tiny clearing at the top of Rocky. After signing in at our third canister, we rested and shared snacks. It wasn't easy getting back up again; I knew my limit had been reached. Matt found a level spot with ample room for the tents. I've been over the route many times since, but I have never come across the spot again.

It was 6:30 PM and we had been moving since morning. I had hoped we could make the saddle between Rocky and Lone to be closer to water, but a personal sacrifice of great magnitude saved the day. Jim and Patrick volunteered to take all our canteens down to the creek in search of water. Exhausted, they were back an hour later. Their quest had taken them down 500 feet and a half mile before enough running water could be found. To this day I remember the gratitude I felt for their service "above and beyond." Thanks to their efforts, we not only had another great meal, but also had water for the rest of the trip. We hit the sack during an early-evening shower.

Awaking at dawn to the sweet song of the white-throated sparrow is joy itself. We breakfasted in patches of sunlight filtering through the translucent leaves of moosewood. That wonderful scent of rain-drenched spruce and fern was everywhere. We broke camp and pushed laboriously through blooming hobblebush toward the summit of Lone. The rain of the previous night made the going slippery, while at the same time glistening on the beautiful faces of painted trillium and bunchberry blossoms. Now in the third day of the Long Six, we felt we could hike forever. It takes two good days with a pack to get your muscles in shape. Compared to the other peaks, Lone's canister tree was in a meadow. I remember how we sprawled out on the sunny, aromatic carpet of green to rest and snack beneath a cloudless sky.

Patrick was singing about a "yellow submarine" as he and Matt led us down a shoulder of Lone into the saddle to begin the climb of Table. The going seemed easier. Just before we reached the flat top, we found a place to sit and view the magnificent profile of Slide and the peaks we had so recently climbed. The air was cool and clear, and the mountains of the Devil's Path and Blackhead Range were clearly visible. The panorama from this spot is one of the best in the Catskills. We were surprised to find a path leading to the high point of Table's summit and our fifth canister of the trip.[1]

Finally came the knee-wearying, three-hour, 2,600-foot descent to Peekamoose Road, where Jim's father was waiting. Amanda, Matt, and I relaxed with our feet in the clear cold of Rondout Creek, watching a trout in a deep pool, the sweet scent of hawkweed in the air. Oh, how good it felt after that long downhill! And how proud I was of my "child," Amanda, who had done the whole trip in those heavy shoes without complaint. A veery filled the glen with rich, downward-spiraling notes. I reminisced about our camaraderie, the humor, the feeling of accomplishment we all shared.

Then, as counterpoint, there was the terrifying eternity, or so it seemed, when the brakes failed on Sid's car and we went racing down Peekamoose Road. Sid had to force the emergency brake to save our lives.

Last of all there was that unforgettable view when we crossed the spillway of the Ashokan Reservoir at sunset—the silhouette of the Long Six against a burnt orange sky. 👫

---

[1] The blue-marked DEC Peekamoose-Table Trail now extends from the Phoenicia-East Branch Trail at its 1.2-mile point from the Denning trailhead, over Table Mountain and Peekamoose Mountain to Peekamoose Road, County Route 42. The canister was removed.

4

THE LAST OF THE WINTER 35ER'S

SEVENTEEN HOURS OVER EIGHT MOUNTAINS

Dan D. Chazin, #556, #214W

It was 8:20 AM on Sunday, March 14, 1991, and we were about to start our climb of the first of eight peaks: Peekamoose, Table, Lone, Rocky, Balsam Cap, Friday, Cornell and Wittenberg. My friend Steve Dundorf needed all eight of these peaks to complete the requirements for winter membership in the Catskill 3500 Club. They all appear in a relatively straight line on the map, and the total distance covered would be no greater than about fifteen miles—certainly achievable by itself in a day hike. But, having climbed all these peaks previously—although never more than four on any one day—I knew that the terrain would make this trip a challenge. Indeed, I wondered whether it was possible to do all eight peaks in one day. But I figured we'd give it a try.

If we had any hope of getting out of the woods before dark, or some reasonable time after dark, we would have to get an early start. We would also need two cars, since the plan was to start at Peekamoose Road and end at Woodland Valley. Steve was only sixteen, so he couldn't drive. But he arranged for his older brother Jim to come along, and Jim had his own car. Steve and I arrived at Woodland Valley at midnight; Jim soon arrived and slept on top of my Isuzu Trooper. I slept in the Isuzu and Steve set up his tent.

We awoke at 6:30 AM, had a quick breakfast, and drove in my Isuzu to Peekamoose Road, leaving Jim's car in Woodland Valley. We started our climb at 8:20 AM, and the climb up Peekamoose was quite easy. Up to 3,100 feet there was little snow or ice, and even above this elevation you could walk around it. Only above 3,400 feet did snow and ice cover the ground, at most a few inches deep. We arrived at the summit at 10:30 AM and lingered for ten minutes. In another half hour we summited Table, enjoyed the beautiful viewpoint and headed to Lone—one of the easiest bushwhacks in the Catskills. With little snow or ice below Table's summit, it took us only fifty minutes to reach the canister on Lone. It was now 12:25 PM and we all felt that we were doing fine in terms of timing.

Here the hike became more difficult, but Steve did a fabulous job of avoiding the worst of the spruce and leading us directly to Rocky's canister, where we arrived at 1:45 PM and spent twenty minutes eating lunch. Then we were faced with what

I've always considered one of the most difficult bushwhacks in the Catskills—the trek from Rocky to Balsam Cap. Twice before, it took me two hours to cover this one-mile stretch. The map is deceptive, showing little elevation change and relatively gentle grades. In fact, the descent of Rocky is very tricky. There are cliffs to descend, and on the way up Balsam Cap you encounter thick spruce and large blowdowns around which it is difficult to maneuver. We managed to descend the cliffs without great difficulty, but it took us an hour to get to the col. It was now 3:00 PM, and we still had four of the eight peaks remaining!

Checking our bearing, Steve pointed to a mountain slightly to the left. "That's Balsam Cap," he said. I recognized its shape, and a check with the map confirmed that the mountain was Friday, not Balsam Cap. Steve agreed and recalculated the bearing to Balsam Cap, visible to the right. Jim glanced at his watch. "We still have four peaks to go, with only three and one half hours of daylight left—and I don't have a flashlight!" We were at the midpoint of the hike, with no easy exit no matter which way we went. Jim realized that time could be saved if we bypassed Balsam Cap and Friday, taking the most direct route to the Wittenberg-Cornell-Slide Trail. This was still no breeze! It required a bushwhack down to an unmarked trail that runs along the East Branch of the Neversink River, which would then be ascended to the marked trail.

"I'm going back the most direct way," announced Jim. "I've got to get back before dark." Steve took the diametrically opposite approach: "This is my last chance to finish the 3500 Club winter peaks this year; I've got to do it!" There was no way to dissuade Steve, but Jim was equally adamant that he must turn back. This put me in a difficult situation. Three of us were already fewer than the generally accepted minimum number of four for winter mountaineering; to split up was almost unthinkable, yet there appeared to be no alternative. If each was insistent on going his own way, whom should I go with? Jim was an Eagle Scout, with previous experience hiking in the Catskills. He didn't have a map or compass, but I could give him mine. He was twenty-five years old and seemed mature and experienced enough to find his way back. Steve was only sixteen. His navigational skills were outstanding, but he was taking the more difficult route. There was no question— I'd have to go with Steve.

I gave Jim my map and compass and a pair of instep crampons. I would've liked to have given him a flashlight, but I only had one, and it seemed more likely that I'd need it than he. "If you don't get back by 8:00 PM," Jim said, "I'll call the police to report you missing." I figured that five hours should be sufficient time to get back, but I said, "How about making it nine o'clock instead?" Jim agreed and soon was on his way.

Steve and I continued up Balsam Cap. We had no trouble finding the canister, but it took nearly an hour to arrive at the summit. I knew that the route from Balsam Cap to Friday was not exceptionally difficult and hoped that we wouldn't have trouble getting from Friday to Cornell. If it took an hour for each segment, we'd be on the marked trail by 6:00 PM and it would, I hoped, take us no more than three hours for the rest of the hike. The hike from Balsam Cap to Friday ended up being surprisingly easy, with not too much spruce. The only real obstacle was the cliff on the south side of Friday, which can pose serious difficulties, but we found a way around it. By 5:10 PM, we were at the summit and found the canister. We had over an hour of light left and only about a mile—with little change of elevation—to the blue trail.

The first part followed the open ridge down to the Friday-Cornell col and was easy, taking only twenty minutes. We appeared to be right on track! Then, things changed. We hit the worst spruce I've ever encountered in the Catskills, a nearly impenetrable thicket. Every step required us to pause and push aside branches; progress was excruciatingly slow. At best, we were going half a mile an hour. Once, my leg slipped into a hole and it took several minutes to get it out. And it was getting dark. At 6:30 we turned on our flashlights, but we still could barely see ten feet ahead of us and we had no real sense in which direction we were traveling.

Two things reassured us: we were following a north compass bearing that had to lead to the trail; and we were following a ridge with a drop on each side. My altimeter consistently read 3,620 feet—just about the elevation shown on the map for the correct route. But I knew from experience that it's not easy to find a trail after dark; markers appear only intermittently on the trees and it's easy to walk right past the trail without noticing it. But a break in this impenetrable spruce would alert us that we had reached the trail. Finally, at 7:30 PM, Steve announced that he had found the trail. It had taken us an hour to hike one-quarter mile, and this was with a very fast hiker!

Another problem arose: my flashlight was now almost completely dead. Luckily, Steve had a fancy Arctic headlamp that gave much light and came equipped with batteries that lasted several hours, even in very cold weather. Both of us were now dependent on Steve's headlamp. Steve would go for a short distance, turn around, and shine the light on the trail. I'd catch up, and we'd repeat the process. We were on the trail, but the trail was a sheet of ice! We both had full crampons. It would have been nearly impossible to climb up (and especially down) Cornell and Wittenberg without them. Unfortunately, my crampons were very dull and sometimes slipped on steep slopes, so I proceeded very cautiously.

On the way up Cornell, we noticed a paper bag from the Wyckoff Bakery on the trail. Inside were an apple and a brownie. There was no note, but I was virtually certain that Jim had left the bag. That meant that he had gotten at least this far. I think it's the first time I ever ate a frozen apple, but it tasted pretty good under the circumstances!

We stopped briefly to enjoy the nighttime view from the summit of Cornell, and then continued to Wittenberg. We had to descend a ten-foot sheer drop through a cleft in the rock. This spot is difficult to negotiate even in good weather, and now we had to descend it in the darkness when it was covered with ice. After Steve got down without difficulty, I was able to wedge myself in the rock cleft and descend with the help of my crampons. At 8:40 PM we arrived at the summit of Wittenberg—the last of the eight peaks that we had set out to climb. The view was spectacular, with lights visible over the Ashokan Reservoir.

The nine o'clock deadline would soon be on us, and we had several more hours of hiking to go! Jim would probably call the police, who might order a search, and he would also call his parents. We had no way to contact anyone and report that we were fine. All we could do was continue down, going as slowly as necessary to avoid injuries. The descent of Wittenberg is very steep in places. It is not an easy hike under ordinary conditions, and the darkness and ice made it much more difficult. Even with crampons, the going was very slow. The ice ended at 3,100 feet, and we took off our crampons. This was the only point at which I got somewhat cold on the hike, despite the fact that the temperature was about 20° all day.

From there, the going was easier. For stretches I followed Steve without his having to shine the light back at me. We arrived at the Terrace lean-to junction at 10:15, and all went well for the next hour. Then, at 2,500 feet, the blazing was poor and we couldn't find the trail! We now had another, potentially more serious problem. After five hours of continuous use in these below-freezing temperatures, Steve's headlamp was getting low and would soon go out. But leave it to Steve—he had packed a spare battery! It was pitch black, however, and we couldn't change the battery without some light. Fortunately, the batteries in my flashlight had built up just enough power to provide weak light—enough to allow Steve to change his battery.

We couldn't find the trail, but we knew where we were and where we had to go. We had a map and compass, so we bushwhacked down. The route was often steep, but entirely downhill, and the ground was clear of snow and ice. At the bottom was a stream, and I crossed it. "What are you doing?" asked Steve. "Isn't this Woodland Creek?" I replied. "We have to cross this stream to get to our car, right?" Steve responded that I was not right. The map showed that we had encountered a tributary that led down to Woodland Creek. So I crossed back. Shortly before 1:00 AM we finally arrived at Woodland Creek. I saw lights across the stream and knew there was a bridge nearby, but after walking for a few minutes, we still couldn't find the bridge.

Now I was getting impatient—all we had to do was get across the stream! I decided to walk across. The water was deeper than my high Sorel boots, which got completely soaked. And the temperature was 20°! Steve had walked a few hundred feet farther along the stream and found the bridge, so he stayed dry. We found Jim's car unlocked. A note on the windshield read: "When you didn't come back by 9:00 PM, I called the police, and they called the Forest Ranger. If you don't get back before dawn, they're going to start a search for you. If you do get back before dawn, call the police. There is a phone at the end of the campground." I left Steve in the car and walked down to the phone. No phone number was posted for the police (this was before "911"), so I dialed "0" and asked for the police. The operator responded, "Is this an emergency?" "Well, I guess it is," I replied. "Okay," she said, "which police do you want?" "I don't know which police I want! I'm calling from the Woodland Valley Campground, and here is the number I'm calling from."

I was connected to the Phoenicia Police, and they put the Forest Ranger on the line. The ranger was Pat Rudge, whom I had encountered several times. She was pleased to hear that we were fine and put Jim on, who told us that he would call his parents to let them know we were safe. Pat said that she and Jim would be there in half an hour.

I returned to the car and found Steve sound asleep. I could not wake him. I ate some food that had been left for us and took off my soaking wet boots and socks. Even the wet Sorel boots had kept my feet relatively warm. There was clothing in the car, but no socks, so I wrapped up my feet in anything that I could find. At 2:00 AM, Pat arrived with Jim. I expected a strong rebuke from her. True, we were both fine and no search had to be conducted, but we had violated a number of standard safety rules, wasted several hours of her time, and undoubtedly had caused great anguish to Steve's and Jim's parents. Pat got information from me and said, "I just want to ask you one question: did you have matches with you?"

Matches were not something that I normally took along on a day hike, and it never occurred to me that we might want to build a fire. But the previous morning I used matches to light the stove, and I had put those matches in my daypack. So I could truthfully respond, "Yes, I did have matches." Pat asked, "Are you too tired to drive?" We both replied that we could drive home. Satisfied, Pat drove off. It was now 2:30 and we still had to drive to my car.

There was one question that still puzzled me. It had taken us ten hours to get back from the Rocky-Balsam Cap col, where Jim had left us. Six and one half of those hours were spent hiking after dark. Granted, Jim took an easier way to get back to the marked trail and presumably got there much faster than we did, giving him additional daylight hours to hike out. But the ice-covered slopes of Cornell and Wittenberg were extremely treacherous, and Jim had only my instep crampons—of limited value on steep, icy slopes. There was no way that he could have followed the Cornell-Wittenberg-Slide Trail back to Woodland Valley in only three and one half hours from the time we left him. And he could not possibly have done any significant hiking after dark, since it was very dark out and he had no flashlight. Yet, somehow, Jim was here, and obviously had arrived some time ago. How could this be?

I asked Jim, and he replied: "Yes, I had a lot of trouble getting up Cornell on the steep, icy trail. I knew that I could never succeed in safely descending the steep slopes of Wittenberg. More importantly, by the time I reached the summit of Cornell, I had only an hour of daylight left, and I realized that I could never complete the intended hike route in that time. The map showed an unmarked trail that led from the Cornell-Wittenberg col down to Moon Haw Road; I figured this two- to three-mile trail was my only hope of getting out before dark. The slope faced south, so I thought that it probably would not be ice-covered. Sure enough, I found this unmarked trail and, as I hoped, it was largely free of snow and ice and I made good time; it took about two hours. Just as it was getting completely dark, I reached the road and saw house lights in the distance. Someone was pulling out of his driveway and offered me a ride to Phoenicia. Someone else gave me a ride to Woodland Valley."

Wow! I said to myself. *In all the years I've hiked in the Catskills, I never hiked that trail. I've never even been able to find it! And here Jim can find it when the top portion is covered with ice, and somehow follows it all the way to Moon Haw Road.* If Jim hadn't made it out before dark—and he almost didn't—nobody would have looked for him there. As amazing as our story was, Jim's was even more incredible; it was a miracle that he got out of the woods safely.

Shortly after 3:00 AM, we arrived at my car. The adventure was over! But a dangerous part of the journey was still ahead. I told Jim to follow me until we got back to Route 28. While I had felt very much awake up to this point, once I started driving I began to get very sleepy. I started seeing strange lights ahead of me and barely stayed awake to Route 28. I could drive no farther, so I pulled into a parking lot and promptly fell asleep. I woke up in a few minutes and tried to continue driving, but in another mile I had to stop again. It took me four hours to get home, a distance which can be covered in two hours if there's no traffic (and there wasn't any). I finally arrived home at 7:00 AM.

Why, I wondered, with all the potential for disaster, had this hike ended so well? Our preparations, training and experience helped. Moreover, Steve and I each corrected the mistakes the other made. But I believe that the most important factor was our attitude. We kept calm the whole time and were able to think and reason. Although we never doubted that we would make it back to the car, we took our time, realizing that it was better to go slowly and carefully than to rush and possibly get injured. I think that our attitude was the most decisive factor that made the difference between the happy ending of this hike, and the far less pleasant endings of other hikes. 🏃

5

THE ESCARPMENT TRAIL: A JOURNEY

WHY DO I DO THIS?

Michael J. Molinski

The beginning of the trip was rainy and foggy. Each little drop felt like it was pounding on my pack and on my body. I could feel the ripple effect flowing into my mental well-being. Not the impression one would like to have at the start of a grand journey.

Windham High Peak is the first summit, and as I walk up the mountain run-off, I can feel my heart pounding through my chest. The blood coursing through my jugular feels as though it is going to break through my skin. For the first time in a while, I think, *I AM ALIVE!*

Many thoughts run through my head as I walk alone through the woods. I play out various situations in my mind's eye of "what ifs"—pretty much worst-case scenarios. The first symptom of thirst hits me ever so slightly. Rather than reach over my shoulder to find the tube of my Camelbak, I turn my head up to the treetops and try to catch the drops of rain. The hood of my poncho deflects the water before I can taste it. Humored, I move on.

The Escarpment Trail zigzags its way across the mountaintop with grand vistas of the Hudson Valley and Berkshire Mountains to the east, and several peaks of the Catskill Forest Preserve to the west. I keep myself mentally occupied by singing lines of country songs in my head—the same few words over and over and over. It annoys me that I can't remember entire songs, but there is nothing I can do about it except try to find ways to merge into other songs. Going from George Strait to Tom Petty to Tenacious D in a few short minutes is a feat in itself.

Just before the halfway point, a sign at the Batavia Kill Trail junction reads that it's just 0.9 miles to the top of Blackhead Mountain. Only that far? I check my map again and try to calculate the altitude change, but the almost merging contour lines make it difficult. This is very steep! A wave of depression hits me like a runaway boulder down the hillside. My legs aren't working as efficiently as I would have expected. A month and a half of drinking and partying has betrayed my body. I can't get more than a few yards up the mountain before I have to rest. I ask myself, *How do we climb mountains?* With no one around to hear me, I say aloud, "One step at a time."

North Point, view of North-South Lake. Photograph by Carol White.

With that little self-encouraging statement, I make it a few more yards before I have to stop again. I can feel my heart trying to beat out of my chest. I am sure every vein is popping out of my head and neck. The lack of food and water is also taking its toll on my withering body. I brought only 1.5 liters of fresh water, some Christmas cookies, and one MRE.[1] Having eaten all but one cookie, I plan to save the last one for breakfast because I know I am not getting out of here before dark.

This is the longest 0.9-mile journey of my life. An hour has elapsed since I passed the sign. I might be halfway there—no way to tell for sure. I hear a raven nearby. I mockingly say out loud, "Even death is taunting me." Fresh tracks in the mud tell me people are not far away. They probably climbed out of Batavia Kill. I can't tell if I am hearing voices in the distance, or if it's the wind or just my imagination. Within minutes a father and son team walk down the trail. We exchange greetings and move on. Well, at least *they* move on. I am still catching a rest on a nearby fallen tree. The compounding effects of adding a third of my body weight onto my back and having consumed little food and water is acting like a great negative synergy.

I reach the peak and feel like crying, but I can't. I bop myself in the nose to initiate the body's natural watery-eye response. It works. I just forgot *how* to cry. I celebrate my summit with the dessert portion of my military-style meal, which has been in my basement for years. It has to be at least fifteen years old, but delicious, nonetheless. For instant energy, I pour mouthfuls of orange-flavored drink mix. I assume the jolt of pure sugar will kick my body into overdrive and I'll make up some lost time.

Thirty minutes after my "lunch," the muscles in my thighs start to quiver and then knot up. The once fresh and oxygen-rich blood that fueled my muscles has turned into concrete mixed with lactic acid. I can no longer walk, and fall to the ground. It feels like a bad dream. Even thinking of moving my legs sends shockwaves of pain up my torso. I roll to the side and see coyote dung. I can't wait to get out of this hostile territory. I waste half an hour of daylight this way, and then get back on the trail heading down to the Dutcher's Notch Trail, putting one foot in front of the other and resting periodically before an incline. I will now refer to this method of hiking as "the zombie walk." I am not thinking about anything except where my next step will be—usually about sixteen inches in front of the last.

After getting past the notch, I gain a small amount of altitude and plateau for a mile. I turn my cell phone on and am surprised to find that I'm in service. I get bombarded with voicemails and text messages. I take another shot of orange-flavored sugar and press on. Within minutes I find myself in paralysis again. I lie down next to a half-rotted log and make a few calls. I have to let my dad know what an idiot I am and that I have sabotaged myself twice in the last two hours. I glance over my shoulder and see another pile of coyote dung—the bad dream continues, the one where you're running from some faceless person or monster but you can't move fast enough. Only this isn't a dream and there's no one chasing me. I am stuck out here by myself. Depression hits again.

On my feet again, with another half hour of precious daylight wasted, I make more calls and set up a pickup time and place for tomorrow at noon. I mention to bring snacks if they feel like it. My body screams for nourishment and fuel. I make my way past an old plane crash site on Stoppel Point in the dimming twilight hours, hastily trying to make it to familiar landmarks. North Point is where I plan to camp, if I can make it before it gets too dark.

I run out of water about a mile away and find a small stream. As if on cue, the skies darken and light rain starts to fall. It's only a drizzle and stops by the time I close my water bottle. I make it to camp—a small rock ledge where I can set my poncho to block out the elements—with minutes of light to spare. My eyes have adjusted to the dimming ambiance, so I take little notice that night has fallen. I hastily set up camp. If there had been enough light, I probably would have taken the rocks out from under my bed. My solo tent is not self-supporting, and with no soft ground to stake it upright, I stuff my sleeping bag into it mummy-style. Taking off my wet boots and socks, I add a clean shirt to the mix and I jump in, ready for dinner.

Now I'd like to take a moment to mention how much I dislike tuna. I absolutely hate it. Just the smell of a tuna sandwich makes me want to vomit. That night, tuna and noodles with a packet of salt and mini Tabasco sauce never tasted so good, even if it was as old as I am.

I sleep in short periods throughout the night. The jagged rocks and howling wind make it hard to sleep peacefully. Every falling leaf or snapping twig makes my eyes jolt open, my hand clutching my machete at all times. I feel a light burning in my eyes and open them to see a half-moon beaming directly at me. I must have rolled onto my poncho and half ripped it down. I check my cell phone, and it's 12:45 AM. I adjust my camp and try to go back to sleep. Later I wake in the darkness with the small pitter-patter of rain hitting my face. This time I truly mummify myself under my sleeping bag and tent material. Only my nose is chilled by the atmosphere. Finally I drift into a semi-comfortable sleep.

The winds pick up and temperatures drop below freezing. The rain mixes with snow, and I try to bury myself deeper into my comfort zone. I only end up banging my head against the cliff, leaving myself a little souvenir. Sleep.

I snap awake to find my surroundings covered in white and the grayish sky turning pink at the horizon. I hastily make my way out of my sleeping bag, throw on a fresh pair of socks, pull on my boots, and scramble back up to the summit to catch the sunrise. For the second time in my life—less than three months after the first time—I will watch the sun slowly fill up the Hudson Valley from the mountain range.

My camera batteries have frozen dead in the night. I even try sticking them in my mouth to warm them up, but to no avail. I make my morning calls to let everyone know that I am alive and well. I have a few messages from friends during the night, talking about some party. If they only knew I was still stuck miles away from home! It takes less than twenty minutes to break down camp and be back on the trail. I am on a perfect pace to reach the extraction point by noon.

At the North-South Lake Campground, two miles below the summit, I make calls to see what my friends are up to and to make sure I still have a ride out of here. Then I make a wrong turn somewhere. I don't know what it is about paved roads that screws up my sense of direction. My body must have been happy to be walking on smooth ground and to be going slightly downhill. I waste about twenty minutes before I get myself back on the right path. And again, I am out of water.

I feel myself falling into the zombie walk again when the trail starts to make a steep incline. Scrambling boulder after boulder to Boulder Rock, I find a small puddle. It's too shallow to dip my bottle into, so I take my hat off and use it like a sponge to soak up nature's life source and wring it into my container. I sip half the bottle away during the hike's next couple of miles.

Hunger has taken its hold. I don't have any food left, and I haven't eaten since the tuna banquet fifteen hours before. From what I have read, pine needles contain high amounts of vitamin C. The next long-needled tree I see, I pull a handful off and stuff them in my mouth. The taste is bitter, yet satisfying. Or maybe not. I chew for a few minutes, swallowing it down with mouthfuls of water. It's not long before I am out of water again. And I was being so good at rationing my water! My natural urges are getting the best of me. Luckily, the night's rain has provided enough runoff to let me fill my bottle for the last time. The sight of dirt and muck floating in it doesn't bother me. I trust my filter. Every sip tastes like pine, however.

One step at a time, I find my way to Inspiration Point. I could really use some inspiration right now. I talk aloud to myself out of boredom and manage to stir up some motivation. I remember I had one more Christmas cookie left that I had purposely saved. It's a bunch of crumbs now, but applying a little muscle, it takes the form of a zip-lock bag corner. To add a little more joy to my life, I also find two crackers and some fortified cheese in my pack. I celebrate Inspiration Point by eating the last of my food and resting for ten minutes. Only an hour before noon, and then the trip is done.

If I were moving any slower, I'd be dead. I make it to the top of Kaaterskill Falls and look down a cliff of about 170 feet. There is no official trail from the top to the bottom, and it's treacherous. That's how I fell and got that really cool scar on my forearm. A small trail half a mile long leads from the bottom of the falls to a main road. Now looking as beat up as I feel, I slowly climb down the ravine and make my way to where people are gathering by the road. I sit and stare at the lower falls for half an hour before people start to make conversation and I get an idea of what time it is. No cell service makes for a bad clock. Apparently I had arrived at the extraction point fifteen minutes ahead of schedule. Maybe their car broke down?

I share stories of my experience with others, and the majority of the responses are that they had just eaten, but if they'd known I was starving they would have saved me something. I just smile and say I am fine. If my appetite could be personified, it would have punched me in the face.

I leave the falls after one o'clock and make it up to the parking lot above the trailhead. I have covered almost exactly twenty-four miles in the last thirty hours. I have gained over 5,800 vertical feet and descended about 5,300. That's like taking the stairs up and down the Empire State Building four times—with the added weight of a pack and boots.

In conclusion, this trip has changed me a little. I can't explain why I do the things I do; sometimes you just have to pick up your things and go. Life won't wait. I hope you enjoyed this journey, as I have. Maybe someone out there can find inspiration in this.🏃

---

[1] The Meal, Ready-to-Eat (MRE) is a self-contained, individual field ration in lightweight packaging procured by the United States military for its service-members for use in combat or other field conditions where organized food facilities are not available.

6

THE ESCARPMENT TRAIL END-TO-END

A Challenging Backpack
(distance, 24 miles; total elevation gain, 5,184 feet)

Kathleen Balthazar Heitzmann, #520, #230W

I left the village of Catskill at 9:30 AM with Scott Fiore, an eighteen-year-old with whom I work. We dropped a car off at Haines Falls on Route 23A, and then drove to the Windham terminus of the Escarpment Trail on Route 23. We were on the trail by 10:50, on a windy, sunny day in the seventies. We passed wild thyme, witch hazel, white pine, beech, striped maple, paper birch, and hemlock on the 450-foot climb to the Elm Ridge lean-to. After a short rest and water, we hiked through an old stand of spruce that gave us a feeling of peace as we treaded under the tall trees on pine needle groundcover. Climbing another 1,350 feet, we summited Windham High Peak at 1:00 PM, finding pin cherry and mountain ash at that elevation. Our lunch was an apple; Scott was yearning for a Big Mac! Leaving High Peak at 1:40, we picked blueberries and enjoyed beautiful mountain views from Burnt Knob and Acra Point.

After eight and a half miles we were so tired we decided to leave Blackhead Mountain for tomorrow. Scott's shoulders ached from his cheap backpack, and my arthritic hips ached from the weight of my pack; I'd carried most of our 5.5 quarts of water. I knew what an arduous hike Blackhead was, while the Batavia Kill lean-to was just a quarter-mile down the yellow trail. We arrived there at 5:45, gathered firewood and got water from the nearby stream. Scott was starving, so the tuna-noodle one-dish supper I'd learned to make on camping trips tasted good. I showed him how to use sand as an abrasive to scrub the pots. Finally, we were just sitting by the fire. I lit candles and began reading *The Hobbit*. I heard snoring; Scott was fast asleep.

I walked down the trail to enjoy the evening, but a new moon left no light and a flashlight provided no atmosphere, so I went to bed. At 3:00 AM a racket woke me up. I shone the flashlight onto four porcupines. They froze, but with constant light on them they ambled off. I built the fire back up, hoping I'd seen the last of them; they returned, but kept the noise down. We slept until 7:00 AM, and after a quick breakfast and lousy coffee (I must get my camp coffee-making skills up to par), we tackled the 1,100 feet up Blackhead, peaking in an hour after some very stiff hand-over-fist climbing.

Lunch was a grapefruit and water; Scott wasn't used to these light lunches! Next time he'll pack in emergency supplies like peanut butter and jelly sandwiches. He was drinking water for both of us, and I worried that we'd run out. We went in search of water from a spring four-tenths of a mile down from Dutcher's Notch; a frog was playing in the trickle that formed a small pool. I got enough into a small water bottle and gave it to Scott.

There's a Cessna plane wreck just below Stoppel Point, beyond which is a nice lookout to the Blackhead Range. This large, level area is sheltered in spruce. From there, the remaining nine miles were relatively easy. The weather was cool, but our T-shirts were soaked with sweat. North Mountain came up fast, and we could see scenic North Point. After a sardine supper, Scott wanted to call it a day, but I decided to go on. I left Scott at 6:30 with only one and a half hours to beat the dark; I descended as fast as I could.

At North Lake I found a phone and called my daughter to pick up Scott there, plus some things I'd emptied out of my pack to lighten it. I sometimes ran, not relishing the idea of hiking in the dark. Along the escarpment edge it became windy and scary. Lights came on across the ravine at Twilight Park. I was slowing down, so I pushed myself harder after Layman's Monument. It was 7:40—twenty minutes of daylight left. I could see Scott's car below. Wouldn't it be funny if I made it out before he got to my car? It was 8:00 PM with just 0.68 miles to go, but under the canopy of trees the trail makes an abrupt left, and it was hard to see trail markers. I could use the sound of Kaaterskill Falls on my right to guide me, but I didn't dare miss the turn ahead, so I took out the flashlight, straining to see those markers and wishing I was out—wishing I'd gotten up at six instead of seven. I finally saw a light—a headlight. I was almost out! I just had to see my way over those rocks … I leapt over them and almost missed the tree I reached out to grab.

Out at Last

Then, I climbed over the guardrails and up Route 23A to Scott's car. No Scott. His car had a flat tire! I looked for his keys, but he had forgotten to give them to me. I hitched a ride to a diner in Haines Falls and waited for him to pass in my car. Finally, I saw my little blue VW bug and jumped up and down waving my hands wildly—but Scott drove by. I rapidly explained the situation to the diner owner, who had been eyeing me suspiciously, and begged him to drive me down to Scott's car. He agreed! The look on Scott's face was indescribable when he saw me.

I don't think Scott had ever changed a tire, so after getting a jack from my car, I changed it and off we went. The next day I was way too sore to take my usual run! 🏃

Part II:
MISADVENTURES

I fell backwards and headfirst down the crack between the outer rock and the main cliff. A hiking buddy saw this, leaped to catch me, missed, and ended up spread-eagled on the outer rock looking over the edge. I, on the other hand, was wedged upside down between the outer rock and the main cliff, looking down two hundred feet to treetops and up at the bottom of that outer rock. … My partner couldn't reach me; I was too far away and the rock was too icy. No ropes, no other people on the trail, no help.

Steve Boheim

Photograph by Larry Gambon.

HUNG UP ON A CLIFF

THE RAPPEL WAS LONGER THAN THE ROPE

Ann L. Clapper, #13, #21W

My husband, Pete Fish, and I were experimenting with rock climbing and especially with rappelling. We would look for likely spots on the topographic maps and then go out and play with the rope. I found that I could do it pretty well, but I never quite got over the fear of going over the edge at the start, and I never tried a free rappel. Pete was very good at it, and he did it with ease and a good deal of flare.

Pete had always wanted to rappel Newman's Ledge near North Lake. We had looked at it, and it was definitely a free rappel and looked to be about 100 feet. Pete decided to try it on a Sunday afternoon in the late fall. The weather that day was cool and very windy. The plan was that Pete would rappel down and then walk south up an incline and connect with the trail. He fastened the rope to a sturdy tree and very carefully instructed me as to the proper way to coil the rope after he was down. I watched him go over the edge. As soon as the rope was loose, I worked on the project of coiling it properly and then fastened it to the pack and took off to meet him at the assigned spot on the trail. It took quite a while to coil the rope. I knew that he was very fussy, so I took the time to do it properly.

When I arrived at the meeting place, he was not there. I called to him, but the wind was blowing and I could not hear any reply. I waited for twenty minutes and then decided that he must have come along earlier and gone down to the car, so I hiked out. When I got to the car, he was not there and I started to get worried. It would be dark in an hour. I had no idea what to do. There was no one in the campground. I phoned my dad from a payphone at the ranger's cabin, and he said he'd come and help me find Pete. My dad prepared for the worst and put together flashlights, ropes, sleeping bags and other gear. My brother was coming as well.

Meanwhile, Pete had been in trouble. The rappel was longer than the rope! He landed on a ledge twenty feet above the ground with no apparent way to get down. He called to me, but I had already pulled up the rope. I could not hear him above the wind or see him from the top. All I could think about was taking care of that darned rope!

Pete stood on the ledge thinking about what to do. He had a lightweight length of rope around his waist with a carabiner attached. He took the rope off and used it to snag the upper branches of a nearby tree and pulled the branches in to him. He used the rope to tie the branches to a small shrub on the ledge, and then he leaped over onto the main part of the tree. He untied the rope, the tree sprang back, and he retrieved his rope and shinnied down the tree to the ground.

On the way back to the meeting place, he encountered more cliffs and searched for an easy way up. Unfortunately he ran into some "rotten" rock (pudding stone) and got hung up again. He could not go up; he could not go down. He stayed there for quite a while thinking about it. Finally, with much difficulty, he made his way up to the trail and descended to the car just at dusk. I ran to the phone and managed to stop the rescue mission just in time before they left home.

This was just one of the times that we made poor decisions in the woods as young people. After Pete became a forest ranger, he often shuddered as he remembered our arrogance and foolish lack of concern for our own safety. 🏃

Newman's Ledge, 1.3 miles north of North-South Lake Public Campground on the Escarpment Trail. Photograph by David White.

8

A REAL CLIFF-HANGER

HANGING BY A THREAD FROM GIANT LEDGE

Steve Boheim, #112

My first Catskill—or any 4,000-footer—climb was Slide Mountain, on Christmas Eve 1967. I bare-booted it from Slide Mountain Road, and caught the peak bagging bug. Most of our peak bagging was done in the summer of 1970. My hiking partner, from Syracuse, knew this guy from Forestry School … a PhD candidate named Mike Kudish.[1] We got lots of trailless trekking tips from Mike and did some of the trailless peaks with him. Mike could tell you the altitude plus or minus 200 feet just by looking at the vegetation (his 1971 thesis was "Vegetational History of the Catskill High Peaks"). Hiking with him was very interesting, educational, and successful—but there was a price: we'd bushwhack for a mile or two, then stop and he'd run a one-hundred-foot line in the woods and catalog all the vegetation on that line … from moss to trees. He knew all the Latin names. We learned a lot about trees, flora, and geology hiking with him. Thanks, Mike!

I had a crew cut and my hiking buddy had long hair, so when we wanted to get permission from landowners to hike on their land (e.g., to North Dome), we soon learned that I should do the talking and my buddy should stuff his hair up under a cap and keep his distance from the landowner. Apparently the "hippies" liked to arrive in Volkswagen buses from New York City and party naked in the streams, scaring the cows. We didn't see any naked hippies or scared cows, but we did get to bag various peaks with the landowners' okay.

We climbed Doubletop—our first encounter with coniferous blowdown, which we had to crawl under for extended distances—and Big Indian and Fir on a hot August day. We ran out of water halfway to Fir, and headed south-southwest from its summit to hit a tributary down to Biscuit Brook. Finding the beginnings of a stream, we drank our fill. Back then, on trailless hikes where water first emerges out of the mountain, we thought nothing of doing this and never had gastrointestinal repercussions. I was sitting there re-hydrating, idly dangling my hand in this nascent stream, and I found, well submerged, a capped Coke bottle, bubbles within, ready to go, just like it had come out of a vending machine. We put it back, amazed.

The Memorable Finish

In January 1972 my last climb to finish the list was Panther, in winter, over Giant Ledge. After admiring the easterly view from Giant Ledge and turning to head off to Panther, my foot slipped on the ice and I fell backwards and headfirst down the crack between the outer rock and the main cliff. My hiking buddy saw this, leaped to catch me, missed, and ended up spread-eagled on the outer rock looking over the edge. I, on the other hand, was wedged upside down between the outer rock and the main cliff, looking down two hundred feet to treetops and up at the bottom of that outer rock. What saved me were my WWII surplus canteens with hip belt, which had jammed me into the crack. My partner couldn't reach me; I was too far away and the rock was too icy. No ropes, no other people on the trail, no help.

So, I did a lot of praying, then turned myself around, right side up, and tried to chimney up that crack, which was all ice on the eastern, main cliff side. I got myself right side up without falling, though to this day I have no idea how I did it. We tried to use my hiking belt with canteens as a rope, but we dropped it and it plunged into the trees below. I somehow got myself up the crack by pressing against the ice with my back against the outer rock, and up I went. I got out and waited for my heart to slow down. Another hiker came along and said, "Nice view." Little did he know what we had just been through. Then we headed off to finish Panther, uneventfully. I don't recommend this method of seeing Giant Ledge in the winter! 🏃

[1] See "First-Growth Forests vs. Ski Slopes."

View from Giant Ledge. Photograph by Larry Gambon.

A HEART ATTACK IN THE CATSKILLS

GOOD HEALTH IS A PRECIOUS THING

Bleecker Staats, #272
from Autumn 1984 *Catskill Canister*

There is an awesome stillness on Round-top this morning, and the clear, thirty-degree air is just what we had hoped for. It is 5:30 AM, May 17, as we slide out of our sleeping bags, grab our cameras, and head toward the ledge. Only the crunching of our boots on the frozen duff[1] breaks the stillness. Cold as it is, the scent of balsam is heavy in the air.

Peter, my freelance writer friend, his St. Bernard named George, and I spent yesterday ascending via a circuitous route from Platte Clove. Despite the intermittent snow showers, a myriad of peppermint-faced spring beauties and blue violets burst forth everywhere. Bushwhacking our way over slippery slabs and getting under, over, and around the numerous blowdowns was not easy. My pack frame seemed to catch on every limb and root as we scrambled up the ledges. By later afternoon we had reached the summit and had anchored the tarp against the wind and lingering snow showers. The venison stew by a small fire topped off a good day's hike. It was not long before tired muscles, full stomachs, and the wind in the balsams brought deep sleep.

Now the time has come when we will view dark and massive Kaaterskill High Peak against the sunrise. And there it is, the distant bright-orange dot finally appearing against the pale sky. The first rays are gilding tiny clouds around Mount Greylock in Massachusetts. Now the golden glow begins to tint the shoulder of High Peak and spills into the valley below. It reminds me of a painting done from this spot by Thomas Cole over a century ago. It is time just to sit and watch this beautiful scene change from dark tones and shadows to rosy pinks and slate blues. It is time, too, for personal reflection and to feel grateful just to be here at this glorious Catskill sunrise.

My last backpack was eight months ago, and on that late-September day the weather was sunny, cool, and clear. Pete, "Uncle Ben," and I were the advance party of ten hikers named "Bleecker's Creepers" by Ben, because we take our time. We were headed for Deer Shanty Brook lean-to and had driven in through Claryville. I had carried my pack for about five minutes when the pressure on my upper body caused a sickening, aching tightness in my chest and neck. Although the pack was no more than forty-five pounds, it seemed to me to be too much for a fifty-four-year-old who works at a desk all day. By the time we reached the lean-to, I thought that I was going to vomit. Removing the pack, I sat down. Soon we moved farther upstream to a larger, more private area for our weekend camp. I did not mention my discomfort to anyone, for we had only a short distance to go, and I was convinced that either the waist strap was not tight enough to take the weight from my shoulders, or my body was telling me that I was no longer a young man. What a relief it was to get that pack off again and to set up camp. We had it all done in fifteen minutes, and by then my discomfort was gone.

The next morning we ate a late breakfast beneath the hemlocks. With only daypacks we began to climb up Table Mountain. We rested at every place there was a view and ate lunch on the sunny top of Peekamoose Mountain. I had never seen such a large crop of mountain ash berries! The red clusters were beautiful against the clear blue and green of the Catskill landscape. Later, the view from Table was the best I had ever seen it. Twenty-five of the other 3,500-foot peaks and the Ashokan Reservoir seemed a ten-minute hike away. Excited as I was to be capturing all this on film, it was hard to realize that less than a day earlier I had felt so miserable.

Charged with the sight of Lone Mountain, Carolyn led the bushwhack to our destination. This was her last peak needed to qualify for membership. We gave her a big round of applause when she signed the canister register at the summit. After a short rest we descended between Lone and Table to our Neversink campsite for a champagne toast to Carolyn. It had been a long, happy day, and it didn't take long for the low gurgling of the Neversink to have us all fast asleep.

Ten days later, my first sip of coffee at my desk suddenly brought that sickening tightness again. My left arm began to feel numb. I headed to the medical department and felt better while lying down and getting an EKG. Next was the sort of fun experience of my first ambulance ride to a local hospital for more tests. A cardiologist informed me that I had experienced a myocardial infarction (MI) and would be admitted to the coronary care unit immediately. Tests also indicated that I had experienced a worse MI within the past two weeks; did I recall the last time I had experienced angina? I mentioned my Catskill weekend and the discomfort I had felt. The staff was appalled that I had not taken the angina more seriously and that I had climbed three mountains the next day.

In two weeks it was another ambulance ride to the Westchester Medical Center, where an angiogram indicated a blockage in the coronary arteries. A cardiologist recommended open-heart surgery to improve the blood flow to my heart. If everything went well, I would probably be back in the Catskills in half a year. A team of surgeons spent seven hours performing a quadruple bypass on me. How could it have happened to me, I wondered? I'm not overweight, I don't have high blood pressure, my job doesn't seem stressful, I climb a lot, and I sit around very little. I learned that arteriosclerosis was the cause of my problem. Recuperation was in the form of resting, reading, and walking. I started with about a fifty-yard walk, three times a day, and each day added to the distance. By the time of my physical stress test in April, I had worked my way up to a daily jaunt of five miles in ninety minutes. With the doctor's approval, I was on my first Catskill hike on April 27. We took the Escarpment Trail from North Lake to North Point for lunch, and back through Mary's Glen. I had no chest pain at all, but there were times when I wished that they had done a bypass on my knees as well.

On this mid-May morning on Roundtop, the sun has climbed higher, lighting the eastern horizon on both sides of the still-dark Kaaterskill High Peak. The shadowy valley below is split by the pale blue ribbon of the Hudson River. Below, resting quietly in purple velvet, the mirror surfaces of North and South lakes reflect the glory of the dawn. I am reminded how thrilled and thankful I am to be present in this Catskill setting. From here everything seems so far away. Far away, too, seems the time of the heart attack.

In the March–April 1992 *Canister*, Bleecker wrote: November 16th was a crisp day with patches of snow among the leaves and rocks as Bill Tucker and I climbed into the cloud cover of North Dome. If it weren't for the compass, I would have headed us in the opposite direction to Sherrill out of the saddle. After a brief lunch amid mossy, icicled boulders that protected us from the northwest wind, we ascended to the summit of Sherrill—not just my 165th climb of a Catskill 3500-foot peak, but my fifty-sixth climb since a quadruple bypass heart operation in October 1983. Today marked the point where I've climbed all the Catskill 3500 peaks since the operation. Maybe it's a first? Is there a Catskill 3500 patch with a little red heart on it? Good health is a precious thing. We should work at it in the amount of exercise we get and, most of all, in what we eat. On the way down I thought of my personal triumph and thanksgiving, and wanted to share the joy of my accomplishment with all my fellow climbers. 🏃

---

[1] Partly decayed organic matter on the forest floor.

10

NOT JUST ANOTHER DAY IN THE WOODS

BROKEN BONE ON PANTHER MOUNTAIN IN WINTER

John Swanson, #592, #187W
from April–June 2002 *Catskill Canister*

December 26 started out like many other winter days. My friend Nan Giblin was leading a group of seven hikers up Panther Mountain. The temperature was below twenty degrees, but not bitterly cold. After a brief introduction and gear check, we headed up the trail at a steady pace. There wasn't enough snow to require snowshoes—bare ground showed through in places. The trail was a little slippery, but we easily skirted any patches of ice. Two and a half hours later we reached the summit of Panther, where we stopped to snack and enjoy the view.

I fell into my role as the sweep when we started down. About 400 feet below the summit, I heard someone yell. I couldn't see what had happened, but could tell something was wrong. The upbeat, jovial conversation had changed to concern.

I had just completed a wilderness first-aid recertification course given by Jonathan Silver, Chairman of the Wilderness First Aid Committee of the Appalachian Mountain Club, and felt a need to rush to the scene to help; I had to restrain my urge to run. The first rule of rescue went through my mind: don't make yourself the second victim. When I got to the group, one of the hikers, Russ Bebb, was sitting on the ground. He had slipped and fallen while stepping down a short, rocky section of the trail. Nan thought Russ' arm might be broken and asked me to look.

We were in a situation most leaders hope they never have to experience. A participant was injured, miles from the road, in winter conditions. I knew we had to act in a controlled manner to prevent things from going from bad to worse. The good news: we had a strong group with adequate gear, it was not bitterly cold, and we were on a modest incline that posed no additional risk to the group, the patient, or me.

In times of crises at home, we can pick up the phone and dial 911. In the field it's different. While it's possible to call for help with a cell phone, the response time is likely to be several hours. We needed to provide Russ with immediate first aid. Handling a wilderness emergency efficiently requires teamwork and leadership. Many tasks need to be done simultaneously. Resources must be assigned to provide first aid and support the first-aid effort, as well as to plan and execute the evacuation. The group must be informed, nourished, and protected from the elements. While Nan managed the accident scene and directed the group, I focused on the patient.

I started with the basics—A, B, C, D, and E: Airway, Breathing, Circulation, Disability, and Environment. I confirmed that the first three were fine, then considered the possibility of spinal injury. We were fortunate, however, and this was not a serious accident. Russ had simply slipped and fallen, injuring only his arm. As for Environment, we had to keep Russ insulated from the cold. Cold ground sucks life-sustaining warmth from the patient at a rapid rate. In ten minutes he could begin the deadly slide into hypothermia and, more importantly, shock. I asked him if he could move himself onto his pack if we helped. He thought it was possible, and John, another hiker, and I helped Russ off the ground. Now, we needed to ensure that he stayed warm. He was already wearing all his layers, so Nan wrapped him in her expedition-weight parka.

Priorities addressed, I reached into my pack and pulled out my first-aid kit, which is about half as big as a one-liter water bottle. It looked awfully small and inadequate, but I knew we could put together what we needed. The name of the game in the field is "improvisation." Next, we had to work on the diagnosis and treatment of Russ' injuries. I keep an accident form in my first-aid kit to use as a guide and ensure that I get all the details recorded. I questioned Russ and found him to be alert and oriented. I did not uncover any important medical conditions. I looked for other injuries that might have been masked by the pain in his arm, but I found none.

I never doubted that the arm was broken. Russ was in serious pain, and the arm was crooked. It needed to be splinted for support and immobilization during the evacuation back to the cars. I had no SAM splint (a common commercial splint), so I started with a small foam pad. This being too small, I tried my crampon bag, which had a rigid plastic liner. That worked better, but more padding was needed, so I decided to use the foam and a small towel that someone offered. I made a sling from a triangular bandage, inserted Russ' injured arm, and tied it to his body with straps so the arm would be immobilized. Then adjustments were made to alleviate any discomfort.

We helped Russ to his feet. I asked him to take a little jump to test the splint. He jumped and confirmed that the splint felt secure. On the walk out, I supported Russ with his uninjured arm draped round my shoulders. Keeping our balance was difficult, so I shed my pack and the contents were divided among the group. I put on crampons for better traction, and we started again. Along the way we talked, told stories and jokes to pass the time and keep up our spirits. At 1:30 PM we reached County Route 47. Once in the hospital, the doctor confirmed that Russ' arm was severely broken.

We had been lucky in being able to perform a self-rescue. Had our efforts uncovered more serious injuries that prevented self-rescue, we would have called or sent someone out to get help from the Department of Environmental Conservation. 🏃‍♀️

Lookout Ledge on Panther Mountain. Photograph of David White by Carol White.

11

NOT IN MY BACKYARD

ADVENTURES IN A 300,000-ACRE BACKYARD

Laurie Moore Rankin, #1337, #531W

"**N**ot in my backyard" is a phrase that brings to mind things like landfills, jails, new malls. But for me, fortunate enough to have grown up in the heart of the Catskill Mountains, NIMBY means I was going to reconsider becoming a member of the Catskill 3500 Club because I'd have to climb the dreaded Slide Mountain in my "backyard," not once, but twice. Slide Mountain, to those of us who have lived here, is the proverbial "tourist trap" of the mountains. Hoards of people seem to be there at all times, and many lack outdoor skills. So, if I were to meet the 3500 Club's criteria, I would go there only on a weekday when the trails are quiet.

Thus it was that I set off one bitterly cold February Tuesday morning in brilliant sunshine. Waiting anxiously at the door the moment she saw the backpack was my faithful little beagle, Jenny. Every square inch of her was wagging along with her tail.

There was only one other car in the parking lot. The stream was covered with so much ice that it was difficult to even notice that it was there; the usual wildly flowing waters could not be heard. It was a pleasant day, but I was anxious to complete this required hike. I climbed with Jenny on her leash to the 3500-foot elevation point. The first scattered balsam firs begin about here, and so did the first of the snowshoe hare tracks. Barely noticeable to the human eye in the fresh snow, the sparse hare's tracks were an exciting thing to a beagle's nose!

Shortly beyond the 3500 foot elevation, the trail swings quite sharply to the left and you begin to enter the balsam forest in earnest. The balsams were covered in a layer of ice and then snow, brilliant in the sunshine and providing jewel after sparkling jewel to the human eye. With each step the firs became heavier and heavier with ice until finally they bent completely over the trail, creating a living tunnel of firs, ice and snow. We were not the only ones to hike through here. Under the cover of the frozen firs, the snowshoe hares had developed a series of interstate highways that caused me to laugh out loud at their tracks—and Jenny to eagerly ask to be let off the leash! Occasional breaks in the fir tunnel allowed us to see the deepest-of-deep blue sky that can only be seen on a cold winter day.

Under continuing sunshine, the temperature had climbed; with barely a breath of air stirring. I was greatly surprised by the breaking of ice on a branch overhead, allowing the fir freedom, showering me with ice, and filling the air with the most wonderful aroma. This phenomenon continued beyond the junction with the Curtis Ormsbee Trail, and soon we were not only smelling, but I think even tasting, the balsam as more and more of the broken ice fell on us. We reached the viewpoint that looks north, and what a treat for the eyes, with several of the Catskill high peaks framed by frozen balsams. We soaked in the view and turned back to the trail, where we were surprised by a gentleman who had spent the night on the summit and was just returning. He said hello to Jenny and me and warned me not to try to go off the summit toward Cornell, for it was very icy on the trail.

That left the summit for just us to enjoy. I reflected for some time on this special place in my backyard, where all my preconceived ideas had been dissipated by the mountain. I was humbled that all this beauty is waiting for us in our backyard, if we only take the time to find it, and I was glad that the 3500 Club required this peak to be climbed twice, including once in the winter. I have returned to Slide Mountain every winter to see how things are in my back yard, to see if maybe, just maybe, there could be another climb like that first one with a special joy for all the senses—and the mountain has rarely failed me.

One cold March day with those bright deep-blue winter skies, I was fortunate enough to see a bald eagle soar overhead. On another March day, my son and I thought we could climb the entire Burroughs Range and not get caught in the predicted snowstorm. We did get caught in the storm, but what an awesome view we got of its approach from near the spring! Another March day found me at the summit in dense fog and pouring rain. The stream crossing was impossible and upon returning to the trail head, and while looking for another crossing, I came upon a flock of several hundred snow geese. They were so camouflaged in the snow that I heard them before I saw them, despite their great numbers.

Then there was the humblest of winter hikes to Slide, the one that I led for the 3500 Club one March. It was a great group of hikers, all with winter experience. We had a wonderful time climbing to the summit of Slide and beyond to Cornell, where we enjoyed endless views and some great "butt sliding" along the way. The toughest part of the climb, the "chimney" between Cornell and Wittenberg, was managed with a rope and the assistance of a very well-placed tree. All of the hikers grabbed the rope and made their way to the bottom unharmed. Then it was my turn. After breathing a sigh of relief that they had all descended unharmed, I swung onto the rope—not paying attention—and my snowshoe caught in the ledge. I felt my knee rip with great pain, and I fell none too gracefully to the bottom of the chimney.

Slide Mountain summit in Winter. Photograph by Andrew Moroz.

I told the group that I was fine, and limped along to the beautiful summit of Wittenberg with its excellent views, hoping to "walk off" the pain in my knee—but knowing there was no way that I was going to. We stopped there to eat, and I sat down to take the weight off my knee. That was a big mistake, in retrospect, as the pain when I put my weight back on my knee afterward was tremendous. I smiled and told everyone that I would "sweep," meaning that I'd be the last in line, not letting anyone else get behind—but in this case it was so that I could cry quietly as I limped along.

I gave serious thought to telling the group that I had really hurt my knee and might need help to get off the mountain, but we were in the middle of nowhere, some 4.6 miles from the nearest trailhead, when I hurt my knee. Being a hike leader means that you have the responsibility of everyone's welfare, and I felt that it would put the others in jeopardy if they had to try to carry me off that mountain. I also felt that it was best if I just kept moving. Stopping at the summit of Wittenberg was the toughest part of the day, and I firmly believe that if I had not had snow to put some "padding" between myself and the ground on every step, I would not have made it off that mountain without assistance.

The next day the orthopedic doctor was amazed at what I had done, as I had torn the meniscus in my left knee. Thankfully, it did not call for surgery, just a brace. With that and several weeks of physical therapy, I was back on the trail in a few months.

Childhood Memories

Other parts of the Catskills and I are great friends as well. My father was the fire observer on Balsam Lake Mountain for several years, including the years that I was growing up. I have many fond childhood memories from that mountain, and a few scary ones as well. I can still hear the sound of a bobcat "screaming" near dark just below the cabin. We kids were always outside just before dark, enjoying the last few minutes. My father identified the sound right away and thought it came from the area of the big swamp. He assured us that the bobcat didn't want to have anything to do with us, but I was not convinced and did not play outside near dark for a few days!

My father would always point out clawed or bitten trees or telephone poles along the road to the tower where bears had marked their territory. He would stop the jeep and look new ones over, and talk about how large the bear likely was that made the mark. I knew, just knew, that I would be having an encounter with a bear that day, and I stayed well within the boundaries of the summit clearing in hopes of not getting eaten. I never saw a bear when I was on that mountain, however.

We didn't walk the road often; we usually rode in the jeep unless checking telephone lines. This could be slower than walking, depending on the jeep's temperament. I was always fearful that we would roll over on the steep hills. My father sometimes drove without brakes; he would just turn the ignition off at the top of the hills and coast down. I was so terrified that, for a time, I refused to ride in the jeep and got out and walked instead, getting back in at the bottom of each steep grade. Occasionally my grandmother came with us, and she always joined me in walking those hills. The jeep never did roll over while my dad was behind the wheel, but later, as a hiker, I came across a jeep that had rolled off the next-to-last hill and was leaning against a tree. This jeep had gone around the locked state access gate, and was an illegal use of a motorized vehicle on state land.

Every April for my birthday I got to go to work with Dad for the day. I always looked forward to this. One April day the tower, including each individual step, was completely encased in several inches of ice. My father said that I didn't have to go up to the cab, but I insisted. I don't remember ever being fearful of climbing the tower, except for that morning. I was so very relieved to reach the cozy cab, with no wind and no ice and my Dad's thermos of coffee to share.

Having spent much of my childhood wandering around the summit of Balsam Lake and nearby Graham, one would think I could lead a hike to the summit of Graham, right? Wrong. If I hadn't been talking so much, I would've looked around instead of blindly following previous snowshoe tracks—which led to nowhere. Highly embarrassed, I explained that the old jeep road to the tower had very steep hills, which in spring would be covered with ice until late May. To reach the tower by jeep, Dad would go around these hills on "bypass roads." We had followed someone's tracks at the top of one of the bypasses and ended up nowhere.

Eventually summiting Graham in deep snow, we ran right into an ice storm! The old tower base on that mountain provided shelter from the biting ice that was falling. We later had to break through ice to get into our cars! 🏃🏃

12

BREAK ON BIG INDIAN MOUNTAIN

BROKEN LEG ON A REMOTE BUSHWHACK

Bleecker Staats, #272
from September–December 1991 *Catskill Canister*

The phone rang; it was Marlene. The beautiful April morning had changed her mind and she decided to join us on the hike to Fir and Big Indian. At the trailhead the temperature was already in the upper sixties. In no time we reached the Biscuit Brook lean-to, where we stopped for a snack before starting the bushwhack up Fir Mountain. The now 70° temperature made the climb a hot one. We signed in at Fir's canister and over lunch recalled the last time we had hiked here, with "Uncle Ben." It was Ben who had labeled us "Bleecker's Creepers" because of the pace at which we hike.

On our way to Big Indian, we crossed a large patch of snow, and an impromptu snowball fight broke out. I can't recall ever having such fun in the snow while wearing shorts! Negotiating the hobblebush and spruce was a challenge, but soon Big Indian's leafless summit loomed ahead. We were at 3,440 feet, a half mile from our goal.

Then it happened. Marlene slipped on leaf-covered frozen ground and exclaimed that her leg was broken. The lump above her left ankle seemed to confirm this. Janet, an X-ray technician, knew the best position of the injury to reduce the pain, and a space blanket and extra clothing were placed under Marlene to make her as comfortable as possible. It was decided that five fast hikers—Piet, John, Shawn, Catherine, and Bill—would go for help while Alice, Janet, Loraine, Mary, Paula, Gordon and I stayed with Marlene. It was 3:15 PM. Logistics alone meant help might not come for hours.

Piet drove to the nearest house, where the occupant telephoned the State Troopers and the Department of Environmental Conservation. Soon Claryville and Grahamsville Fire Department volunteers arrived at the house, joined by Frost Valley employees and DEC rangers—all ready to begin the rescue.

Back on the shoulder of Big Indian, we slid a plastic tarp under Marlene, piled on more clothes, and took turns supporting her leg. When it began to rain, we covered her with more plastic and started a fire. Marlene was as cheerful as she could be under the circumstances, and expressed concern for our uninformed families and for the risk to our own well-being in staying with her. Not one of us, of course, would've considered leaving.

About 11:00 PM, Bill came out of the night with the advance five-person rescue team of rangers and paramedics. They wasted no time in putting a splint on Marlene's leg and sliding her into a sleeping bag and tent. After beefing up the fire, they tied space blankets together to keep out the wind, and gave us fresh water and food. The rescue team then radioed our condition back to the Frost Valley command post, and from there it was relayed to our families. Janet got a little sleep with Marlene in the tent. The rest of us spent the windy, 48° night warming ourselves in front of the fire. I recall looking across the fire and seeing a row of nodding figures seated on a log against a backdrop of space blankets, tree trunks, and a starlit sky.

About 4:00 AM a message crackled on Ranger Rudge's radio: the main rescue team was on its way up. They arrived three hours later, carrying a litter, food and thermoses of hot drinks. They blanketed Marlene and strapped her into the litter. This was then attached to a backpack adaptation that allowed the rescuers to carry Marlene with her weight suspended from the centers of four pack frames. It took two and a half hours to negotiate the half-mile, 200-foot descent to the Pine Hill-West Branch Trail, where another group of rangers and volunteers waited with a wide-wheeled platform to attach to the bottom of the litter.

Frost Valley volunteers provided us with sandwiches, fruit and juice at the lean-to. Meanwhile, an ambulance was awaiting the arrival of Marlene's litter. On our way home, Alice and I stopped at Kingston Hospital. Both bones in Marlene's lower left leg were broken, and the doctors recommended a cast for six to eight weeks.

All of us will remember with gratitude the kind help of those volunteers who gave up their weekend to rescue us. Although I was not the one carried down that day, I witnessed enough caring in those volunteers, rangers, and my fellow hikers to carry me through the rest of my life. ⚐

13.

CATSKILL ADVENTURES AND MISADVENTURES

LESSONS FROM A SOLO HIKER

Ken Metzner, #1543

When I climbed the thirty-five Catskill 3,500-foot peaks and the four required Catskill winter peaks between May and December of 2004, I planned and prepared my outings carefully—or so I thought! My previous hiking and climbing experience had mainly been at higher altitudes above treeline, starting with hikes with my father and brothers in the Alps more than sixty years ago, and then more recent hikes in the American West. So perhaps I was a little cavalier approaching the lower-altitude Catskills.

Senior Moments

My first Catskills trip was in the May 2004 buggy season. After a three-hour drive from my home in Manhattan, I bushwhacked up Vly Mountain in light intermittent rain and got thoroughly soaked, hiking boots and all. I had rubber boots, but left them in the van. Descending, I took a "shortcut" without checking my compass, with the result that I veered south instead of west and had to circle back. No big deal; I was back in less than three hours. (I have always had what my wife Judy calls "adventures," so I am not allowed to take any shortcuts when we hike together.)

I stayed in a Prattsville motel that night, although I almost always ate and slept at the trailheads in my trusty VW EuroVan Camper equipped with stove, sink and fridge. The next morning I had to return from the trailhead to the motel to retrieve my forgotten wallet. I then bushwhacked up Bearpen Mountain wearing my rubber boots—much better for trudging through puddles. Above the early morning valley fog it was a sunny, bird-singing day.

In the afternoon I bushwhacked Halcott Mountain from Route 42. Partway up I put my glasses on a log to bug-spray myself and forgot to put them back on. I discovered the oversight ten minutes farther up through the trailless forest. Careful hiker? Right! I doubled back, trying to recognize that log, and lo and behold, I did find them, gold frames spotlighted by a ray of sunlight. Lucky this time. Descending by a shortcut again, I missed the trailhead by only (?) half a mile.

First lessons: check around for personal items before leaving after breaks; take better care with the compass.

A Bonanza of Peaks and the Canister Search

Over two days, I climbed Black Dome, Thomas Cole, Blackhead, Windham High Peak, Kaaterskill High Peak and West Kill without major mishap, except that I was greeted by a thunderstorm on Windham the first day and got thoroughly soaked again on the second day in thunderous rain descending West Kill. I met some other hikers for the first time.

On the third day my plan was to bushwhack up Southwest Hunter Mountain to find a canister nailed high on a tree with a logbook, and sign in. Rain-soaked and filthy, but warm, I was at a place where all directions led down. The summit, right? But I couldn't find the canister, even after thrashing around for twenty minutes in the undergrowth getting filthier and wetter and losing all sense of direction for the descent. In a clever move I pulled out my compass for the first time, but somehow the needle had gotten stuck. Again I was lucky: The sun came out and my watch was working, so I got a directional fix and found my way back to the trail.

In September I went back, and even in good weather I had to do the half-hour bushwhack twice before I noticed the cairns mentioned in the guidebook and found the darn canister. Of course the Canister Police go around regularly to all thirteen canister peaks, copy down all names and take them back to the Canister Verification Bureau to correlate with later applications for the coveted 3500 Club membership. Woe betide any cheaters. That was my paranoid fantasy as I hiked these lonesome trails. Just because I'm paranoid doesn't mean they're not after me.

Lesson: don't just bring essential equipment; check that it works and review how it works.

You may ask, "Why does he do this?" Why not enjoy a relaxed retirement, read, go to movies, plays, and concerts? I enjoy all that, but the lure of the mountains, the need to "get away," is built-in, perhaps imprinted in the genes. As a working adult with two sons, and then with second wife Judy and our daughter, there were ski trips and family outings, and I would sneak into the hills on business trips, but it was never enough. Now in retirement I have the time, and even though dreams of Denali have faded for lack of funds and the fading of youthful strength, there is an endless supply of mountains I haven't visited yet and peaks I haven't challenged.

My Van is Broken Into

Misfortune threatened on my next trip. I arrived late on a lovely June afternoon at the Spruceton Road trailhead at 2,100 feet, bound for 3,680-foot Rusk Mountain. It was going to be a short hike: a half mile on a very good trail, and then about a mile bushwhack to the summit. I got to the top okay, but the sun was setting. It was a new moon and I had forgotten to bring a flashlight, so I could not read my compass or map. I had also forgotten my trekking poles, so I had to make a pole from a fallen branch and feel my way down with it.

It took me so long, going carefully, to get back to the trail that it was pitch black by then and the trail was only a very faint whitening of the blackness. I kept crashing into bushes at the side of the trail, but at least there weren't any cliffs. The trail is an old road with a locked iron gate at the bottom, which I wouldn't be able to see in the blackness. Nearing it, I pulled out my keys to click on the headlights of the van, and had a weird thought that I might bang into the gate and drop my keys. And, precisely at that moment, I did smack hard into the gate and did drop my keys! I couldn't find them, searching on my knees in the blackness amongst the leaves and gravel. Spare keys were in the car, so I broke into my own car (I won't explain how easy that was). I didn't find the other set of keys until morning.

Lessons: check on sunset time, and sunrise for that matter, and the current moon phase when planning a hike; always take a headlamp; don't forget your hiking poles; and put spare car keys in your backpack.

Marc, Evan and Elena on Cornell Mountain summit. Photograph by Ken Metzner.

How to Avoid a Twenty-Mile Road Hike at the End of the Day

You would think I would've learned something by now and been more careful, but the next day was worse. My plan was to bushwhack straight up North Dome from the north (Spruceton Road), and then bushwhack west to Sherrill and back down to near my starting point. I made North Dome fine, but on the traverse to Sherrill I immediately ran into cliffs. I tried going around them to the south, but I didn't recalculate my compass bearing, going by feel in a dreamy kind of mood on that hot, humid day, which is really stupid when you can't see very far through the trees. I had planned to be back at the van by two o'clock, but I finally figured out that I was more than 90° off course—probably in Peck Hollow—going south instead of west, with my van on the north side of the mountain. It was a buggy 90° day, my water was running low and I was getting tired.

I decided to forget about Sherrill and continue south to Shandaken on Route 28. The place seemed like a ghost town. A motel sign said OPEN, but there was nobody there. A Coke machine and a public phone were both out of order. A shutter flapped in the wind. It was a twenty-mile road hike back, and my throat was parched. I spied a hotdog stand a quarter of a mile away. I got there as the guy was closing up, and he sold me three sodas. He was originally from Greece, and one of my daughters-in-law is also of Greek extraction, so we chatted and exchanged some life stories that ended with a deal for him to taxi me back. Lucky me, again.

Lessons: start using your compass *before* you get lost; on a hot summer day take twice as much water as usual.

Sleeping under the Stars

In July my wife and I toured the Canadian Maritime provinces, and in August my daughter Veronica and I climbed Mount Adams and Mount Rainier in Washington. Back in the Catskills in mid-September, three days of climbing passed without misadventures! By October I had only climbed sixteen of the required peaks, but warm sunny fall weather brought me to the Catskills again. Starting at 7:15 AM, I bushwhacked off the Seager Trail up Drury Hollow, reaching Graham Mountain at 9:20, hiked to Balsam Lake Mountain by 10:55, returned to Graham by 12:30, bushwhacked to Doubletop by 3:00 and to Big Indian Mountain by 5:35. I couldn't resist bagging this last peak, and it only added about twenty minutes, but I soon regretted it.

Worried about nightfall, I ran down several miles in the waning evening light. I came to an intersection with a dirt road. In the gathering dark I didn't see the trail continuation, but took the invitingly broad dirt road. Fifteen minutes later, after the road petered out with several stream crossings, I realized my mistake, but got lost feeling my way back across the streams. It was now pitch black, no moonlight, no flashlight. Unbelievable, you say? Yes, *déja vu* all over again. Only this time there was no safe, wide path; I was stumbling around on a slope in the woods. I fell over a rock and picked myself up. Then I tumbled head-first two or three feet down a little cliff, landing on my face. The dirt didn't taste great, but it was better than rock. Luckily I didn't break any bones or my glasses, but I realized I had to stay put—can't risk falling down a bigger cliff. It was about 7:30 PM. Never daunted, I felt around for a small level area, scratched some leaves together for bedding, put on my spare shirt and fleece jacket, wrapped my windbreaker around my hips, and curled up in fetal position. At first I was still warm from running and the temperature was a balmy 55°. But my feet had gotten soaked in the stream crossings, my body cooled, the temperature dropped, and I settled in for a long, shivering, cold night with short, progressively more nightmarish dreams.

When I awoke I marveled at glimpses of starry sky visible through the black canopy, and sometime later moonshine bathed everything in a comforting ghostly glow. After eleven hours the blessed sun rose behind the hills, and I saw a dirt road fifty feet down the slope! Less than half an hour later I was back in my van drinking hot chocolate, having breakfast and settling down for a short nap.

Lessons: don't go down a trail if you can't see the trail markers that you know must be there; absorb and observe all previous lessons! 🏃🏃

14

DUTCHMAN'S PATH

The Mountains and the Mind

Robert L. Gram, #1400

The morning of January 10, 2003, was clear and cold when we arrived near the end of Moon Haw Road. Through bare trees we spied 3,780-foot Wittenberg and 3,860-foot Cornell, our twin destinations; we would then descend to Woodland Valley where we'd spotted a second car. At 9:30 the morning light sharpened the contour of the range and magnified bare rock. In the woods a solitary stone chimney, beige-weathered and nearly camouflaged by surrounding trees, testified to past human life. Ted, the Catskill historian, suggested that the chimney was once attached to a lodge or Adirondack-style great house. He thought that the caretaker, a Mr. Van Benschoten, had forged the Dutchman's Trail, the path we were hiking. Perhaps Van Benschoten had notched and painted the trees to help hunters reach the col between Wittenberg and Cornell.

I was the newest member of the trio. David and Ted had hiked extensively in the Catskills. They had shown me the remains of a plane downed after World War II on the flank of one mountain, as well as a large cave on another that was suitable for bears or bivouacking humans. Our discussions as we hiked were wide-ranging; it is wonderful and a bit daunting to accompany individuals who are well-versed and sure of themselves. Even boring hikes become interesting. We would discuss the best brand of snowshoe and the worst presidential administration. As we gazed upon the chilly scene, we retained hope that our government's noncompliance with the Kyoto Accords had not affected our small region of winter paradise. Global warming is not something a Catskill hiker appreciates, unless he or she is an aspirant trying to attain the winter Catskill 3500 merit badge under easier conditions.

Strapping on snowshoes, we slogged down a steep embankment and forded a narrow snow-clotted stream that had developed a film of ice overnight. Even slight gusts kicked up delicate snow clouds; they hovered briefly before disappearing in the morning light. The snow had the consistency of talc as we broke trail. Even with snowshoes we sank knee-deep and took turns ploughing the trail; we found ourselves in cursing mode by midmorning—early for us. We often lost sight of the hand-painted blazes low down on partly buried trees. The strange beauty of trees twisted and sculpted by snow captivated us, further slowing our pace: pine and spruce boughs lost their natural arc with great snow slabs atop each one; fir trees resembled arrowheads pointed toward the sky. Spindrift twirled past us; nature seemed sentient because of these diaphanous miniature tornadoes. The deep snow blanket created rolling white hillocks; I had the illusion of plodding through Sahara dunes. Apart from the steady knocking of an occasional woodpecker, we felt alone in the woods.

Discussion ensued about what and where we would eat and the prices. As the grade steepened and the sun rose, the snow began to melt and stick to our snowshoes. We were forced to raise weighted legs, stork-like, and remove snow by batting the edges of our snowshoes with ski poles. We bent forward as we bulldozed through white drifts. My calves began to ache. Sweat trickled down my chest in the dazzling noonday sun. Yet it was too cold to remove layers. As we toiled up, I followed high-altitude advice: I've climbed mountains over 18,000 feet, and it is thought that one conserves oxygen in depleted zones by breathing deeply and then holding the breath before exhaling. Sea level breathing never seemed tougher.

Initially we moved more quickly than prudence might dictate. An Ecuadorian guide once told me two rules to effective mountaineering: the first is to go slow; the second applies only after you've mastered the first—now, go slower. I often wonder whether our initial burst had something to do with a form of machismo or one-upmanship we three adopted hiking together over the years.

The mountain steepened as we approached the col, and we were reduced to a scramble. We hoisted ourselves over exposed roots and through snow-choked, narrow rock crannies; at times, we had to remove knapsacks to squeeze through. We crawled around and under stunted spruce and pine, often liberating skeins of snow that trickled through neck openings. We shouted to one another: "Is this Friday Mountain?" As we found ourselves on nearly perpendicular faces, we realized that we had lost the ill-marked path. We were too tired to go back down and reroute ourselves. My altimeter indicated that we were about 300 feet below the path's ending on the col.

Although fatigue overtook us, we bulled through, crawling and hiking in a half-stoop up the mountain, knapsack canvas scraping exposed rock. Unexpected branches snagged our beanies and lifted them off our heads. The air smelled of resin. Stumps spotted with amoeba-shaped mold broke under the pressure of my pull and emitted a sawdust smell, reminding me of spring. The unconsolidated snow grew wetter at midday, so that on steep rock it would give way with a whooshing sound. We removed and then reattached our snowshoes. Increasingly we relied on arm strength to forge forward; sweat stung my eyes. At times we crawled on hands and knees through thick brush and low-slung branches. It shouldn't be this tough, we told ourselves. We stopped on a patch of rock and snacked. The snow-covered landscape seemed an alternate world where reality was uniformly white.

David was the first to reach the col, at 1:30. The snow was hardpack and slick as ice on the meager path. The tops of trees, wound tightly with ice, arched to the ground like croquet wickets. We felt we were in a tunnel. Ted found a rock and removed sweaty layers. He noted that the last 150 feet had been hell; unconsolidated snow created a situation of two steps forward, one slide backward. I noted that there's the Hiking Two Step and the Texas Two Step: one is a dance of life.

David and I decided to bag Cornell's peak. The trees were weighted with more snow near the summit, and the tree tunnel was more constricted. We found ourselves in a perpetual stoop. Shims of ice fell all around us, producing a sound like the tinkling of wine glasses. The trail reached the icy fifteen-foot cut in the rock; even with crampons we would need ice axes to ascend. We sought to bypass the pitch, but the embankments were lined with impenetrable thickets. The frost had locked everything in place, and even the narrowest branch possessed the hardness of metal. After a round of curses and a philosophical excursion into life's unfairness, we retreated and rejoined Ted on the summit of Wittenberg, where the view of the Ashokan Reservoir and the Hudson Valley lay before us unhindered by haze. We could see Connecticut past the Kingston-Rhinecliff Bridge. In spite of the cold we were warmed and lulled by the sun. We munched trail mix and scoffed down sandwiches, while engaging hikers who were heading down.

We should have begun our downward trek to Woodland Valley, but the summit views invited us to sit still and observe. In the distance Overlook, Indian Head, and Twin had begun to darken. Cobalt-colored Samuel's Point seemed higher and more Alp-shaped than I remembered; to the south, the mountains blazed in direct sunlight. It was easy to believe that life still operated on Daylight Savings Time. In all seasons I underestimate the time it takes to descend Wittenberg before darkness falls. I find myself fumbling down its flanks, the beam from my headlamp moving from one tree to the next to discern night-camouflaged blazes. Is it simply the beauty of its summit views that causes delay?

Wittenberg is beautiful for more than its views from the top, however. Spied from a distance as one travels by car on Route 28 west of Phoenicia, it looks higher than its 3,780-foot listing. One gets the impression of a giant thumb-shaped peak from this vantage. The mountain leans toward the Hudson River like a cresting wave, its energy poised to spill over and engulf the Ashokan Reservoir. On a warm day I'll pull out my portable canvas chair and do nothing but stare at the mountain. Transfixed by nature's great artwork, I get in trouble with tailgating motorists. Gazing at Wittenberg, I understand how Monet could paint the same haystack from various light perspectives throughout the day.

View from Wittenberg. Photograph by Larry Gambon.

I fell in love at age five with the beauty of Ramapo High Torn, a prominent bump in the Ramapo chain. As I stared at its precipitous, rocky, southwest face, I thought it was the highest point on earth and believed the gods sported on its summit. In time I came to believe in the Christian God and went so far as to spend my vocational life as an ordained Protestant minister. I never forgot that early connection between divinity and mountains, however. I've always relished the idea that Jesus spent much of his time in the hills. During a theological examination after my initial graduation from one seminary, a conservative pastor asked me who I believed Jesus to be. I thought a minute, and because I was too brash to deliver the "correct" answer, I said, "Galilean Peak Bagger." In spite of my flippancy, I passed the licensing examination.

The summit of Wittenberg produced languor, and we roused ourselves with difficulty. We followed snowshoe tracks, grateful that we no longer had to break trail. Long tree shadows now intersected our path; our world became colder by the minute. Soon in darkness we inched our way down, grasping pine branches and stepping delicately; often we eased off a shelf in the rump position, hoping not to turn an ankle as we landed blindly on a snowy floor. The cold penetrated my waterproof bibs. We checked our watches often, and said nothing. Beams skewed across the downward path. The world was silent.

I was leading when I heard the crack of breaking branches. I saw Ted tumbling head over heels down the steep slope behind me, kicking up rooster tails of snow. David and I backtracked quickly. Ted's snowshoe had snagged in something. He was "not the worse for wear," as he put it, but he seemed too calm; I think Ted had begun to suffer from the cold. His emotions had begun to recede.

Soon, feelings would escalate. David had taken the lead. We had worked our way down a particularly steep stretch composed of exposed, ice-encrusted rock.

Our beams illuminated the blue tinge of ice. We removed our snowshoes and negotiated the face, employing arms, legs and rumps. My gloved hands slipped on pointed rocks on which I could not see the filmy ice sheath; we moved glacially. Exhalations crystallized in ovoid shapes. Cold nipped at fingertips and ears in spite of insulated gloves and a woolen beanie.

David was the first one to arrive at the base. He reattached his snowshoes and proceeded on the relatively flat terrain, then stopped, looking down, very still; his headlamp focused on the snow, then upwards and back and forth. He started to curse. "There is no path!" he yelled. "There is no frigging trail!" The tracks had simply ended. The snowshoes had tamped down a rough circle in the snow. The anonymous hiker we had followed unwittingly had been airlifted from this snowy plateau, or so it seemed. Virgin snow blanketed the downward slope. There was no sign of a blaze. Our light beams raced back and forth, producing the effect of a spotlighted movie premiere. For a moment I hated the anonymous trailblazer, then angry thoughts soon turned inward upon myself. Somewhere up the mountain we had ignored the signs and focused on the snowshoe trail in front of us.

We argued and found fault with one another's route finding and hiking abilities. Each in turn tried to be the calming presence for the others. We pored over maps and consulted compass and GPS. The stars were out, but were of little help in orienteering. We tried to retrace, but decided we would waste too much time on the slippery ice face. Best to bushwhack down. "Let's get our asses out of here!" David yelled, now frightened. We were getting colder. There was a stuttering quality to our speech; was this the sign of hypothermia?

We ploughed through drifts, breaking trail. Our snowshoes often sank to mid-calf. The night cold hardened the first snow layer; each footfall crunched through it into deep snow. I was almost in a half-run, panting, exhalations hoarse and ragged. My throat burned. We snaked around thick stands of trees and brush, trying to find the path of least resistance in the trackless forest. The night sky was star-dappled. Our single beams of artificial light produced loneliness and a heightened sense of lost-ness, surrounded by darkness. Mostly, our visual focus lay three feet in front of our snowshoes; I practically fell over because I followed the angle of my light beam.

I crossed a snow-packed area and noticed the change only after I began sinking again in soft snow. I retraced and realized that we had stumbled across the trail! We were supposed to hike west, but we started east—the incline we had just negotiated was on our right; shouldn't it be to our left when hiking out? We checked our compasses and pronounced that we were traveling in the right direction in spite of this seeming topographic anomaly. The trail flattened, and soon we realized that we were hiking in drifts above the swampy section that preceded the T junction. We consulted compasses a second time, and continued in the wrong direction until we spotted the wooden trail junction sign in the distance, 2.6 miles from the trail-head. Curses and accusations all around. "Are we trying a second time to find the Wittenberg trail?" Exhaustion produced my jest. One of my friends issued a threat, so I ditched the humor.

We responded to each other through a miasma of cold and fear. And hope. We were moving in the right direction now—finally. We would get out of here eventually if we followed the blazes very carefully, but this is not easy in the dark woods. Now we didn't trust our orienteering skills. Just follow the blazes. There was a period after the snowshoe prints ended that I played with the idea that we wouldn't make it. And I thought to myself: "What a way to go." The idea of mountains and divinity had informed my entire life. Perhaps it was the only consistent idea that unites the child to the man. How fitting for a life to end where, in some sense, it had spiritually begun.

Rationally I sensed we wouldn't die; we were prepared to bivouac for the night. The extreme cold had loosened theological thoughts, however, and the possibility of demise seemed written on the pinched, cold-bitten faces of my partners. My toes had grown numb. My fingertips ached and felt raw, as if mountain sprites gnawed on them. We emptied our knapsacks and ate our remaining food. Finishing our reserves was a challenge to ourselves: we didn't want to think of storing food in case of a bivouac. I put on two extra layers of fleece. The extra bulk, accompanied by fatigue, affected my balance. *Here's the Sixty-Four-Thousand-Dollar Question*, I said to myself: *will the Pillsbury Dough Boy make it down the mountain?*

On the descent, fatigue may have produced a sharpening of the senses. I noticed large fir trees with huge green "wingspans." Great fallen oak and tulip trees were snagged in the branches of other great trees, creating geometrically straight hypotenuses. Rocks were covered with mold, fungus and moss. What would it be like to be a simple one-celled organism living the sedentary good life on a rock? I spotted rabbit and deer tracks, sensed the yawning space of the Woodland Valley. Our descent steepened, and at times we lost the trail. With every step my trembling quadriceps entreated me to take a seat in the snow and rest for the night. Then, our spirits lightened when someone said, "Hear it?" It was the faint sound of moving water. Woodland Creek.

Later, when I asked Ted about the experience, he noted that it was tough going. "But there were others that were much worse for me." David refused to comment when I e-mailed to get his response; he wanted to forget about the Dutchman's Path. For me the hike was both terrifying and sublime. "Wittenberg Peak Bagger," I whispered, gazing at the night sky for some recognition or spiritual confirmation before entering the car.

I didn't receive it. 𝄞

15

DON'T GO BEYOND YOUR LIMITS

NO CONNECTION BETWEEN AGE AND STRENGTH

from Cy Whitney, #266, #93W, as reported to Carol White

A twenty-five-year-old newspaper reporter was assigned to accompany a club-sponsored hike and was pleasantly relieved when he saw mostly middle-aged participants. A short way up 3,843-foot Peekamoose Mountain, the reporter was surprised when the hikers left the trail. He found the footing tricky over uneven, slippery rocks under fallen leaves. After an hour and a half, the group arrived at debris from a twin-engine Piper Aztec that had crashed two years previously.

I was twice the reporter's age, but I noticed that the young man had slowed down on the steady uphill trek through rugged terrain. I gave him an energy-boosting candy bar and advised him to bandage a "hot spot" that might become a blister.

The trouble began when the group started side-hilling around a steep slope of 3,200-foot Van Wyck Mountain, where the uneven footing feels precarious—a fast fall could occur should one lose one's footing. The reporter's legs were giving out fast; it took him a half hour to ascend 100 feet. Bill Riemvis and I stayed with him. It was another 450 feet to the summit of 3,847-foot Table Mountain, which the rest of the party had already reached.

The sky was darkening with impending rain or snow, the temperature had dropped, and the wind was increasing. Now, it was farther to go back than to proceed ahead. If only the young man could reach that summit, we'd be on a trail! But the reporter could climb no more—his legs were in knots. Riemvis went up to the others to report the impasse, and the hike leader descended to assess the situation. No one was prepared for a night out. The hike leader told me to continue around Table Mountain to another trail that descended to the Neversink River; part of the group would meet us there. The others would continue over Table and Peekamoose and down to the cars, and get help to the other trailhead in Denning.

Club members helped carry the young man between them, gave him hot liquids and two pain pills, and found a Y-shaped walking stick, which helped somewhat. In two hours they descended 1,200 feet to the Neversink, where two logs had to be scaled over branching sections of the river. The reporter managed to walk another 1.5 miles out to the trailhead, where a police and rescue vehicle had just arrived. It was 7:30 PM, ten and a half hours after the hike had begun.

Lesson: Don't go beyond your limits. Understand fully what you're getting into. This hike was billed as "moderate," but what is moderate for seasoned hikers is an ordeal for the uninitiated. 🚶‍♂️🚶‍♀️

Rondout Creek, the Blue Hole near the Peekamoose Mountain trailhead. Rated one of the top ten swimming holes in the United States by Backpacker *magazine. Photograph by Larry Gambon.*

16

THE HIKE FROM HELL

HEAVENLY IN MEMORY ONLY

Evelyn Drapkin

Eight of us met at a motel on December 20 in order to leave early the next morning to climb Slide, Cornell, and Wittenberg mountains on the first day of winter. We drove up to the town in a heavy downpour and met before dinner; many of us were meeting for the first time. The group consisted of three women and five men, joined by our common friendship with Dave and Naomi Sutter. My husband, Bill Drapkin, and his friend George Solovay were aspirants to the Catskill 3500 Club. We were planning a linear hike over the range, so some of the men spotted cars at Woodland Valley State Park where we would finish the traverse.

The next day dawned cloudy and uninspiring, but it wasn't raining. We were on our way bright and early on this shortest day of the year. We climbed Slide without incident, reaching the summit ahead of schedule. The snow necessitated that we don crampons as we continued to Cornell. The going was fairly easy; summiting Cornell was uneventful. Then we reached the descent between Cornell and Wittenberg, where we encountered a ten-foot ice-covered vertical descent to a ledge; the ice had obliterated all hand- and foot-holds. Several minutes of exploration failed to yield an alternative route down. What to do?

Dave always carries a length of rope in his pack, but has never had occasion to use it. This would be the day! The rope was looped around a tree and Dave descended first, followed by George. I was next. My fear of heights was kicking in, and if I waited too long for my turn I would never go down. I wrapped the rope around my hand and, with encouragement from below, began to slide down. Before reaching the ledge there was a foothold that had to be reached in order to back off the decline. By sheer force of will, I did as directed and found myself on the safety of the ledge. As I was congratulating myself, Naomi came down with a flop onto her back. She was unhurt; I'd gone to her aid and missed Bill's descent until he, too, fell.

It was evident when he got up that all was not well. We spent time determining that he did not have a life-threatening injury, but he did have pain in his lower back and butt. We stopped as long as was practical, but time was passing and we still had Wittenberg to climb and descend—4.6 miles and many more steep ledges. The going became very slow with Bill in the rear looking very pale. We were at a point where there was no turning back.

We managed to summit Wittenberg with only two stops to minister to muscle spasms. We were way behind our planned times. As the light faded we each took out our flashlights, but didn't use all of them in case we needed backup. The night was warm for that time of year and the sky was clear. Our eyes adapted amazingly well to the night, but not enough to see the blazes. Our map indicated a stream crossing, and its sound became louder and louder as we descended. It was now 6:30 PM and fully dark as we arrived at the stream. We needed to find the bridge to

Infamous V-cut ledge near summit of Cornell Mountain. Photograph by Carol White.

cross this large stream. We watched the water race along over the rocks while Dave Kocian and Brian went to the left, and Dave Sutter to the right, to search for the bridge. After fifteen minutes they all had come back without finding the bridge. We were discouraged and tired and wanted this hike to end! There didn't seem to be a safe way across.

Suddenly Dave Sutter said in a commanding voice, "We're crossing." The stream was swiftly flowing and deep, but we had no alternative. Hildie was in front of me when she slipped down into the water; somehow I didn't follow her down. Behind me I heard Bill hit the water. Finally we all had crossed, and at seven o'clock reached our cars; now we had to drive twenty miles back to the Slide trailhead to get the rest of the cars.

Hours later, back home and asleep, I was awakened at 3:30 AM by a crash in the bathroom. Bill spent the rest of that night and the next in the hospital. He had fractured his coccyx in his fall, which caused bleeding. When he got up in the middle of the night, his blood pressure dropped, causing unconsciousness.

I've not been back to any of the three mountains we climbed that day, but Bill has, many times. He also completed his winter and summer peaks the following year. In retrospect, we had a fantastic day on that "hike from hell" that has yielded many hours of conversation and laughter. We survived! ⚇

Part III:
WILDLIFE ENCOUNTERS

*I heard some crashing from up above me. …
Rocks, logs, leaves and debris were falling toward
me. I didn't have time to even think of what could
be causing this before I saw it: this huge black bear,
probably 400 pounds, was rolling, sliding, tumbling
and falling right toward me! He actually looked like
he was having fun falling down the most dangerously
steep part of the notch.*

Anthony Versandi

Photograph by Paul Misko.

17

BEAR SLIDE!

FOUR HUNDRED POUNDS OF FUR HAVING FUN

Anthony Versandi, #1488, #637W

It was the first week of May, but there was still patchy snow on Halcott Mountain. This was to be my thirty-fourth peak, with only Plateau remaining. I had soloed all the tougher trailless peaks, so Halcott should be a piece of cake. I found my way to the top without any problems, took photos of myself at the canister with a tripod, and just enjoyed the warm sun. When I began to pack up my camera and gear, my peaceful day started to change. I got myself all riled up when I realized that my brand-new, never-before-used $65 filter unscrewed from my lens and fell somewhere in the brush. I frantically searched and got myself worked up into a crazed state. Being so mad at myself and wondering how I could have been so stupid, I headed down the west side (the wrong side) of the ridge, away from Route 42 where I'd started.

After about an 800-foot descent I heard a stream rushing. That's when I knew I had gone the wrong way. Time to climb back up the ridge! My next mistake was following the ridge too far to the north. I figured this out only after I headed east toward the road and found myself sliding down the steepest part of Deep Notch. I used a thick stick out in front of me as a brake to slow me down until I reached a point that seemed safe, checked out the next "controlled" slide route, and then on to the next point. I continued to make my way down methodically when, suddenly, while resting at a small ledge, I heard some crashing from up above me.

I turned to see what was happening. Rocks, logs, leaves and debris were falling toward me. I didn't have time to even think of what could be causing this before I saw it: this huge black bear, probably 400 pounds, was rolling, sliding, tumbling and falling right toward me! He actually looked like he was having fun falling down the most dangerously steep part of the notch and sending a mess in my direction in the process. He kept coming, and slid past me maybe eight feet away, down the notch and out of sight! I don't think he even knew I was there.

So what started as a simple, not very difficult bushwhack, wound up to be a very memorable trip. Boy, was I glad I lost that filter! ⚑

18

TWO BEARS

BEARS IN THE CATSKILLS

**Rev. Ray L. Donahue, #23, #1W
from Autumn 1968 *Catskill Canister***

During July of 1961, I explored the trails around North Lake Campground. Near Inspiration Point on the Escarpment Trail, I heard an animal crashing through the woods to the north of me. When I finally saw what was making the noise, it was not a deer, as I had thought, but a half-grown black bear. Since it was running directly toward me, I let out a war whoop that changed its direction of travel. That frightened young bear crossed the trail less than a hundred yards in front of me and then rolled and crashed over the edge of the escarpment into Kaaterskill Clove. I still laugh as I think of the wild flight of that bear going off South Mountain. (It wasn't hurt by the fall.)

The only other bear I've seen was on the shoulder of Big Indian that leads to Fir. It was in the fall of 1963, when I first began my Catskill peak bagging. I was a little uneasy as I left Big Indian for Fir, because this was one of my first solo bushwhacks. You can imagine how startled I was when a full-grown bear rose from the ground right in front of me. That bear must have been more startled than I, because it thundered off the ridge without ever looking back. Since then, I have been on many bushwhacks, but none have been as exciting as the one on Big Indian.

Bears are seldom seen, for they are shy creatures, but throughout the mountains their droppings and tracks can be seen. Just this spring, one bear left its mark by destroying the newly installed canister on Rocky. With all these bears in the Catskills now, I hope to write someday about the "Three Bears." 🏃

19

BLACK BEAR TALES

HOW TO ENCOUNTER A BEAR IN THE WILD

Mark Schaefer, #209

Many hikers have told me that they have never seen a black bear while hiking in the Catskills, and I did not see any bears, either, during my first five years of Catskill hikes. On my first sighting all I saw was its back as the bear dived into the dense bushes near the muddy pond on Bearpen Mountain. It was another five years before I saw another. I saw two that day along the Escarpment Trail atop Arizona Mountain. They were about a hundred yards apart and appeared to be three-year-old siblings. Both were grazing on berries. I met them separately, a few minutes apart. Each immediately stood up, looked at me for a few seconds, and then turned tail and ran away into the woods. This was followed by several more years of no sightings.

These early sightings gave me several keys to finding bears. Bears love berries. Knowing locations of berry patches and when they ripen is important. Acorns, nuts, and grasses are also on their menu. Hiking solo will greatly increase your chances of seeing a bear. Groups of hikers will inevitably make more noise, and black bears will usually leave at their first sense that humans are approaching. Hiking on lightly traveled trails or midweek also helps. Bears are more active in the early morning and late afternoon. On warm sunny days they will often stay in their dens to avoid the heat of the day. Cool, overcast, breezy days enhance your chances. It is also possible that the breeze rustling through the foliage will conceal your approach. You might be just as surprised as they are when you stumble upon a bear.

The last two years I have made an effort to hike at times and in areas where I expect the bears will be. I spotted six bears in 2004 and well over a dozen in 2005. On a breezy, midweek September day in 2004, I came upon a bear walking toward me. It was on Bearpen amongst the infamous mud wallows on the ridge-top road northwest of the summit. I spotted him about ten seconds before he saw me. I stopped to watch, and he continued toward me. I was impressed by how similar we were. Like me, he was gingerly walking around the mud wallows, apparently not wishing to get his feet wet. And we were both there to feast on blackberries. At about thirty yards he stopped, perked up his ears, started to sniff, and looked

Catskill Mountain black bear. Photograph by Paul Misko.

in my direction. Bears are shortsighted, so he probably could not focus on what I was. But he knew something was there. We stared at each other over the mud wallows for several minutes. I concluded this might go on all day, so I took a step in his direction. As expected, he immediately turned and scampered back on the road from whence he had come. Bearpen and the neighboring Roundtop have provided the most prolific numbers of my bear sightings, but midweek is essential because of heavy ATV usage on weekends.

On an overcast, breezy, and chilly Father's Day 2005, I was hiking up the Cathedral Glen trail on Belleayre through a deep and beautiful hemlock glen. Normally, I am constantly scanning the woods looking for wildlife, and this kind of day was ideal. That day, however, I was climbing at a good clip, had my head down, and was deep in thought when I heard some rustling off trail. I looked into the woods expecting to see a deer, perhaps, but was surprised to find myself only twelve feet from a very small bear foraging away from me. She appeared to be a three-year-old cub. Within a few seconds I saw a teddy-bear-sized cub in tow, and then another cub. I stopped to allow the bears time and room to move on. The mother was no more than forty inches long. I was almost tempted to ask her, "Aren't you a little young for this?" Multiple births are somewhat rare for first-time bear mothers, but I suspect these were her first cubs. I later learned that females are capable of mating as early as two years of age. The encounter was surreal—she never once looked toward me, although it is hard to believe she was unaware of my presence. The cubs also paid no attention to me. They climbed a small tree, so I thought I must have spooked them, but they immediately scampered back down. They were just playing. Despite it being Father's Day, Papa Bear was, of course, nowhere to be seen.

You might see black bears anywhere in the Catskills. I have seen bears on multiple occasions on Huntersfield Mountain, on the southern half of the Huckleberry Loop trail, on St. Anne's Peak (the summit west of West Kill), and on Ashokan High Point (on both summits and along Kanape Brook).

There are some well-known precautions to take. Never approach bears or attempt to feed them. Be careful not to come between a mother bear and her cubs; slowly back away if that happens. Take precautions with food while camping, such as using a bear canister for storing food. Fortunately, black bears in the Catskill backcountry are still quite shy. They do not exhibit the aggressive tendencies that their kin have acquired near human habitation. Unlike when encountering grizzly bears out west, never play dead. If you feel threatened, your best defense is to stand tall, make a lot of noise and, in the rare case you are attacked, fight back. You can neither outrun nor outclimb a bear but, fortunately, they will almost always run from you. I have never had a bad experience. I enjoy every encounter, but I maintain caution.

There were an estimated 1,500 bears inhabiting the Catskills in 2005. That is up from 600 in the 1970s, so your opportunities of seeing bears are increasing. However, if you hike in groups, on popular trails, at midday on weekends, or in warm sunny weather, you will likely miss them. Or, more correctly, they will easily avoid you. With luck, caution and common sense, you will enjoy any bear encounter, as I have. Maybe you, too, will have a bear tale or two to tell! 🐾

20

ENCOUNTERS WITH WILDLIFE

BEAR ENCOUNTER

Elie Bijou

Bear on Plateau

In July 1970 I set off for a hike up Plateau and Sugarloaf mountains. In those years, Catskill lean-tos were located on mountain summits. My plan was to hike Plateau, drop my gear off at the summit shelter, then hike Sugarloaf and possibly Twin. As I traversed the long mesa of Plateau, the weather worsened; the sky darkened as I descended Plateau. I decided to wait for the thunderstorm to abate under an overhang on the Mink Hollow side. My companions on that humid day were a hunting knife, a borrowed metal canteen, and tropical Hershey bars.

My mother did not approve of my hiking. She had often told me stories about campers who were mauled by bears, but what she failed to tell me was that almost all of these occurrences happened out west, in parks such as Glacier, Yosemite and Yellowstone, and involved grizzlies. To mothers, a bear is a bear.

It was raining lightly and drops were dripping from the overhang. I heard an unmistakable thrash and crash in the brush. Suddenly a black bear about five feet in length appeared twenty feet below me. I froze in sheer terror, unaware of what to do. The only thing that ran through my head was "Camper Mauled in Catskills." The bear sniffed to the left, then to the right, and finally his snout pointed directly toward me. We stood there for about twenty long seconds. My heart was racing. I placed my hand on the hunting knife and flicked off the snap protector. The sweat beaded across my brow and the hand that gripped the knife handle, rolling off of my palm and into the furrows of the antler grip. Thoughts raced through my mind. I debated whether or not to bolt, but I was captivated at the same time by the sight of this rarely seen Catskills creature. Finally the bear backed away, turned tail and ran into the woods.

In my excitement and youthful exuberance, I jumped down from my perch and raced into the woods looking for the bear. I do not know what possessed me to follow him. Twenty feet in, still clutching the knife handle, I stopped cold without a plan of action. Was it to confront the bear *à la* Daniel Boone and wrestle it to the ground, cutting its ears off as my trophy? No, I had just wanted to see where the bear was headed. Finally I came to the conclusion that I was just as fearful as he was and it was best to leave him alone.

Shakily, I walked back to my perch and waited for the sun to come out. When I felt confident that the bear was not milling around, I slowly ambled to the stream—keeping a watchful eye on the surrounding woods—and refilled my leaky canteen. My hike up Sugarloaf would have to wait for another time. 🏃

View from Orchard Point on Plateau Mountain. Photograph by Larry Gambon.

21

THIS HIKE WAS FOR THE BIRDS—LITERALLY!

IN SEARCH OF THE RARE BICKNELL'S THRUSH

Tom Rankin, #1503, #627W

My son David is a bird-watching enthusiast. In his early teens, he had already observed over 200 species of birds. I love to hike, and in 2001 was working on becoming a member of the Catskill 3500 Club. An organization that caters to both interests is The Vermont Institute of Natural Science. Its program "Mountain Birdwatch" monitors birds such as Bicknell's thrush,[1] the black pole warbler, and the white-throated sparrow. The 3500 Club owes its start in part to the study of Bicknell's thrush by people like Dan Smiley, who compiled a list of the highest peaks in the Catskills from which they could observe and study these rare birds.

My son is athletic and likes to hike occasionally. This would be a perfect way to introduce him to a true scientific research project, and hike at the same time! He liked the idea of participating in the study. He had never seen a Bicknell's thrush, so he wanted to go for that reason as well. We sent away for the educational materials. David studied them and prepared. In this study, you can either see or hear the birds in question, as long as you are positive you have identified them. For this reason we were sent a tape of bird songs and pictures of each bird. We had been assigned Black Dome and Thomas Cole mountains as our observing area. We had to be at the summit by sunrise, and this was early June, so we knew we'd have to get a very early start.

A few weeks later we got up at 1:30 in the morning and drove to the trailhead at the end of Big Hollow Road, arriving at 3:15. The moon was a few days past full and did not cast much light under the trees, so we kept our headlamps on. I had never been up this trail, so I was constantly scanning around to make sure I didn't take wrong turns. I heard and then saw something moving! Was it a bear? Fortunately, it was only a porcupine. It waddled away into the brush, but we got a good look at him. Other than the occasional rustle of porcupines (we did see a couple more that morning), the woods were calm. We could hear the stream below us as we climbed higher and higher. Eventually the stars faded as dawn began to lighten the sky. In the col between Black Dome and Blackhead, it was light enough to put our headlamps away.

We rested briefly in the saddle and then prepared for observing. I carried David's notebook, and he carried his binoculars. The blood-red sun was just rising over the Hudson Valley as we reached the summit of Black Dome. We heard several birds singing and soon saw them flitting from tree to tree. David is a very keen observer and soon he had found his first Bicknell's thrush. He identified it both by sight and sound. We established five observing points near the two summits and saw various birds at all of them. David sighted several more Bicknell's thrushes and even pointed one out to me. (Most of them all look alike to my untrained eye). We duly recorded all the information that the program requires—date, time, temperature, wind speed, tree height, etc.—so the institute would have a good baseline for our observations.

It was great to see so many Bicknell's thrushes on our trip. After climbing Thomas Cole, we returned to the first saddle. I also summited Blackhead, while David rested. As we walked back down the trail, we looked around at all the sights we had missed as we climbed up. A young ranger met us just before the trailhead and chatted with us. He was very interested in birding as well, and encouraged David to continue in his hobby. Later, David enrolled at the SUNY College of Environmental Science and Forestry, studying to be an ornithologist.

We got back to the car at 9:30 AM. We had climbed three mountains and participated in a scientific study, all before many people had even gotten out of bed! 🐾

---

[1] The June 2004 Catskill Centennial issue of the *New York State Conservationist*, the official publication of the New York State Department of Environmental Conservation, highlights the Bicknell's thrush in an article written by Bill Rudge, on page 11. This rare bird was discovered on June 15, 1881, on Slide Mountain by twenty-one-year-old Eugene Bicknell. He heard the song of the Swainson's thrush and then heard an unfamiliar song more reminiscent of a veery. Bicknell shot a thrush-sized bird and sent the specimen to the American Museum of Natural History, where experts declared it a new subspecies of gray-cheeked thrush. In 1995, when DNA analysis completed the examination of evidence, the American Ornithologists' Union bestowed full species status upon the bird, naming it the Bicknell's thrush (*Catharus bicknelli*). We now know that the Catskills are the southernmost part of its breeding range. In New York State the Bicknell's thrush is listed as a Species of Special Concern. In 1997 the Catskill Peaks region was identified by Audubon New York as an Important Bird Area because it supports a significant proportion of the state's Bicknell's thrush population. In 2000 the Catskill Forest Preserve peaks higher than 3,500 feet were designated part of a state Bird Conservation Area.

22

PORCUPINE SHOWS EXOTIC TASTES

THESE GUYS EAT EVERYTHING

Richard Levine #852
from January–March 1994 *Catskill Canister*

I was awakened at 1:00 am by an *oom-oom*, followed by some clicks. I unzipped the flap of my tent and, looking out into the bright night, saw silhouettes of trees and little else. Suddenly, the light from Tom's flashlight moved swiftly, followed by the sound of a rock striking the ground.

"Did you see anything?" I asked.

"It's the porcupine we saw earlier in the evening. God, it's an ugly creature."

Tom Dinceco, Bill Murphy and I were camped in the col between Slide and Cornell, and next day planned to bushwhack north down the mountainside to our cars at Woodland Valley. It was quiet now, and Tom and I crawled back into our sleeping bags.

As I was dozing off, the animal sounds started again. This time I was the one who got out and threw something. This brought silence, but not for long. It was obviously a losing battle. The animal could outlast us any time. I ignored its sounds as best I could, and eventually fell asleep.

In the morning we looked over our equipment and took inventory. We had known enough to hang our food out of reach; but, undeterred, the porcupine had sampled the brim of my cap, Tom's toothpaste, Bill's insect repellent and parts of his backpack—in fact, anything that bore the salt of our sweat. Porcupines have even been known to eat the fan belts off cars.

This was our first encounter with a porcupine. During many years of hiking, we had encountered mice, voles, weasels, even a bear or two—all of them interested in food. The porcupine had shown us it had more exotic tastes.

23

THREE DOG DAY

DOGS ON GORP AND POWER BARS

Steve Herrmann, #1064, #425W

I have been hiking in the Catskills since the early 1980s. Originally from Long Island, I always loved coming upstate for the woods, rivers and solitude. In 1975 I came to Oneonta and have stayed ever since. For a carpenter, this has been a great place to work. My wife and I have raised two daughters here and built our own house in 1984. Being close to the Catskills was nice, and we took advantage of this whenever we could. With my work being somewhat seasonal, I learned to enjoy the winter months for cross-country skiing and snowshoeing. I got hooked on snowshoeing and found that to be my favorite way of enjoying the mountains. (After climbing twenty peaks you also get hooked on wondering what all the other peaks are like.) This was the beginning of becoming a Catskill 35'er.

Once the Catskills are conquered, the next logical step is the Adirondacks. I still enjoy going to the Catskills, especially when I take someone new to the mountains. Then I can take a different trail or bushwhack so the day is enjoyed by all. I have had many good adventures in these mountains and made some lifelong friends on the way. Over the years I have climbed mountains all over the country, but the Adirondacks and Catskills are still my favorites.

One hiking adventure will always stick in my mind. My plan was to hike Eagle, Haynes and Balsam mountains from Seager one day in September. There was a light drizzle in the air as I hiked to the sign-in register. Three dogs ran towards me: a large yellow lab mix, a mid-sized long-haired collie type and a mid-sized shorter-haired mutt. They followed me, and when I reached the lean-to two miles up the trail, it was raining pretty hard. I figured these dogs had had enough and would soon turn around and head home. But as I climbed the steep approach to the Pine Hill–West Branch Trail, the three dogs followed my every step. (Actually, two followed me; the yellow lab had been running on the side as dogs usually do. He would run ahead a few hundred feet and then come back, and then lope off for another run.) Reaching the trail junction, I was on my way to Eagle Mountain. The rain persisted and the three dogs were still keeping me company. It was a fairly warm day, just very wet. This was a great test for my Gore-Tex gear.

When I reached the col below Balsam, it was raining pretty heavily, and I wasn't sure if I should continue since these dogs were now over six miles from home. What if they wouldn't return with me? Well, I really wanted to climb Balsam and, since my encouraging the dogs to go home was not working, I figured I'd let them come along for one more peak. We bagged the peak, and on the return I shared my power bars and gorp with the dogs, now soaked to the skin. The two mid-sized dogs would not leave my side. They stayed just inches away and moved as I moved. The yellow lab was still running up and down the trail like a maniac.

Finally we reached the parking lot, and the expressions on the smaller dogs' faces were definitely of relief. I think the yellow lab was glad to be back, too, as he must have been exhausted. I had hiked fourteen miles that day, and I'm sure the lab had done two or three times that. As I got into my truck and slid into some dry clothes, the three dogs just sat in the parking lot. When I drove away, the three of them looked at me as if to say, "Good-bye. We'll see you again!" I'll never forget their wet faces and what good companions they were for a great Catskill hike. 🥾

On the trail to Balsam Mountain. Photograph by Larry Gambon.

24

ENCOUNTER ON SHERRILL MOUNTAIN

TRACKS, CLAWINGS, SCAT— MAMA AND CUBS

Hilma L. Volk, #619
from Autumn 1987 *Catskill Canister*

One day last September I set out on a solo bushwhack to knock off my 27th and 28th peaks. From the access area of NY 42, I set my compass for a direct line to the top of Sherrill, although I knew I would use the creek for navigation. The wide trail I intercepted paralleled the north side of the stream for a while and then veered off to the left. Not knowing its destination, I bushwhacked on course, slowed by the jumbled terrain along the slope of the brook's V-shaped valley. After traveling that way for some time, I crossed the creek, seeking better footing. There was a trail there, built long ago and, judging from the placement of rocks, with considerable work. On the other side of a side stream, the understory became a field of bright green nettles showing signs of recent trampling.

In a wet seepage area, the imprint of a foot caught my attention. Picking up a leaf, I expected to see a boot print. Instead, it was a wide, stubby footprint with toes. *Good-sized bear*, I thought, touching the toe marks. The steep, sharp impressions indicated that the prints must have been made that day. Gazing around at the tall slim tree trunks and the seemingly inedible low growth, I wondered how the big animals found enough to eat here. Nearby was what had to be bear scat, but it was atypical, as if the bear had diarrhea. It was full of wild black cherries. But the odd thing was that most of the skins were intact. Perhaps the bear had thrown up? As I climbed I noticed more tracks and fairly fresh scat. There were toe and claw marks where the moss had been peeled away during a scramble up the rocks. Now and then I'd see little toes. Since it had rained hard all day Sunday, I knew that the tracks had been made since then.

Closer to the top, I checked for tracks under an overhang of one of the numerous sandstone outcroppings, but found only a tin can lid, a couple of old cans, two smashed liquor bottles, a stash of gathered wood, some reflective material stuffed into a natural shelf, and bird tracks. Hiker or hunter? Most slobs in either category were not this ambitious. At the summit canister the log confirmed that a group had been up there Saturday. Big letters on the top of one page said, "Rainy." Their other page was headed "Rain!"

Now I set the compass for a line to North Dome. With the mountain in sight, I stopped to pick some blackberries, surprised that the bears had not gotten them. A snorty whistle broke the silence. Casually I glanced over to watch a young buck bound out of sight. Once on North Dome, I meandered around until I found the canister. Part of the party on Saturday had made it there.

Reversing the compass direction, I knew that that heading should take me back to Sherrill, but it just did not seem right. Pulling out the map and replotting the course confirmed that same direction. Unlike the trip to North Dome, I could not see Sherrill because of the foliage. It did not appear as if any peak was directly ahead, but I followed the compass heading on faith. Back on Sherrill, I took a compass heading that would lead me to just above the old trail. It was now ten minutes to five; the round trip from Sherrill to North Dome had taken three hours. The route passed cherry trees small enough for bears to eat from them. There were more tracks and more fecal material, but nowhere did I see the claw marks on the trees that male bears make.

As I traveled down to the south edge of the field of nettles, I reminisced about my days working for the U.S. Fish & Wildlife Service in upper Michigan. One day, driving around a bend in the refuge, I came upon a mother bear and twin cubs. One "woof" from mom sent the kids scrambling up a tree. I was remembering this when I heard a branch snap. Looking below and behind me, I marveled at the tall black body standing on her hind legs staring at me. She was about 200 feet away. Then a cute little black head popped above the nettles, then another one.

On a signal that I didn't hear, the cubs started running. I expected them to bolt up a tree, but they did not. One took off in a direction about eleven o'clock from me, but the other was running directly toward me through the three-foot-tall nettles. Then it veered off, shooting by me about thirty feet away and disappearing past thick trees where the slope became steeper. It surprised me that the little guys were still so small. Fat and squatty and just plain cute, you might have stuffed the two of them into a big garbage sack—if you could catch them.

Now I faced the interesting situation of having to walk between mother and cub. Across the sea of nettles, the bears had performed their almost magical disappearing act. I proceeded slowly. The nettles obscured the footing on haphazard rocks covered with soggy moss that slipped off under the weight of a boot. And I kept an eye out for mama bear.

I'd like to report on an eventful encounter that ensued, but unfortunately—or fortunately—I cannot. The dimming light had transformed much of the forest to shadow, and I did not see the shadow-like animals again. Picking up the old trail, I made great time back to the car where the really unfortunate event had occurred—a flat tire. 🐾

25

THE THREE PORCUPINES

THE LOWLY PORKY IN HIS ELEMENT

William B. Lawson, #78, #39W
from Autumn 1980 *Catskill Canister*

On May 16, 1979, I spent the night near the beautiful "Ed West" lookout on the Escarpment Trail just south of the top of Blackhead Mountain. As the sun set at 8:15, a solitary white throat called to say, "Good night!" A nighthawk shot up past the lookout, and the resident porcupine waddled around the big rock to investigate the food situation, which for him was rather poor. To keep him occupied, I left an empty beer can at the lookout, then retired to my sleeping bag well off the trail. Though the sky was clear, it was a bit too cold to remain up long.

At 3:00 AM I was awakened by something brushing my sack. The resident porky, which I spotted with my light, apparently could not finish his rounds without investigating me. But he had done me a favor, for I could now see the waning moon in all its glory in the clear cold sky before going back to sleep. I got up at 4:30 to find an ice crust on my outer bag. Then, to the morning song of many white throats, the sunrise began and continued spectacularly. Just in front of the escarpment, a magnificent curtain of mist clouds allowed the sun to beam through occasionally as they moved past the lookout. The curtain split over Arizona Mountain, with some clouds passing over Stoppel Point and others heading into the East Jewett Valley.

After a bite to eat, I enjoyed the view and then stowed things away, including the gnawed beer can that my companion had enjoyed during the night. I hiked over Blackhead and down its north side over Acra Point. A winter wren cheered my trip with his beautiful warbling song. Acra Point was full of black-throated blue warblers, which croak enthusiastically rather than warble! As always I paused at each of the lookouts, and especially at the rocky one facing the Blackhead Range before the descent to the col with Burnt Knob. The peace and beauty of the mountains were especially wonderful that morning.

When I started down the red trail back to my car in the valley, I spotted a second porcupine in the trail ahead. Thinking of old Nessmuk's dictum—"And do not despise the fretful porcupine; he is better than he looks"—I decided to give this one a merry chase to see if I could have caught him for meat. In fact, I could have easily had him before he scrambled up a tree. It is worth remembering—for emergencies, of course—that porcupine is the easiest food to catch in the woods.

Back in the car, the motor turned over but it would not go. I am no mechanic, but after an hour's tinkering I was convinced that no gas was getting to the engine. The reason, I discovered, was that a third porky had gnawed a short stretch of flexible tubing in my gas line to shreds. He had also chewed on the axle and gas tank, but those were of good Swedish steel.

A kind fisherman gave me a ride to Maplecrest, where I obtained tubing and clamps. During the walk back to Big Hollow, aided by another friendly ride, I pondered the lowly porcupine, who sometimes amuses us, but who can also show us our place in the scheme of things in the mountains. Further, he aids the cause of conservation by annoying slovenly campers.

Later that summer I saw a message in the sign-in book in Big Hollow: "Don't run over the porcupine at the parking lot." Reading this gave me mixed feelings but, after all, it is *his* home. 🚶🚶

Porcupine climbs cliff. Photograph by David White.

Part IV:
WILD WEATHER

At about 3,650 feet, I found an overhang and threw myself under it as the first bolts of lightning hit all around me. … This was not good at all. This storm was way too intense for anyone to be where I was. I was shivering hard, but I don't know if it was from the cold wet clothes or from being quite scared. I know the hair was standing tall on the back of my neck. I'd never heard thunder so loud!

Dean Macgeorge

Photograph by Andrew Moroz.

26

A WILD ADVENTURE IN THE NEVERSINK

SCOUTING FOR ADVENTURE

Dean Macgeorge, #1174, #456W

This hike had all the trappings of winter hiking that I have experienced over the years, all rolled into one weekend. At the time I was an assistant scoutmaster with the Boy Scouts, and with my usual hiking partner, Bill, we took some of the older boys into the Neversink Valley in the middle of January. We planned to climb Friday, Balsam Cap, Rocky and Lone mountains—as much for my winter patch as for the boys to learn more about the Catskills and winter camping in general. We started out from the Denning trailhead with heavy packs loaded with everything we thought we may need and made our way up the valley to one of the designated campsites.

After setting up camp we headed upstream to climb Friday Mountain. We had daypacks with food, extra layers and crampons. These mountains are all trailless, and we spent the hike teaching map and compass skills to the boys. It was a beautiful day and the conditions did not warrant crampons, so we left them in our packs—except for me. I had them strapped to the outside of my pack. Or so I thought. We found the canister at the true summit, signed in, and then ate our lunches. We headed back down, and when we reached the valley I noticed that my crampons were gone. Dang! I sure didn't feel like going back for them, so we continued on to camp to think it over.

The next morning was clear and cold, perfect for the hiking ahead of us. It was also my birthday. Bill surprised me with the announcement that he would go back up Friday to find my crampons. I was to go with the boys up Lone and Rocky, and then meet Bill on Balsam Cap Mountain. We all started out at the same time and carried walkie-talkies to help find each other. The boys worked together like a well-oiled machine, using map and compass to find the summit of Lone. They were still a little tired from climbing Friday, so they were happy to find that Lone was not a difficult climb. We signed the register and headed over to Rocky, which was less fun than Lone, but the boys did great finding their groove. Rocky came and went, and it was off to find Bill and the summit of Balsam Cap.

For anyone who has been up there, you know how thick it can get, and for those who haven't—check it out, because it can be great fun if you have the right attitude. Our scouts certainly had the right attitude that day—good thing, considering it was the middle of winter and I couldn't think of a more remote place to be. I didn't let on my concerns about finding Bill, let alone the summit. We spent a good deal of time roaming (a polite term) around the top of that God-forsaken mountain looking for the canister. We finally stumbled upon it with relief and signed the register. The boys settled down to have a snack, when Bill called on the radio.

He was very happy to make contact, but he sounded frazzled. I knew we were in for quite a story. He had found my crampons very near the summit of Friday and was on his way to Balsam Cap when he forgot to trust his compass. Let's just say that there were large cliff bands and deep snow involved. Becoming more and more frustrated and concerned, he started to panic. He really had to get hold of himself and apply the skills we had been teaching the scouts. He basically back-tracked and started over, this time trusting his compass. Later, on the hike back to the campsite when we were out of earshot of the boys, he told me how badly shaken up he had really been.

With four difficult mountains under our belts and feeling pretty good about ourselves in general, Mother Nature decided to show up and humble us a bit. In fact, we could have been killed. It was around 4:00 PM, and we had a large fire going when the wind started. We were driven into our tents to cook dinner, which became a chilly chore. The temperature dropped to 2° and soon the wind began gusting up to sixty miles per hour. Frostbite was a concern at this point, but I was way more worried about a tree coming down on one of the tents. The wind sounded like a locomotive starting up the valley and picking up speed as it came towards us. I was scared.

I don't think I slept a wink that night. My four-season tent was seemingly taking a beating, flapping violently all night. When dawn broke, the wind had died down, but it was bitterly cold. It took a long time to pack up for the hike out. We had to keep warming our hands by the fire or they would lose feeling quickly.

A friend of mine had showed up the afternoon before the big blow and had set up camp next to us. He had worn plastic mountaineering boots on the hike in, and had broken through ice and gotten his feet wet. He didn't bother to try to dry the boots out by the fire, so they were basically chunks of ice the next morning. He had a real tough time getting them back on. He ended up with frostbite on his big toes, bad enough to turn them completely black. It was frighteningly cold.

On the hike out we had a few tricky water crossings, but managed to keep our feet dry—until the last crossing. Our oldest scout broke through the ice and got both feet wet. He freaked out. He was running and jumping around shouting, "This is not good!" We were about two miles from my truck, so I threw him the keys and told him to make haste, figuring the fast pace would warm his feet until he got to the parking lot. I also figured, of course, that he would know enough to start the truck and use the heater. To my surprise, he did not. When we got to the parking area, he was just sitting there rubbing his feet. (A year later he got his license.)

As always after a hike, we evaluated how it went. We have a tailgate test that goes like this: you make two piles on my tailgate from what's in your pack; one pile is of what you used, and the other pile is of stuff you didn't use. Then we talk about it so as to better prepare for future adventures in backpacking. We discussed the options we had when the older scout went into the drink. Should he have stopped and put on dry socks? Should we have gotten a fire going and dried his footwear? We decided that we were happy with our decisions and our performance as a team. I asked the boys if they were at all concerned by the violent weather the night before, and they responded that it was a wild adventure that they would not soon forget.

I'll always love the Catskills for the adventures they have afforded me in the past, and the ones I'll get to experience in the future. 🚶🚶

Winter ice. Photograph by Larry Gambon.

27

MY FIRST HIKE IN THE CATSKILLS

A Twenty-Degree Gale on the Burroughs Range on Memorial Day

Walter Gregory, #18, #8W
from Spring 1980 *Catskill Canister*

It was Memorial Day, 1961, and it started fair and warm, with no alarming weather predictions. With an early start to allow time for placing cars for a shuttle, off we went for a great day in the Catskills—Harry Ackerly, Mac Monroe, and I. The goal was to hike over Wittenberg, Cornell, and Slide, leaving one car at the foot of Slide and the other in Woodland Valley. This would be excellent training for my upcoming trip with the Boy Scouts that summer to the mountains of New Mexico. If I was to be a leader of boys where there is much rugged hiking in mountainous terrain, I had better be able to hike and keep up!

Mac, who was in front, took off in so much of a hurry that he ran a red light and was stopped by the State Police. What a beginning! We couldn't tell where they took him. What to do? Well, Harry and I decided to continue and adjust the original plans. "Wait! Who's that? Why, it's Mac!" He had caught up to us on the Thruway; he surely must have traveled hard to catch up. It took more than an hour to spot one car at the Slide trailhead, but we were finally on the trail.

On top of Wittenberg it was cold and overcast, but this was almost summer—it had to improve. Little did we know! We didn't linger on the summit, and before we reached Cornell it started to snow lightly. With the wind and cold I began to feel a little uneasy. We kept on, however, and at the summit there were four inches of snow—and it was coming down harder. This was my chilly introduction to hiking in the mountains. I quickly learned that chinos and a thin windbreaker were not quite proper in these conditions. We found that if we kept moving, however, we could stay almost warm.

Nearer to Slide Mountain, the snow was over our shoe tops, but we had passed the halfway point and felt we should go on. The precipitation had changed to snow and sleet, and with the wind it seemed to be falling horizontally. The trees looked like gaunt figures from dreamland. All the edges of branches into the storm had collected four or five inches of frozen rooster tails, looking for all the world like white fronds or setter tails waving stiffly in the cold wind. It was beautiful and different, but with that weather, surely no place to stop and gaze at the scenery.

The steep side of Slide almost did us in. Harry, with untiring energy, kept climbing ahead to return with favorable reports of "almost there" and other encouraging words. I had always admired him. He was five years my senior, one of those thin, wiry, ageless people who could go up and down and all over the trails with ease.

Boy, were we bushed when we finally reached the summit and the limited shelter of the lean-to (now removed)! It still stormed and the wind seemed much stronger up there. The thermometer registered 20°. I was starting to shiver. The others were all for building a fire (with what?), but I said, "No way! Just half a sandwich and I'm getting out of here. Off this mountain as soon as possible: let's just get pointed in the right direction and *go!*" The snow was now eight inches deep and getting deeper. We met a group of scouts with two leaders going up, their goal the lean-to. They had come up from Baltimore to enjoy a nice warm camping weekend, and where did they go but to the highest mountain? What a surprise they had!

View of Wittenberg Mountain from Cornell Mountain. Photograph by Andrew Moroz.

It seemed to take forever, but we eventually reached my car. It was raining and my car was completely covered with snow. Off with the wet shirt, windbreaker, and shoes—thank goodness for the foresight to bring extras. We stopped to buy a dry pair of pants for me. There were no lights because of a power failure, but fumbling around in the semi-dark with my flashlight, I found my size and hurriedly changed. We went for Mac's car, and his had no snow (the elevation was lower.) Then, back to Phoenicia for a hot meal and coffee, and all things seemed good once again.

Since that Memorial Day, I've climbed these mountains many times in all seasons, but never have I had such varying weather as on that day. My gear and clothing is now correct. I know when to turn back because of unsafe conditions, and have done so on several occasions both in the Catskills and the Adirondacks. I feel ready for whatever turn the weather may take. 🥾

28

MY FIRST SNOWSHOE ADVENTURE

ROOKIE'S CHRISTMAS ON THE BURROUGHS RANGE

Craig Mitchell, #161, #394W

I was a camper at the Lake Delaware Boys Camp in Delhi in the summer of 1972, and there I met my friend and mentor, Father Ray Donahue. A 10.9-mile hike was organized, starting from North Lake over Blackhead Mountain on the Escarpment Trail and down to the Batavia Kill lean-to, a total ascent of about 2,500 feet. The next day we ascended Black Dome and Thomas Cole, and then descended down to Maplecrest. I fell in love with the beauty of the Catskills and I couldn't wait to tell my friends on Long Island and come back for more.

Ray and I talked about the Catskills, peak bagging, the Catskill 3500 Club, and snowshoeing. I vividly remember him showing slides of his hikes, especially the pictures from atop Wittenberg of the great Friday slide taken only a month after it occurred. That enormous red-brown scar on the side of a mountain was something I thought only happened in the Rockies, and I tried to fathom the power and destruction of this event.[1]

Before that summer, all of my friends' and my experiences were one- or two-night backpacking trips in Bear Mountain Park and Harriman State Park, mostly with Boy Scouts. When school started, a friend got me involved in the high-school outdoor club. That fall I climbed another four mountains, and we planned a Thanksgiving backpacking trip to the Catskills, but that was squashed by our parents because of hunting season; our next opportunity would be at Christmas.

When Stu, Jon and I planned this hike, one mountain came up—Slide, the biggest! My brother agreed to drive us from Long Island to the trailhead on County Route 47 at Winnisook Lake (the trailhead was later moved to the present location, one mile south). We would spend two nights in the Slide Mountain lean-to (later removed by DEC) and one night at Terrace Mountain lean-to before hiking out to the bus stop in Phoenicia. We never sought advice, nor did I remember my conversations with Ray Donahue about the Catskills, winter weather conditions, and snowshoes.

We did, however, each buy ourselves Optimus 8R stoves (outdated, metallic, blue backpack stoves in a metal case—oh so heavy! But I still have mine, and it still works). For Christmas all three of us received the same brand of snowshoes. It was a complete surprise; none of us had even thought about needing snowshoes for this hike. They were a royal blue plastic (eight or ten inches wide and up to forty-two inches long) with leather bindings and no crampon. We knew nothing about what made a good or bad snowshoe.

The morning after Christmas, off we went with my brother. The clouds thickened as we drove north, and a light, steady snow began. It was cold, but with the snow falling, all the trees dusted and the quiet, it was oh so beautiful. The trail had two inches of fresh powder on a hard base, with about a foot of snow off the trail. As we climbed, the snow got deeper. Here were three beginners in cotton[2] on the Catskills' tallest peak in the cold and snow, putting on brand new snowshoes with full packs. We struggled to get them on, and after only a few steps we were all walking out of them and tripping and falling. The packs came off, and we put the snowshoes back on. That last mile to the summit was torture, taking over two hours!

We arrived at the summit, in the clouds, cold and wet, snow still falling. The lean-to looked so good—until we saw that inside were six inches of snow and ice! We changed into dry clothes and spent the rest of the day cleaning out the snow and trying to stay warm by running around and exploring the summit winter wonderland. We drank a lot of hot chocolate and soup. Everything froze so fast, that

Slide Mountain summit, 4,180 feet, late December. Photograph by David White.

the only way to keep our wet clothing and boots from freezing was to wear them. Fortunately, I did have several pairs of wool socks. That night and the next day, the bitter cold and snow continued. Our bags were rated three-season, probably thirty-five to forty degrees.

After the two nights we headed off Slide toward Cornell. The snow was up to three feet deep and we slid most of the way down, getting wet but still having fun. Cornell's crown was a major challenge for beginners in non-cramponed snowshoes, struggling 600 feet up with full packs in lots of fresh deep snow! We didn't get to Terrace Mountain lean-to until four o'clock when, luckily, the snow stopped and the temperature moderated, because we were wet and cold. Shortly after arriving, we heard the distinctive voice of our friend, Ray Donahue! We had lots of laughs over our adventures. He showed us tips on our bindings and how he made crampons for traction out of nuts and bolts. As darkness approached, Ray bushwhacked off the ridge.

The next day we hiked off Terrace Mountain and walked six miles to Phoenicia for the bus ride back to Long Island. For three nights we hadn't seen one other hiker except Ray; that serenity probably can't be found anymore. The following year I finished my Catskill 3500 Club hikes on West Kill Mountain (trailless then). I continue to hike and snowshoe in the Northeast and have gone through two pairs of wooden modified Bearpaw snowshoes, one Tubbs, and now use either Atlas or newer Tubbs. And my clothing has been upgraded, too! Moral of the story: hike and snowshoe, but be prepared, try out new equipment before you get to the trailhead, don't wear cotton, and have fun. 𖧧

---

[1] See "Something Happened in the Mountains."

[2] Cotton doesn't dry well. It clings and stays cold when wet, and therefore can cause hypothermia. Wool remains warm even when wet. Newer synthetic clothing wicks away sweat, is lighter when wet, and dries quickly.

29

WEATHERWISE OR OTHERWISE?

YOU NEVER KNOW WHAT WILL HAPPEN ON A CATSKILLS BACKPACK

Bleecker Staats, #272
from Winter 1987 *Catskill Canister*

The forecast was: "Occasional showers on Saturday; clearing on Sunday. Possible snow in Buffalo." I was glad we were headed for the Neversink Valley in the Catskills, and not to Buffalo. At the Denning trailhead we loaded our packs with all the supplies we needed for our group and headed up the yellow-marked Denning-Woodland Valley Trail (now Phoenicia-East Branch Trail). We were the first of ten hikers on this "Bleecker's Creepers"[1] weekend. We packed in along a trail where aroma and color were forecasting the coming autumn. Some of the crossing logs were rotted away, and getting across the Neversink River with heavy packs was tricky. The place we picked to camp was a quarter-mile upstream from the lean-to along an unofficial green trail. There, we formed a "kitchen" from stones of an existing fireplace and picked sites for the five tents. The prospect of spending the night snuggled in sleeping bags beside a forest stream is always exciting. Day hiking is surely enjoyable, but overnight camping is the ultimate Catskill experience.

In an hour John came up the trail, and then Tim, as the sun was setting. Our stomachs were reminding us that there were spaces that needed filling. At last the rest arrived, their approaching flashlights twinkling like fireflies. A candle lantern on a hemlock branch showed them where to cross to our camp. We soon had a great dinner going. We ate our planned fare in courses, starting with soup and salad and then on to the main course of macaroni and cheese with hamburger and gravy. There is nothing like a good hearty meal to add to a campout. My only disappointment was that I had forgotten my backpack oven, so the cake planned for dessert never was baked. Ah well, no one is perfect. Drinking tea, hot chocolate, fresh coffee, we chatted around the cheery fire. Later, in a tent filled with the mixed aroma of evergreens and campfire, I crawled into my sleeping bag thinking what a nice place it was to camp and what nice people with which to be camping.

The sun shone briefly during our hot breakfast, and we made plans for the day. Four elected to stay at camp—reading, exploring the stream, or doing whatever

A Catskill Mountain stream. Photograph by Larry Gambon.

seemed pleasant. In high spirits the rest of us crossed the Neversink and started off on an unofficial red trail. What a lovely walk this is, even if the "occasional showers" predicted were turning into a steady drizzle. Up along the rushing stream we filed through dripping beeches and maples. A blue jay called above a beaver meadow. We passed crystal pools dotted with fallen yellow and red leaves, a trout's paradise. It was still raining when we chatted with a couple camped upstream, and later on when we took a break.

At 2,600 feet, Bill and Ed took a compass heading that would bring us within ten feet of the canister on Rocky. When climbing through the wet forest, wonderful smells of damp moss, rich bark, mature ferns, and balsam permeate the air; you can tell your elevation by your nose. Whoever planted all those "Christmas trees" up there surely put them close to one another! We were soaked from below as well as above. It rained even harder at the summit. When signing the register, we had to switch from pen to pencil to keep our signatures from smearing.

It got wetter and colder as we descended to the col between Rocky and Lone, where we ate a brief lunch. Some returned to camp from there; Bill, Ed, and I proceeded up Lone to the canister. It was windy, wet, and cold when we signed in, and it was a relief to get moving again down to camp. The going was slippery, and my thin gloves were as soaked as my jeans and shirt. I wished I'd put on my Gortex jacket before I reached the wet balsams on Rocky.

The campfire greeting us on our return to camp was a welcome sight. How Marlene and Carolyn got it going in the rain was a feat in itself! I shivered so much that I could hardly hold my cup of hot chocolate. It was half an hour after changing clothes and getting into my sleeping bag before the shivering stopped.

About 7:00 PM, I awoke from a nap and the "occasional showers" had now turned into a windy deluge. Although Bill had put extra logs on the fire, it was fading fast. Everyone was snug in tents with snacks, so I didn't feel bad about the big planned dinner we were missing. A chocolate bar just hit the spot!

Nature called at 3:00 AM. The wind was blowing, and the sound of rain had given way to something plopping hard against the windy side of the tent. I could hear large branches slowly cracking and falling to the forest floor. I soon realized my suspicions were right when I shined my flashlight out through the tent flap. What a shock it was to see the light beam shining into a blinding blizzard! There was an inch of snow on everything. Tree trunks looked like so many marble columns. Was this October 4?

Around 8:00 AM there were five inches of blowing snow and no sign of it letting up. The word was passed for all to be dressed, ready to leave in fifteen minutes. We would leave our gear behind. It would be hazardous to attempt a crossing of the swollen Neversink; leaving by the green trail would be wiser. Following this informal trail proved easier said than done, however, because the snow on the tree trunks obliterated traces of green paint. We worked our way around the tributaries of Deer Shanty Brook, through bent beeches and over fallen trunks. As we bent under and stepped over blowdowns, I was glad I'd left my heavy pack behind. Finally we ascended to the yellow trail, now hardly recognizable. We had to walk off the trail often to get around downed beeches and moosewood.

To unlock and un-jam the doors of our snow-encrusted vehicles, it was necessary to chip away the crust. I discovered that I had left the window on the passenger side of Judy's car open. There was a drift of snow from the window ledge down across to the driver's seat. Fortunately, she is a forgiving soul. Back home in Red Hook, the power was out because of the storm.

Monday dawned sunny and bright. Ed, Bill, and I met for breakfast and then drove back to the trailhead. Most of the snow had melted, and trees had dropped their snowy burdens and sprung back up. At our campsite, at least five additional inches of snow had fallen after our fast exit. The swollen Neversink was still crystal clear. After two trips, with lunch in between, we finished loading the last of the wet gear and left for home at 5:40 PM.

I will always be reminded of those four days whenever I hear a weatherman say, "Occasional showers on Saturday." ❧

---

[1] So-named because we take our time.

30

DRENCHED ON DOUBLETOP

FROM CALM STREAMS TO RAGING TORRENTS

Walter L. Gregory, #18, #8W
from Spring 1978 *Catskill Canister*

Despite the rain, seven stalwarts started from Seager on a scheduled Catskill 3500 Club hike to climb Doubletop and Graham. The group included myself (leader), Donahue, Hentschel, Mitchell, Lindo, Bachli, and Virginia Durso. We expected the rain to stop soon, but it rained very hard all day, much as you would find in a tropical storm or even a hurricane.

When we started, Dry Brook was its usual calm stream. (Its name comes from the German, *drei*, meaning "three"—it is never dry!) We easily crossed Drury Hollow Brook and the north and south forks of Flatiron Brook by hopping rocks. About three-fourths of the way up, we encountered snow that became two feet deep at the summit—Bachli and Ginnie didn't have snowshoes with them. Each step was like stepping into a pothole. Being soaked inside and out, the plan to climb Graham was scrubbed.

Whereas the climb was a wet and miserable slippery ascent, the descent was a wild, challenging experience. Water runoff and the melting snow made the return dangerous—below the snow line all was mud and slide and slip … and more mud and slip and slide. The placid brooks were now raging torrents! The south fork of Flatiron Brook was now about four feet deep and fifteen feet across. After much discussion and worry, the first group reaching it joined hands and formed a chain, carefully making this crossing through deep, rushing water. Drury Hollow Brook was also a raging torrent and forced us to form another chain to get safely across.

The second group, slowed by lack of snowshoes, arrived forty minutes later to these crossings. Bachli and I ranged up and down the banks in search of suitable logs, while Ginnie calmly awaited our return. We traveled way upstream to cross the south fork. This was the first climb in the Catskills for Ginnie, and through it all she showed much grit and stamina. It was quite an introduction for her! Despite all that water above and below and around us, we enjoyed the day with the usual amount of fun and nonsense that erupts on every trip. 𝕏

31

STORM HIKING

MOTHER NATURE PUTS ON A SHOW

Dean Macgeorge, #1174, #456W

My son Chris was working at Camp Trimount, a Boy Scout camp in East Jewett, and I drove up each Friday night to pick him up for the weekend. One weekend I decided to mix a hike into the event. I called my favorite taxi driver in Greene County and asked him to pick me up at the camp at 2:30 PM and drive me over to the trailhead for the Blackhead Range on Big Hollow Road. The weather started to deteriorate as we drove over, but I was prepared because I had checked the forecast earlier that day. As he dropped me off, the lightning and thunder exploded onto the scene and I made a run for the Batavia Kill lean-to, one and a quarter miles up the trail. I waited in the lean-to for the storm to let up, which it soon did. I hustled up Blackhead Mountain and then started over to Black Dome.

As I reached the lookout on Blackhead, I could see the clouds gathering strength. I love the stretch of trail between those two mountains, and made haste covering it. As I topped out on Black Dome, I could see the clouds swirling around near the top of Thomas Cole Mountain. I knew I'd better put the hammer down or I'd be in the thick of it sooner than I really wanted. I was tripping on all the rocks and roots because I was watching the weather rather than the trail. And the weather was worth watching! Those clouds were getting darker and turning a menacing shade of purple. I was starting to worry—purple is *not* good. I hit the summit of Thomas Cole and dropped off on a faint trail leading back to the camp (and dry clothes). At about 3,650 feet, I found an overhang and threw myself under it as the first bolts of lightning hit all around me. Holy crap! This was not good at all. This storm was way too intense for anyone to be where I was.

I was shivering hard, but I don't know if it was from the cold wet clothes or from being quite scared. I know the hair was standing tall on the back of my neck. I'd never heard thunder so loud! This went on for over an hour. I decided that I was going to have to make a run for it sometime before it started to get dark. I determined that 6:00 PM was the cut-off time for getting out before dark. That was at 5:15. The storm raged continuously up until 6:00 PM, when I started down a totally soaking bushwhack. It was really dicey going. It was so wet and slippery that thoughts of a broken or twisted ankle started to occupy my mind.

Luckily the storm let up as I made my way down to camp, and I even had time to stop and pick some juicy raspberries. Sweet rewards! As I made my way through camp, I found my son in the dining hall. He said that he had heard that I was up there, but he wasn't concerned. He'd hiked with me plenty in the past, so he knew how it went sometimes.

I had brought along a fresh change of clothes, and made use of the showers. Boy, did that feel grand! I then ventured down to Palenville for a nice Italian meal before picking him up later that evening.

The most amazing times I have had in the Catskills are when Mother Nature puts on a big show. 🥾

Black Dome Mountain from Blackhead Mountain. Photograph by Larry Gambon.

32

SOMETHING HAPPENED IN THE MOUNTAINS

A New 2,300-Foot Slide Route to Friday Mountain

Rev. Ray L. Donahue, #23, #1W
from Winter 1969 *Catskill Canister*, originally titled
"Historia Naturalis de Montis Ruina"

After a week of rain, the downpour on May 29, 1968, was by far the heaviest. This was the kind of day that keeps even a woodsman inside. Nelson Shultis, owner of the Wittenberg Lumber Company, certainly had no intention of going out that morning, but the log truck from Dolgeville had arrived to be loaded. So there he was, loading logs in Moon Haw Hollow. He was wet, muddy, and unhappy. And so was the truck driver.

The ridge that rises above Moon Haw and Maltby hollows in a giant semi-circle is one of the most rugged in the mountains. On its crest are four of the major Catskill peaks. Its face is extremely steep and is well known for its ledges and cliffs. The days of driving rain were beginning to leave their mark on this ridge. Here and there along its great arc, the water-logged soil was slipping down the smooth rock of the ledges, only to be stopped by the firmly rooted earth below.

Four miles away from the ridge and three thousand feet lower is the hamlet of West Shokan. There, the water in the main gauge was rising rapidly. It was well on its way to the record reading for the day of 4.88 inches. The time was 11:00 AM., and the loading operation in Moon Haw Hollow was nearing completion. Both men were thinking about dry clothes and hot coffee. Suddenly, the truck driver pointed to the stream and yelled, "Look at that!" It was no longer water, but a fast-moving chocolate pudding of mud. Sniffing, he added, "It smells just like freshly-plowed earth. What's going on here?" Mr. Shultis did not have to think of an answer; he knew what had happened back in the mountains.

Unlike at other places on the ridge, the movement of wet earth on the easterly arm of Friday Mountain was not stopped. After pulling away from a small outcropping rock, it was guided on its downward plunge by a small gully. As the slide gained momentum, tons of mud and hundreds of trees were hurled down the mountainside. At several spots the slope's grade eased a bit, but this only caused the slide to become wider before continuing its relentless descent to the stream between the eastern tongues of Cornell and Friday. Fortunately the main force of the slide was dissipated within 300 yards after reaching the streambed, and the remainder was neatly channeled to the Ashokan Reservoir.

During the Memorial Day weekend, the weather cleared. As the clouds lifted, a 2,300-foot scar with a vertical rise of 1,000 feet was unveiled on the northeast flank of Friday Mountain. Mr. Shultis and his crew were the first to make an on-the-spot investigation of the slide's track. The mud on the slide track has long since turned to hardpan. Mountaineers are discovering this new route for the ascent of Friday.[1] It is a challenge, and it is a climb with continuous views. Far from being an ugly scar, the slide track on Friday is a beauty mark on the face of the Catskills. 👣

---

[1] See "A Winter Slide Climb."

View from Blackhead Mountain in November. Photograph by David White.

33

BLACKHEAD FROM THE JONES FARM

THE COLDEST HALF HOUR OF MY LIFE

Franklin B. Clark, #33, #23W
from Winter 1982 *Catskill Canister*

On the first Saturday in November 1927, the Greene County Boy Scouts organized a hike up 3,940-foot Blackhead Mountain. The scout executive led boys from Athens, Cairo, and Catskill up the trail from the Jones farm; the Maplecrest scoutmaster led his boys up the trail from Big Hollow. They would all meet on top for lunch. I was sixteen, had never hiked anything but roads, and had looked forward to a 3,000-foot climb with a sense of excitement tinged with apprehension.

It was spitting snow when my father dropped off the Athens contingent. The first part of the hike was up a ridge, which presented no problems for anyone. When we came to the section that was once a log chute, there were plenty of trees to grab. We were proud to reach the high shoulder below the summit. On top we found a wild winter day. We were dressed for fall in the Hudson Valley, and here we were in a snow cloud with a raging north wind. The spring was covered with four inches of ice. The trees were so coated with hoarfrost that we had great difficulty in starting fires to cook the food we had brought. It was the coldest half hour of my life.

Almost forty years passed before I went near Blackhead again. In January 1967 the Catskill 3500 Club designated Black Dome and Thomas Cole for its first winter hike. On the way back, Bill Leavitt led those of us who needed to climb Blackhead in winter up the old trail from the col. A sleet storm carried on a south wind had reached us before noon. This time, however, dressed in a parka, warm mittens and boots, I found it an enjoyable experience. Blackhead has since become one of my favorite mountains. 🚶

Part V:

WINTER ADVENTURING

Stretching down from a handhold, I let go. No problem to the first spot. Jumping off that, my gaiter string catches on a branch halfway down and I'm suddenly hanging headfirst. It's too high to reach up and free it, and the tension of the string is too strong to wiggle it free. … Dave says I resembled a side of beef hanging in the butcher's cooler.

Carol White

Photograph by Tom Rankin.

34

ENGULFED BY NATURE

THE OUTER AND INNER JOURNEY

Manuel A. Peraza #1373, #566W

On March 9, 2003, I arrive at the Seager Road trailhead parking lot at 8:30 AM to find my friend Robert "Rocky" Walberg already waiting. He will be the one leading me on this last of my 3500 winter peaks, to the summit of Doubletop Mountain. There couldn't be anybody better than he to join me on this hike.

This is a real winter day—cloudy, cold and windy—the kind of day I wish I were in my bed in Staten Island instead of here, three hours away in the middle of this range of mountains. Don't get me wrong: I love the outdoors, but today my thoughts are influenced by the not so pleasant experience of the solo hike I took before this one on Plateau Mountain eight days ago. At the same time, however, I feel great excitement at the prospect of finishing the last of the winter 3500 peaks, finally. These feelings are like two forces pulling in opposite directions.

The warm ambiance inside the car makes me slow down a bit in putting on my boots and gaiters. After the final pack and equipment check, I lock up the car, and I stand ready to start hiking. Rocky, who is ready before me, starts to check his car carefully. He opens the hood and looks inside, then looks under the radiator, and I hear him saying something about a leak. I will never forget the intense color of that yellow-green antifreeze, enhanced by the white snow, splashing on the ground in a steady rhythm. "Well! I don't want to get stuck out here, Manuel," he says, with a very serious expression. "You'll have to climb the mountain by yourself. I saw some snowshoe tracks; they may help you. Just point the compass south and go. You know where to start, right?" "Yes, I do," I answer. "Bye, and be careful," he says, then jumps in his car and takes off fast, leaving a narrow trail of that psychedelic-colored antifreeze on the frozen ground.

All of a sudden here I am standing in the middle of the parking lot alone, feeling kind of puzzled and realizing that things are not going exactly right—first the car leak, and now the wind picking up and the snow, just a trace before, intensifying. But I have a mission to accomplish, so I'd better put on my snowshoes and get going.

The first mile on the Seager Trail is great for warming up. After crossing the creeks and kills with their ice- and snow-covered rocks, I feel nature slowly engulfing me with its subtle and invisible veil. It seems as though I am looking through a diffuser photo filter into the panorama, accompanied by the stillness and the sounds of water and wind. It is part of the eternal forest symphony, broken now by the *click, clack* of my plastic snowshoes.

Now I see the bridge where I have to leave the trail and bushwhack to Doubletop's summit. I set the compass and can see barely visible snowshoe tracks here. *Where are my trekking poles? Here they are! Now, my first step into the real hike. They say a hundred-mile journey starts with a single step … well, what about a two mile journey to the top? That sounds much better. I better stop talking to myself and pay attention to what I'm doing.*

The snow and wind increase in intensity. While trying to follow almost nonexistent tracks, I recall that when I climbed this mountain with Madame Marguerite for the summer peaks, there were some distinctive features of the terrain. I hope to identify these as I go along. I try to stay at the center of the ridge, especially at the lower part of the mountain. This mountain, like many in the Catskills, looks like a staircase with giant steps on the way to the summit. I still have to reach the first giant step … Ah! It is time for a sip of water and a little break. The beauty of hiking solo is that you can enjoy the moments of solitude and contemplation without distractions. I am not a forestry expert or a botanical whiz kid, so I just enjoy the beauty around me. My tree knowledge is average, with some exceptions—like being able to recognize spruces. I can also recognize Scotch pines and Douglas firs, not only because those are the types of trees I have seen the most of, but also because I use them at home at Christmas.

As I climb higher, the snow is becoming deeper and powdery. I am slowly reaching my points of reference and the giant steps in an orderly manner, although by now the faint tracks on the snow are all but gone. I am completely energized, like the Duracell bunny. I just have to scout ahead more intensely and check the compass more often, because the visibility is poor. One wrong move and I may get lost. In certain areas bushwhacking gets thicker and harder than before, but the idea is to keep pushing toward the goal. Emerging from one of those thick patches, my eyes catch an open space ahead; the clear area turns out to be powdery snow. With every step I take, I get deeper into it until it reaches my waist. Well, just another small, difficult spot! I reach a more level area where I can stand comfortably, have a water break, and look around to study my next move. I check the compass and start walking again in a southbound direction, as the crow flies. The snow is now knee deep and the climb is getting steeper. My educated guess is that I'm about seven to eight hundred feet below the summit, which is not bad.

I think about what I'll do after I finish my 3500 winter mountains, when all of a sudden—in a flash—I find myself buried in snow up to my neck. For a few seconds

I'm in shock, paralyzed, my mind totally blank. Then my instincts for self-preservation propel me into action. I try to get out by using what resembles swimming strokes, but I cannot move my lower body. I am trapped. A spruce trap! Now reason enters the drama. I stop unnecessary movement and evaluate the situation. I try to move my left foot. It moves! Now let's try the right foot. It does not move. I try harder. No movement at all. At that instant, out of nowhere, I think of the fall I sustained one week ago a few feet below the summit of Plateau Mountain. One of the points of my left crampon got caught in the right leg gaiter. After a few somersaults in the air and seeing the crampons I was wearing against the background of the blue sky, my fall was finally stopped by a tree, where I lay motionless with my back in the snow, assessing possible injuries. Move one finger, move the other. Move one hand, move the other …

I am in the middle of a blizzard. Spirals of twisted snow rise up as though dancing into the clouds, energized by the strong, howling winds rushing loudly through the trees. I glance at the huge, black, triangular rock two hundred feet above me—very impressive.

I have to start digging until I can reach the snowshoe and try to free it. As I dig into the powdery snow, it keeps falling back into the opening. Finally I reach the end tip of my right snowshoe and pull it hard, but I am not able to dislodge it. I keep digging, but the snowshoe is embedded in the branches. No way can I free myself the way things are right now. My next step is to try to free my foot by loosening the snowshoe straps, but whenever I move it's like quicksand, with nothing solid to hold onto. My left leg is in an off-balanced position, so it is tough to maneuver. With my gloves off, little by little I start to loosen one strap after the other with my bare hands. Finally, my foot is free. What a nice sensation it is to be able to move my rather numb legs again! Now let's pull the snowshoe out. A few side-to-side shakes and pulls, and here it comes. I get out of the trap, put on my gloves and snowshoes, and pack quickly because I'm getting cold!

With my legs numb, I move to the left of the trap, make a right turn, and slowly start climbing until I find myself again in waist-deep snow. *This mountain is not going to stop challenging me*, I tell myself. I keep going, but the snow trap has consumed a good deal of my energy. I have to rest more frequently. All I'm doing is fighting the snow and going aimlessly uphill, so it's time to set course again. *Let's look for a focal point, a landmark. Yes! Where the big black triangular rock is?* I look up, but with so much snow swirling, sometimes I can see it and sometimes I can't. Suddenly there it is! On my right. I have to get to it!

For about two hundred feet it is hard going, and I come to a point where the possibility of quitting crosses my mind, but guess what? By now I am only fifty feet away from the big black rock. It's only a matter of minutes before I get to it. What a sense of relief it is to be able to touch and lean against the rock! I am smiling, proud; I can feel my strength coming back. It is hard to explain the euphoria of the moment. *But wait—I have not reached the top yet! Am I on the right route?* I caress the black rock and proceed to climb an inclined narrow lateral ledge on the side of the rock. To my surprise, at the end of it is an animal path going uphill into the trees. I follow it, switching to other, similar paths looking for the highest point of the terrain. The more I advance, the more numerous the paths become, which inclines me to believe that the mountain summit is not very far away.

I am right, because after fifteen minutes I spot the much-looked-for gray canister. I register in the book and write something to the effect that this is the last of my 3500 winter peaks. After returning the book to the canister and making sure it is properly secure, I start looking for a place to sit, have lunch, and celebrate my birthday and that of my mother, who has been gone a long time. My birthday gift for her is a prayer and Doubletop Mountain; for me, it's the 3500 winter patch. Mission accomplished.

I summon forth the joyful memories of my youth, when our families used to gather together to celebrate our birthdays. There's no better place than this beautiful mountain to revive those moments and to reflect on how the mountains with their magnetism have always lured me into their arms, ever since I was a child growing up in the Andes. I remember getting up at four o'clock in the morning to climb three thousand feet so that I could contemplate the distant glow of the snow-covered peaks at dawn. What an unforgettable sight! I recall traversing the Chihuahuan desert, with its unique characteristics and terrain formations, solo for five days. It was there that for the first time in my life I could—like an animal—smell water from one mile away.

After many years of rock climbing and mountaineering, here I am in the Catskill Mountains—back into the simplicity and sheer beauty of hiking, with its spiritual and physical rewards given to those willing to open their minds and spirits to allow the magic of nature to enter.

After thirty minutes at the top, I start my descent. Five minutes into the descent, Rocky Walberg comes out from behind a bend in the path and scares the hell out of me. He asks me how I am doing, and he looks into my pupils. "You are okay," he says. "I saw where you got into trouble. Congratulations! You really are a mountain man."

At the trailhead box, I check us out in the book as Rocky continues to the parking lot. The new club secretary, Laurie Moore, and Margaret Smith are there, and I join them. Somebody opens a trunk, and to my surprise they have pies and coffee in there to celebrate one of the women getting her winter patch. What a treat!

A last note: I have climbed Doubletop many times since that March 3, 2003, morning, but I have never been able to find that big black triangular rock again. ⚇

35

ROOKIE CRAMPONING

FOUR MISTAKES

Dean Macgeorge, #1174, #456W

Mistakes were made. More than I'd like to admit. I was hungry to do a winter ascent in the Catskills and eager to try using crampons for the first time. I decided to climb Windham High Peak and planned a very early start from my house in the Hudson Valley. It was January 1 and every bit of winter. I told my wife my plans and kissed her good-bye. On the way up the Thruway, I changed my mind and decided to make the hike more interesting by climbing North Dome Mountain instead. It was supposed to be a stiff bushwhack from the Devil's Path, or so I was told. Mistake #1: now nobody knew my plans.

I did not own a pair of gaiters, but I had on a new pair of North Face Gortex pants and didn't think anything about it. I strapped on the crampons at the trailhead and started up the trail to West Kill Mountain. After a half mile or so, you take a right into the woods and start the bushwhack up North Dome. I had my map and compass and the skills to use them, so I wasn't worried about navigation. I *was* worried, however, about the dark clouds collecting as I climbed upwards toward the summit. Soon the snow started coming down in earnest. At the same time the climb became extremely steep, and I was beginning to have trouble getting a purchase with my feet. The first time I heard a rip, my heart sank, as I knew I had just wrecked my pants. You see, the pants were quite baggy, and that doesn't work well with crampons. As my feet slipped trying to get a grip on anything under the two to three feet of snow I was trying to plow through, the crampons would catch my pants and shred them. Mistake #2: not bringing gaiters to protect my pants. Two minutes later, rip again. And then again. I finally used my trusty bandana to lessen the damage to at least one side, but that only gave my crampon something to catch on and trip me up. The fun of this hike was dissipating fast! I found myself on my bum in deep powder swearing up a storm.

If that wasn't enough, the storm strengthened. I decided to turn around. This is the kind of stuff you read about in the papers: "Hiker lost in storm, found dead." Not me. I descended 500 hard-won feet in elevation, and the storm lessened. Great. So I decided to head back up just in time for the storm to intensify again. Back down again. I determined that the storm was really just a bunch of squalls and went back up again. Fifteen hundred feet of climbing to net 500 feet of elevation. I was getting frustrated. Mistake #3: getting frustrated can lead to bad decision-making.

Meanwhile my pants were taking a beating and no longer afforded me much protection from the elements. I felt the snow getting in and chilling me. I quickened the pace to keep myself warmer and soon reached the canister on the summit. I signed in and decided that I might as well pop over to the summit of Sherrill Mountain while I was up there. It was only 9:00 AM, and with North Dome behind me I was feeling better. It was a quick trip to the next summit, and as I signed in I decided to lessen the trip back by dropping down to Route 42 and hitching a ride; I just wanted down … now. Mistake #4: hitch-hiking early on New Year's Day in the Catskills can be difficult.

I decided to go door to door at the few homes along Route 42 near where I finally came out of the forest. There I stood on their front steps looking like I just washed up on the beach after being shipwrecked, by the looks of my pants—totally shredded! The damage was so extensive that it became quite funny to me. I felt like I was wearing a badge of honor that proclaimed, *I survived!* I must have looked like a fool. I found only one house occupied. When the guy answered the door, I got strange looks and the usual questions: "You were where, doing what? You call that fun?" Just then a beautiful girl appeared, and as he glanced at her he told me that he couldn't leave her to give me a ride to my truck ten miles away. He even turned down the $20 I offered. I can't say I blame him.

I started walking. Two hours, but only a few cars later, a limousine, of all things, stopped and picked me up. It was an interesting ride, as the vehicle was only running on six or seven of its eight cylinders. I was beginning to wonder if it would make it, but the driver was unconcerned and took me right to the trailhead. I offered him the $20, but he declined it. I sent the pants back to North Face for repairs, and they sent me a brand new pair! It was a good ending to a crazy day in the Catskills. 🏃

36

THE BOYS ENJOYED A COLD ONE

Sub-Zero Snow Devils and Survival

Joe Herrod

I met Chris Cobbs and Big Mully at the trailhead to Wittenberg Mountain at 8:00 AM. The temperature had warmed up to 20° on a cloudy, windy January 16. Surprisingly, there was no ice and only four inches of snow—no need for either crampons or snowshoes. A day hiker came blowing by us on the steep climb out of Woodland Valley. Big Mully was wrestling a serious chest cold and wheezed, snorted, hacked his way up the trail. Because the wind was blowing so hard, I mentioned that a nice lean-to on Terrace Mountain was just nine-tenths of a mile on a side trail, and maybe we should go there instead of tenting up on top.

At 2.6 miles and 2,550 feet, the trail comes to a "T." Right is a 1,300 climb in 1.3 miles to Wittenberg; left is the 300-foot descent to the lean-to. The wind made the choice: left. Arriving at 12:30, what do we do now? After eating we ambled back up the trail half a mile to a bare rock area, but now the wind is really fierce. It's blizzard conditions—biting cold, a driving snow squall—so we turn around and get blown back to the lean-to where there's not much to do except hunker down.

Big Mully got busy melting snow for our water supply. Two day-hikers arrived on their way to Woodland Valley after starting on the other side of Slide Mountain. They have no emergency equipment, not even a day pack, just camelback water bags! We consider them dumb and lucky. It's a long and potentially hazardous hike over Slide, Cornell, and Wittenberg, and a lot of accidents can happen in a blizzard. With sub-zero cold coming in, they didn't leave themselves any margin for error. They tell us the predicted high temperature for tomorrow is only 5°. This is the first we have heard of the intense cold returning, and it sends a shiver through me. The forecast I had was for a continuing warming trend.

By late afternoon Big Mully has melted all the water we will need. We've drunk hot drinks, eaten freeze-dried dinners, and are ready to settle in for the evening. The weather is clearing, the temperature is dropping fast, and the wind is even stronger. We're thankful that we're in the lean-to instead of in a tent being blown off the top of the mountain. I took the boys outside the lean-to and showed them Saturn and Jupiter shining brightly along with a waxing moon in the cold twilight. They stayed there about eleven seconds.

Here's what I was wearing in my sleeping bag: inner socks, knee socks, fiberfill booties, polypro briefs, polypro long johns, fleece pants, two polypro long-sleeved undershirts, fleece shirt, fleece jacket, Marmot polartec jacket, neck gaiter, fleece hat, poly gloves and wool mittens. All of this was inside a fiberfill bag liner and a down bag—but I use a twenty-five-year-old bag probably rated for no lower than 25°. I felt like I was in a strait jacket. Couldn't move. I once read that if you weren't wearing all your clothes when you went to bed, you had carried too many clothes. I did not carry too many clothes. Big Mully contends that being so tightly bundled actually makes you colder. He highly recommends an investment in a −20° synthetic bag. He slept in polypro liner socks with wool socks over those, full top/bottom heavyweight polypro, and a wool shirt. And he never pulled the sleeping bag hood over his head. He was enjoying the all-night-long snow showers on his face too much!

It was a memorable night. The wind sounded like a dozen freight trains passing through. One good thing about it was that it drowned out Big Mully's snoring. We could hear gusts gathering strength behind the lean-to, and then look out and see snow devils swirling past. The back draft blew snow into the lean-to and all over our gear. We suspected gusts of forty to fifty miles per hour. Chris wanted to put up a space blanket to block it out, but we were too cold and apathetic to fool with it. We didn't have enough tarp to cover the opening, and it might have ripped down anyway.

Chris left his candle burning—just to give some semblance of warmth, I guess. I didn't bother to hang my food; if any animal was determined enough to brave the cold for my Pop Tarts, it could have them. Anyway, don't bears hibernate? If we'd had any brains we'd have been with them, Big Mully adds. I kept waking up as I cooled down. Half a dozen times I did reverse pushups with my elbows and heels and isometric exercises to generate heat inside the bag. It works. I found that I dissipated less heat while lying on my side than while lying on my back. You notice such finer points when you are on the edge. But sleeping on my side makes my shoulders hurt. Later, we found that our down sleeping bags were wet, mostly from perspiration that condenses in the outer layers in cold weather. If we'd stayed out another night, I would've been in trouble.

At the first light, Big Mully is awake and coughing his lungs out, as he has been doing all night. Chris is completely cocooned inside his bag; not even his nose is sticking out. It's 7:15 and Big Mully makes me guess the temperature: −12°. That's the coldest I've ever been out in; with a twenty-mile-per-hour wind, the wind chill is −52°. At 7:30 the sun popped over the Cross Mountain ridge and shined directly into the lean-to, more a psychological than a real boost. A light coating of snow covers us; I had two icebergs for water bottles. Big Mully and Chris fire off their stoves and begin melting snow and thawing water bottles. Breakfast is Pop Tarts, granola bars, and hot tea.

Eventually you have to do it—the hardest part of winter camping: get out of the bag, pack up, and time the disrobing so that you don't freeze before you start. There's the hassle of putting your gaiters on while your fingers freeze. Our toes went numb before we started. Chris walked around the lean-to several times to try to warm up. Off at 10:30, and the temperature has risen to −5°. On the 3.5-mile trek back, the wind was in our faces and ice coated Chris's eyelashes. As the feeling began to come back into my numb toes, the sensation was unpleasant. The footing was lousy—not enough snow for snowshoes, but just deep enough to hide loose rocks. Big Mully couldn't take the slow pace any longer—he was too cold—and took off. The temperature remained −5° as we descended.

My fifty-sixth birthday was in one week, so the boys treated me to a birthday meal when we finally made it back. Thanks. 🥾

Catskill Mountain winter scene. Photograph by Larry Gambon.

37

MOUNTAIN ODYSSEY

FROM "DOWN THE TUBES BY 40" TO WINTER 111 FIRST

Betty Heald, #305, #102W

While employed by the New York City YMCA as Nature Director of a girls' camp near Port Jervis, New York, I was invited by the camp director to be the female leader of a group of ten co-ed campers on a three-day trek from Madison Hut to Lake of the Clouds Hut in New Hampshire. It wasn't until 1971 that I discovered there were hiking clubs; it took me a year to locate one in northern New Jersey. At first I day-hiked, and only on summer weekends. Within four years I was traversing a fifty-mile-plus, hut-to-hut hike of the Presidential Range in New Hampshire's White Mountains.

One December, I attended the Appalachian Mountain Club/Adirondack Mountain Club weeklong Winter School, providing me with the basic skills needed for future winter hiking quests in New York State and New England. I learned how to use Iverson Bear-paw snowshoes and ten-point crampons. I felt prepared to join my fellow North Jersey Adirondack Mountain Club members on winter Catskill hikes.

My enthusiasm for winter hiking grew during that first winter and I made many Catskill climbs. The first climb, in early January, is especially memorable. Doubletop Mountain was scheduled, a 3,860-foot trailless peak in the central Catskill Forest Preserve. When I contacted the hike leader, he was hesitant about allowing a woman to accompany the party. He felt I had insufficient experience and that I might not have the stamina to keep up with a dozen males. He insisted I provide my own transportation to and from the trailhead. If unable to keep up, I would be returning on my own to my car and back to New Jersey. I assured him I would not hinder the group's progress, I would have a hiking companion, and I would arrive and depart independently from the rest of his group.

What a picture-perfect winter day it was! The sky was clear with nary a cloud in sight. The air was crisp and cold, with little wind, a bright sun, and snow several feet deep. It was a large group—all males except for me. Soon, those in the lead started breaking through the snow's crust. My companion and I were lighter than most in the group and moved easily beyond them, reaching the summit ahead of everyone else. Many were panting, perspiring, and complaining of the difficult conditions. Rather than being tired, I was exhilarated!

Soon I was one of the regulars on the Saturday winter Catskill hikes, and still the only woman. I was thrilled by the beautiful snow-covered trees and trails and the camaraderie of the group. I thrived on the challenge of each trip. Despite teaching junior-high students all week, it was no trouble getting up at 5:30 AM on a Saturday morning to meet the group to carpool for the long drive to the Catskills. It was a big letdown for me when, in March of 1979, I completed the requirements for the Winter Catskill 3500.

In December of the following winter, Phil Heald phoned. He and I had met while hiking and camping in Maine's Baxter State Park the previous summer. He knew I was a Catskill Winter 35er and wondered if I'd be his guide on a few hikes in the Catskills during the holiday. Thus began a happy and exciting relationship. By the time the winter ended, Phil had met the requirements for the Winter Catskill 3500 (#113), and I had re-climbed many as his guide. We proceeded to work together on climbing the Winter Adirondack 46er peaks. My stipulation to do this was that equal time be spent in climbing the mountains of New England's 4000-Footers and Hundred Highest.

In November of 1983, Phil and I married at Sturbridge Village, Massachusetts, and in 1985 we became the first husband-and-wife team to climb all 113[1] Four-Thousand-Footers in the Northeast in the winter. From 1982 through the summer of 1994, Phil and I organized and co-led the Appalachian Mountain Club Range Hike. This is a fifty-plus-mile hike, mostly on the Appalachian Trail, hut to hut, from Franconia Notch across the Franconia and Presidential Ranges. After Phil's death in 1994, I once more organized the Range Hike before turning over the reins to others.

Now, back in New Jersey, I am deeply involved again with ADK's North Jersey Chapter. I initiated Thursday hikes that draw a significant number of hikers each week. 🏃

---

[1] There are now 115 peaks to summit for membership in the 111ers of Northeastern USA—the New York-New England 4,000-footers. When Betty entered the club, there were 113 required peaks. Originally there were 111.

38

THE ICE MITES

NEW EXPERIENCES IN EVERY HIKE

Larry Allen, #1277, and Kevin Wagner, #1283

No matter how many times you walk a trail or climb a mountain in the "Skills," you will always be rewarded with a unique and everlasting experience. Our first hike to Panther Mountain was in February 1998, a cold and cloudy day. We had already successfully attempted and bagged our first winter peak and were looking to take our second one. As we reached the top of Giant Ledge, we also reached the base of the clouds. That alone was a unique experience as we then began hiking in a fog, knowing that below us and below the ledge was clear air and views of the distant cloves. On the very same hike on a different day, the landscape and views can change and the adventurous hiker will be introduced to other remarkable scenes of the Catskill Mountains.

The following December we planned an overnight, two-day hike to Panther Mountain by way of Giant Ledge. It was December 18 near midday as we arrived at the Giant Ledge parking area. The temperature was in the low twenties, but we were prepared for these elements. We checked our supplies as we packed up and strapped in: tent, sleeping bags, stove, food, drinks, and a cell phone. Kevin brought along a ridge rest, and Larry had a small homemade square fashioned from foam for an experimental ground pad. Our packs were expectedly heavy. Since it was Larry's birthday, Kevin acted as the "pack mule," carrying the heavier supplies.

The hike to Giant Ledge is normally a mild climb, but with the addition of snow, ice, and extraordinarily heavy backpacks, we were both feeling a little strained on the approach to the ledge. Our crampons helped ease our climb as it prevented us from slipping on the packed snow and ice. On this day, Giant Ledge offered exceptional views. To the south lay Wittenberg, Cornell, and Slide, with Friday just visible in the background. To the east was the Devils Path with Plateau, Sugarloaf, Twin, and Indian Head. We could also see Hunter Mountain toward the northeast and Panther to the north. Next to Huckleberry Point, this area offers some of the most breathtaking vistas in all of the Catskills. Here we stood on Giant Ledge, where the cliff drops precipitously over three hundred feet straight down to treetops. The view almost induces vertigo. As you look down into the trees, they look so close, yet so small. The clean, crisp air and the clear blue sky combined to give us views at their best. Even the ice on the ground and in the trees sparkled.

After finding a suitable camping area, we set up camp near the edge of the cliff. We fixed a tasty dinner of canned beef stew with biscuits and hot coffee as we discussed the day's journey and sights so far. After dinner we explored the ledge more completely. As the sun started to set, we made our way to the cliffs on the western edge of the ledge and took pictures of Fir and Big Indian. As the sun dropped below the horizon, so, too, did the temperature. The ice-glazed Giant Ledge glimmered from the waxing moon as we walked back to camp with the assistance of headlamps.

It was completely dark at five o'clock. Our excitement about winter camping waned as there was now little to do with ourselves. We talked some more, cleaned up around the campsite, hung our food from a tree limb, and then sat on the ledge and watched lights flicker miles away. Boredom set in, and Kevin started to pace to and fro. Larry listened to ice crunch beneath Kevin's crampons. The sound of crunching ice faded into the forest as Kevin searched for firewood. Useable downed and dead limbs were scarce in this part of the ledge. Not only had the available firewood been picked over by previous campers, but what was available was coated with snow and ice. The sounds of that night were of crunching ice and snapping wood. The distant lights were replaced by headlamps searching the night. Kevin shredded paper and made a teepee of the best and driest twigs—well, the least damp twigs. None of the wood was exactly "dry." Larry provided small pieces of waxed cardboard he carried, and the campfire finally poured forth light and heat. Every overnighter needs a campfire. What is a camp without breathing in smoke and having watery eyes? It all comes with the package.

For three hours we busied ourselves dodging smoke as we tried to keep a small flickering fire burning on a sheet of ice. Fun comes in funny flavors. At nine o'clock we burned out along with the fire and crawled into our tent. It was like leaving a freezer and entering an icebox. We tried in vain to keep warm. We were lying on ice with outside temperatures in the single digits. Larry's foam ground pad was almost useless, so it became a pillow. One ground pad was reluctantly shared. Noise filled the tent. Larry snored as he breathed, both in and out—an achievement not many master. We were awake by four, stirring and wanting to get out of the icebox and back into the freezer. At six we enjoyed a breakfast of steamed sausage links and instant coffee. This was straight from our hiking book of phrases: "If you don't like it, take it when you hike." Canned beef stew, steamed sausage, and instant coffee are almost enjoyable while camping, but almost any other time they are just barely palatable. After breakfast we saw the most glorious sight to be seen in the Catskills: the sunrise. The sun brought with it glorious, if relative, warmth. The soft morning glow of the rising sun was a welcome sight. We watched the dawn while sitting on the ledge as the sun rose over Wittenberg.

We took our crampons, lunch, and drinks as we headed to Panther. The ice made traveling tricky as we dropped into the saddle between the ledge and Panther Mountain. As we started climbing Panther, we were able to gauge our progress by looking back at Giant Ledge. Two hours from when we left, we reached the 3,500-foot sign. At 3,600 feet, Panther was the "Land of Ice." The trees—each branch and every needle—was covered with rime, looking like hard candies. The trees bent with the weight of the ice. Our path was narrow and low. We noticed that the ice clinging to the evergreen branches was cylindrical, not teardrop in shape as we would have expected. The balsam needles were united in a rippled coat of ice. The top of Panther was a wonderland of nature's ice sculptures. The view from the summit of Panther Mountain is partially obstructed by new growth, but is splendid nevertheless. The air up there was crisp and cold.

On our way back to the ledge, we stopped for lunch on the south face of Panther. Just off the trail, we found another beautiful vista. Most notable was Giant Ledge rising out of the col. We dubbed this spot, "Triple-A Ledge," a sheer drop of 200 feet into the beginning of Dougherty Clove. It was here, on our "Triple-A Ledge," that we saw for the first time the "ice mites." We stood just below the cloud cover and looked out into the valley and the world below, when we saw the most amazing of creatures dancing in the air.

"Ice mites" are those minute particles of ice and crystallized vapor that we saw floating upwards in the air. The sun-warmed air deeper in the clove rose up through the clove, bringing the ice mites swarming and dancing upward towards us. It was the most incredible sight! The ice mites seemed to be migrating by the millions, alive as they swarmed all around and above us. Reflecting in the sunlight, they clustered and swarmed across Dougherty Clove in front of the cloud shadow. It seemed to us that we could reach out and touch them, but in reality, the ice mites disappeared and melted just before reaching our fingertips. The ice mites were the frosting of our hike, the icing on the cake, so to speak.

We left Panther, Giant Ledge and the ice mites to "Tomorrow's Travelers." It is our hope that the ice mites will be just as alive for you as they were for us. The Catskill region offers more than trails and peaks. The Catskills offer adventure, fun, and new experiences with every hike. And, at just the right time, under the right conditions, there is the elusive ice mite dance every winter for those who are adventurous enough to look. 🏃

39

WINTER HIKE

RHAPSODY IN WHITE

Joan Dean, #360, #135W
from Autumn 1989 *Catskill Canister*

"**Y**ou shouldn't go alone," he said. I was counting on him to climb with me that day. "Can't, yet. Knee's still sore and the back hurts a bit. Maybe in a week or so."

About two feet of new snow had fallen in two preceding storms. I had down-hilled all day in whirling powder during the first blizzard. It snowed again that night. Today dawned cold and clear; the sky was cobalt blue, and I wanted to climb in the fresh, clean, untracked world. Soon after leaving my friend's home, I was at the trailhead and parked my car close to the newly plowed, high banks of snow. I geared up, decided on high gaiters, put sun/wind cream on my face, chose a ski pole rather than an ice ax, and committed myself to the mountain.

I signed in the register and added when I expected to sign out. There were no other tracks, not even animal tracks. No sounds of birds. Just the wind and the swish of my pant legs as they brushed past each other. For the first hour I was in the shade, cold, listening to the wind high above and wondering how high I had to climb before I was in that wind.

The route I'd chosen had some steep side-hilling, but two feet of new snow gives good purchase for snowshoes. At the side-hill area I plunged the ski pole into the snow until it dug into the ice below, took about three steps with the snowshoes, and established my climbing pattern. A small avalanche starts by my right foot. I watch pieces of snow jump and skitter like Mexican jumping beans, gather weight, and smack into a tree. Other little slides take off with every step. I must keep aware, *be* aware of conditions. Twenty-five steps, a ten-second rest, plunge the ski pole in, swing, step, press in—again and again. Any tree a welcome handhold, even any decent branch. Large rock, good stopping place for a hand-ful of gorp, even a sip of hot and honeyed tea from my thermos. Drinking water at each rest stop—replacing water lost in the exertion of the climb, water I don't notice losing because the wind keeps me dry. Ice forms in my water bottle—tuck it in the pack closer to my back; should have brought a wide-mouthed jug and hung it inside my shirtfront.

Ah, the cold, blue sky! The wind! Such sharp contrasts—blue sky, white snow, gray birch, sparkling ice trees, black tree scars. The woods change—more evergreens now. And hoarfrost, a white coating on trees and bushes. A new world hides the trail markers. Wind blows; trees whisper secrets to me. A sudden crack in a tree, a creak, as a live tree moves under the weight of a dead and partially fallen tree. Don't fall now, please. The rock areas are thicker here, the boulders larger, cliffs, fewer trees. Have to use a hand to help my knees up and get that old Bearpaw over and between the rocks. Now an icy rock ledge; I heave myself up, using any inch of dry rock to grasp. The actual peak is a bit onward but, ah! The views from here! Cock-a-doodle-doo! I look quickly around—did I yell that? I've done it! I'm here! Drunk with the climb, drinking in the vast white-gray vista, ridges leading to other mountain peaks and valleys, sky, and the wind.

Another look at the ALL THAT IS and I stroll over to the peak in this fairy world of evergreens and snow. Time to go down now—turnaround time (beyond turnaround time!) Don't get caught on that side-hill down below in the dark. Plunge, slide, whoop, face full of snow, who cares? Get up, brush off, plunge, slide, holler, now slower here, take a break, caution at the side-hill, don't want to imitate the Mexican jumping bean. Off the mountain now. Already? So fast? Stopping to eat the last of my gorp, drink tepid tea, linger in the silence of the woods, colder as evening falls. I sign out in the register at 5:00 PM, not 4:00 as I had estimated.

I drove past my friend's house to tell him I was off the mountain, and met him walking along the road. "It's dark," he chided. "I was coming over to the lodge to see if you were back. Anne fixed a casserole. Come on over for supper and tell us about your climb." I was home. 🏃

40

A WINTER SLIDE CLIMB

SLIDE CLIMB AND DANGEROUS DESCENT

Edward Ripley-Duggan, #1389, #548W

Many hikers have a strong affection for slide climbing. Ascending a peak via a rockslide often means an unrelentingly steep ascent, sometimes coupled with unstable footing, but there are usually good views and a certain amount of scrambling to compensate for the difficulty. The Friday Mountain slide is no exception. Slides in the Catskills are less common than those in the Adirondacks, which adds to their hiking appeal.

The Friday slide occurred in May 1968 after heavy rains.[1] With a roar that was audible several miles away, a section of the east slope gave way; the initial collapse of a sandstone ledge occurred just above the 3,100-foot mark. This mass of rock plowed down the mountain until it came to rest at the brook at the bottom of the slope, 1,100 feet below. In its wake, loose shattered rock was strewn down the slide's path. Birch and other trees now stabilize the upper section, but the bottom 500 feet of the slide remains active, with new rock and dirt constantly breaking loose. The result is a deep, wide gouge below the upper slide. It's a fascinating place, and is easily the most interesting ascent to Friday Mountain.

We left one car at the parking area (that the landowner used to make available) and drove to the end of Moon Haw Road, parking the other car in the snow-plow turnaround before the gates. We climbed the slope above the end of the road (a private landholding that must be avoided), and followed logging roads before reaching a brook originating below Cornell and joining Wittenberg Brook, which flows into Maltby Hollow. We headed upstream toward the Cornell headwall, generally following old roads, until we hit the final approach path to the slide beyond a hemlock grove. In season this gives a wonderful view of Cornell's steep face and Wittenberg beyond.

The three feet of unconsolidated powder above the slide that turned us back two weeks ago had melted and turned to ice, forming a miniature glacier that snaked down the length of the lower slide. This was hard, steep ice, and we stayed to one side for a safer ascent with dry rock and crusted snow. We ventured onto the central ice-covered stream if the footing appeared better, but a slip would have had nasty consequences. A toboggan ride downhill into a boulder is not my idea of a morning well spent—self-arrest on rock-hard ice is a near-impossibility. I found myself thankful that I'd brought an ice axe; David had not grabbed his in the morning rush. This ascent is one of few in the Catskills where an ice axe is a big help.

We hit hardpack, a good surface to ascend the next two sections. After a stiff climb we reached ledges where a great slab of rock stands to one side, seemingly frozen in the act of pulling away. A year, a century, or a millennium from now, and this too will come crashing down, creating a new slide. The area above the ledge was a good place for a breather before ascending the remaining six hundred feet. This is as pretty and open a forest glade as one could wish for. We summited about noon, had lunch, and then descended to the ledge east of the summit and followed the series of ledges down to the col with Balsam Cap.

We had to take care with our footing on that ascent, as there were deep rock traps hidden under the snow. Crevasse country! As usual the summit seemed to have moved farther south than expected. One of us almost walked right past the canister. A safe descent route became the order of the day. This turned out to be the most nerve-wracking portion of the trip. Balsam Cap's ridge is notoriously ledge-infested; some of those ledges are fifty-foot cliffs! In spite of easier alternatives, we elected to take that route. Taking a bearing, we started a slow descent onto what we hoped was the ridge—it is poorly defined on top. There were twenty minutes of anxiety when we hit a spot so precipitous that there was no way down. After retracing we found a steep descent over the ledge that had hung us up. We owed this route largely to an agile and doubtless wily coyote whose tracks we followed. David found a fine viewpoint of the ridge extending directly below us, but the intermittent herd path was hard to follow in deep snow.

Despite the anxieties of the descent, this was a beautiful and challenging hike—nine hours of tough bushwhacking. The combination of the slide ascent, the exquisite and unusual vantages and views, and later, the song of the coyotes as we descended the ridge, was thoroughly enjoyable. This is a great route, offering a significant degree of difficulty in any season.

Note: The route described is no longer available without explicit permission. The present landholders at the foot of Balsam Cap and Friday are now less tolerant of hikers crossing their lands. The parking and access to private property described above is no longer allowed, thanks to significant abuse by a small minority of hikers. Portions of the descent from Balsam Cap cross private land, and it is important to ask permission there as well. 🚶

[1] See "Something Happened in the Mountains."

41

HOW I SUCCUMBED TO PEAK BAGGERS' DISEASE

FEEDING THE HIKING FEVER WITH SNOW-COVERED PEAKS

by Darielle Graham, #654, #262W
from May–June 1992 *Catskill Canister*

Once upon a time I regarded peak bagging with indifference verging on disdain. Peak baggers bored the boots off me. Their talk consisted of the peaks they had climbed and the peaks they had left to climb. They crowed over marathon days that began and ended by flashlight, with barely enough time for dinner and sleep before the next day's peak bagging resumed.

The obsession with peak bagging was foreign to me. I'd hiked in both the Adirondacks and Catskills, but had never kept a tally of my climbs and never needed more than the enjoyment of being outdoors in pristine surroundings to keep me returning.

But I had not reckoned with my ego. When a couple of my fellow female hikers decided to climb the Catskill 3500 peaks in winter, I felt confronted with my own inability and unwillingness to hike in a season that ordinarily sent me scurrying to an exercise class or to the warmth of my office. Having a goal helped; in my case it was a dual goal—going for the winter patch and overcoming my dislike of winter hiking.

Winter barely settled in before I was plodding through foot-deep snow to the summit of North Dome. I followed in the footsteps of my husband, a winter thirty-fiver twice and going for his third. From North Dome, Sherrill beckoned. Like the sun that glazed the trees with gold, I was not yet ready to go home. Next day we bushwhacked to Big Indian and Fir. The trail to Eagle was nicely packed, and the prospect of collecting a third peak lent wings to my legs and sent me flying to the top.

Two weeks later my husband and I signed in at the same motel and climbed five more mountains. Within the week, peak bagging fever struck again. They say you're supposed to starve a fever, but I fed mine with snow-covered peaks. A ritual soon developed of driving up Friday evening, returning home Sunday, and in between bagging at least four peaks. I called in the occasional "sick" day. If we had a commitment in the city, we drove to and from the Catskills the same day. I felt like a fighter pilot: no sooner had I claimed one set of victories than on I flew to the next.

I asked my husband if my compulsive behavior was wearing him down. (True, he'd lost ten pounds, but I attributed that to vegetarian dinners twice a week.) He smiled and said that he remembered being as zealous with his Adirondack peaks; then he admitted winter was his favorite season and that he was delighted I wanted to hike every weekend.

As the number of peaks required for the patch diminished, my fever intensified. In the process I learned to deal with brutal cold, to trust my crampons on ice. The sleet and slush encountered on Balsam Lake and Graham proved no deterrent. Sliding down steep, frozen trails on my backside could be fun. I came to appreciate the usefulness of my husband's ice axe on the slick ledges of Wittenberg and Cornell. Some nights I lay awake dividing the peaks I had left into the number of remaining winter weekends. My husband produced equations more ambitious than mine that left me questioning my ability, yet wanting the challenge.

It came on February 29, 1992. Starting at 7:30 AM from Denning, we hiked up Table, bushwhacked to Lone, followed by Rocky; we were on a roll, so we continued to Balsam Cap, taking almost two hours to bash through a mile of densely packed spruce. Despite the bitter cold and the strenuous bushwhacking, our entry in each canister ended with a "Yahoo!" This would be a day to remember.[1] On the first of March I wrote my last entry, in the Doubletop canister, and checked off the last space on my tally sheet!

This experience made me more tolerant of other peak baggers. Now, when they recount their efforts, I listen with interest, because for a time I too talked of nothing else. I now realize how easy it is to become compulsive. But along the way I remember the contrast of naked trees against the snow, the tinkle of crystal spruce boughs, the sun setting the snow on fire. My husband summed up the end of my peak bagging fever by asking, "Does this mean we can stop living in the Catskills?" ⚑

---

[1] See "A Catskills Winter Marathon."

42

A CATSKILLS WINTER MARATHON

ON A ROLL — UNTIL MOUNTAINS TAKE THEIR TOLL

Darielle Graham, #654, #262W
originally published in *Adirondac,* the magazine of the
Adirondack Mountain Club, Inc. (ADK)

It began at five o'clock in the morning with the discovery that we had no water. The dribble the night before when we brushed our teeth should have alerted us that something was amiss, but our thoughts were on getting a good night's sleep in readiness for the next day. My husband John had brought his stove and was disinclined to waste time melting the ice outside the door. Such labor was expected when you winter camped, but we (sole occupants) were staying in a comfortable, albeit isolated, lodge. The owners did not live on the premises. As a last resort we turned to the toilet tank. When we left, it was empty—its contents boiled and in our bottles. Neither of us cared to speculate as to the taste!

At the Denning trailhead it was brutally cold and windy on a sunny late-February day. John signed the register, turned and said, "Ready?" It was 7:30 AM. All winter we had spent weekends in the Catskills climbing a considerable array of peaks, so this Saturday found us fit and strong for Table, Lone, and Rocky. Balsam Cap, next in line, was also possible. It sounded simple. No more than a mile separated each peak. What the map did not reveal, however, were the notorious balsam thickets, which are especially dense between Rocky and Balsam Cap. The short stretch between these two peaks is generally viewed as one of the toughest bushwhacks in the Catskills.

The warm-up walk along the woods road acted as a panacea against the freezing cold; it was way below zero. Each step forward unraveled the knots in my stomach and steeled me for the union with Table, Lone, and Rocky. Balsam Cap I stored in the cupboard of my mind, like a forbidden food I craved but knew I should sensibly refrain from eating. At the junction with the Table-Peekamoose Trail, a signpost indicated that Table was two and three-quarter miles.

The Neversink River is split into three branches here; they have log bridges. My balance on logs, especially icy ones, is shaky. Fear of falling into deep, fast-running water paralyzes me after a few steps and I am incapable of moving without help. Fortunately the small branches were frozen over, so we crossed on ice slabs instead of slippery logs. Only on the main branch did I have to brave a log bridge, which I managed with a hand from John.

Near the top of Table, where the wind had whipped the powder into knee-high drifts, John had to yank me up with his ice axe to prevent me from slithering backwards. Otherwise, I plodded steadily behind him, admiring the latticework of trees against the snow. Finally the ascent leveled off and we found ourselves pushing through ice- and snow-covered spruce boughs that drooped over the trail. At the highest point, we spared only a second to glance at our watches: ten o'clock. It was too frigid to linger.

At the spot where the trail turns toward Peekamoose, we plunged heads-down into the snow thicket, using whatever openings presented themselves. Soon we reached an outcrop with a view, from which we gazed at our goal. Directly ahead, sharply etched against the cloudless blue sky, lay Lone, while diminutive Rocky peeked out from around Lone's right shoulder. We glissaded[1] to the col leading to Lone. We followed the summit ridge through open scrub and scattered spruce. When the ridgeline turned into cliffs, we detoured to the right and found easier ways up. A northeasterly direction led us straight to the orange canister atop Lone, the only blaze of color in the white landscape. John entered a "Yahoo!" after our names in the register. It was not yet 11:15. We set off to Rocky as eager as kids on a treasure hunt.

In my eagerness I overlooked the fact that John did not suggest a water break. Unlike many people—myself included—who drink too little in winter, John does the opposite to prevent dehydration. Even when freezing temperatures make you want to keep moving, he forces himself to take water breaks. I learned later that he was not enamored with drinking water from a toilet tank.

The crossing from Lone to Rocky is tricky. You must avoid the temptation to head straight for Rocky, as it leads you into nasty hardwood thickets and involves unnecessary loss of altitude. You should stay on the height of land by swinging to the right and threading the line between hardwoods and evergreen. You do reach a point where you have no choice but to bulldoze through, but by staying in the taller trees you can avoid the worst.

The trouble with Rocky is that there is no pronounced high point. Some people have spent as much as an hour thrashing around on top searching for the canister. John relies on a combination of memory, herd-path-following and luck, but I was still surprised when he stopped in his tracks, looked up and announced, "It's up there." After clawing up ledges concealed in the thickets, we emerged into a clearing and, sure enough, there was the canister. We entered our names and another "Yahoo!" in the register on Rocky.

With the third and final peak accomplished, John said he was hungry and asked if I was ready for lunch. I was hungry, too, but not for my cheese sandwich. "It's still early," I replied. "Do you think we could do Balsam Cap? It seems a shame not to carry on." It was 12:15. We both knew we should not ignore hunger pangs, that to do so would only hasten the onset of fatigue. John also knew my impatience would prevent him from enjoying lunch. "Might as well," he relented. "We seem to be on a roll."

Dropping off the summit to the northeast, we picked up a herd path that had been clipped in places and even had blazes. The direction was not exactly right and, when the woods opened up, John noticed we were headed for Friday rather than Balsam Cap. Correcting to the southeast, we then began the toughest bushwhacking of the day. Bushwhacking requires a certain frame of mind. Regard it as a field in which you do battle, and you will never emerge a true winner. View it instead as a chance to wander off the well-trod trail and roam a "road less traveled," and bushwhacking becomes bearable, even an adventure. It never ceased to amaze me that in brush not even a breeze could slip through, a muscular six-foot man, twice my size, seemed able to do the impossible.

Having a goal helped. My eagerness and resolve to reach Balsam Cap enabled me to tolerate, even forgive, the sharp boughs that clawed my face or stabbed my eyes, the tree stumps that ripped holes in my pants, the hidden roots underfoot that sent me sprawling. Snow worked its way into every nook and cranny, and ice formed between our packs and our backs. John got the brunt of it, being in front; I was spared numerous icy showers. At times I became quite trapped. I could not match John for speed, and at times I lost sight of him except for his footprints. Bushwhacking could be a lonely experience. A glimpse of his bright red jacket through the dark tunnel, or the sound of his voice answering my call, kept me company. The southwest slope was covered with fallen trees. Whenever we found a clear path, within fifty yards it became impassable.

Throughout, my resolve never wavered. It took us almost two hours before we finally emerged at the top into open scrub. John used his memory to locate the canister. Another "Yahoo!"—the loudest yet. Now I was ready for lunch! The circle of scrub afforded some shelter from the bitter wind, and we huddled together. By this time we were both very thirsty. That was when we discovered how terrible the water tasted. It was so putrid it was undrinkable except as coffee or tea, and we drank nowhere near the amount warranted by such a long and arduous hike. Our frozen sandwiches were not very appetizing, either.

John decided to head straight for the Neversink River, but several minutes of breaking trail and figuring out which way to go convinced him to retrace our original route. He discovered that it was not nearly as convoluted as it had seemed on the way up; except for the bypasses around fallen trees, it was fairly direct. Once in the col, it was a quick and easy descent to the river. We found two sets of fresh tracks; until then we had seen none. The registers contained no recent entries but ours. We followed the tracks along the river to a green-blazed trail on the north bank. There, they continued along the bank. We stayed with the blazes.

The trail led us a miserable dance as it ascended and descended the bluffs above the river. The torturous route started to take its toll, each uphill earning a curse from John. After spending the day absorbed in route-finding and sniffing out each canister like a bloodhound fox—the things he most enjoyed about hiking trailless peaks—John found a marked trail dull. His enthusiasm and energy had waned. Dehydration was partly to blame for the drop in energy. Any fatigue I felt was overshadowed by my elation at having gained all four peaks. We had only three more miles to go on a hard-packed trail.

When John announced that we could probably shortcut to the woods road, I was happy to abandon the trail and bushwhack up a steep slope. But on the ridge it became clear that we were thrashing unduly in deep snow, so John concluded that better time would be made keeping to the trail. It was 6:30 PM when we reached the parking lot; we had been gone ten and a half hours.

Back at the lodge, the innkeepers greeted us like long-lost relatives and apologized profusely for forgetting to turn on the water. They treated us to cocktails and dinner—nothing was too much trouble for them. 🏃🏃

---

[1] A sliding descent of a snow-covered slope on snowshoes.

43

NIGHT FALLS EARLY

PEAK BAGGING PERILS

Susan Lehrer, #1306, #579W

Winter 3,500-foot peaks can be tricky. That's partly because conditions vary so widely from one year to another and even from one mountain to the next. But mostly it's because getting the winter patch can become an obsession, and there are so few months to work on it. I, of course, would never let this happen, but one winter my good friend Addie Haas decided that the winter patch was within reach. She planned to climb her last winter peak, Cornell, and have a champagne celebration just shy of March 21 and the official start of spring. To get to Cornell, you first need to go up either Slide or Wittenberg. She had already tried both ways, but the weather had not been favorable, so no Cornell yet. We understood her determination, therefore, to get up that final peak before spring.

It was March and longer days appeared to be coming out of the winter's night, but we started the hike later than we planned. A cheery group of us set out up Slide (the easier way, we figured). I took along my dog, a sturdy snow dog who loves a good hike. The snow was all but gone—at the bottom, that is. Sensibly, we still took our winter packs, with crampons, warm clothing and other heavy stuff, but this slowed us down. When we got to the top of Slide, on a beautiful sunlit afternoon, we were running later than we should have been.

The back side of Slide towards Cornell was deep in snow, mushy even on the trail. It was slick going down Slide and up Cornell, and we made pretty poor time through the snow. I was doing well because I'd brought along my super-duper crampons and could move right along on packed snow or ice. I, ever the wimp and worrywart, was watching the time; the day was fleeting by, but no one suggested turning around. We finally got to the top of Cornell and congratulated our friend, but prudently held off on the celebration.

Going down Cornell was tough. (But my dog Teddy was super!) Some in the group, including the new Winter 35er, were considerably slower than others going downhill in the snow. I knew that if we all hung back together, we'd get to the cars well after dark, and those back home would be calling the troops out after us. Three of us, plus Teddy, were doing pretty well ascending the 960 feet back up Slide. We could hear the others way behind us. Bob, who'd stayed on Slide (and who was also the group's champion worrywart), had long ago given up on waiting for us.

I and two other women decided to go down Slide by ourselves. It was twilight already; I was anxious about walking out in the dark, even though I had a flashlight in my pack. Soon it was too dark to see the trail, even such a wide one as that. I learned quickly that my handheld flashlight was just about useless. Luckily, however, one of the others had a decent headlamp, so we could go from one trail marker to the next. (I never knew they were reflective!) I learned how easy it would have been to wander off the trail in the dark.

At one point I couldn't see Teddy and worried that he'd gone chasing after something, so I whistled loudly for him. I heard an answering howl from way off in the woods someplace. As it turned out, Teddy was right there next to us, so I guess I had hailed an obliging coyote. Teddy doesn't ordinarily like to get in the car at the end of a hike, so I usually put him back on the leash well beforehand. This time, however, I couldn't imagine walking down the trail in the dark with him pulling me, so I decided he'd have to make up his mind to get into the car on his own or get left behind. No problem. When the three of us finally got back to the parking area and I opened the hatchback, the dog gladly jumped in, curled up and immediately went to sleep.

We humans, however, were worried about the others bringing up the rear. One woman said that if her husband didn't hear from her by a certain time, he was going to call the State Police—and that deadline was fast approaching. I was the only one with a car and keys; we decided that one of us would wait in case the others showed up, and the other two would go find a phone. We'd have to travel far to find a house, but the woman was adamant, so off we drove. After many miles we found a house with lights on and knocked at the door. The couple that answered the knock looked like 1960s hippies. They seemed accustomed to having stray hikers in distress appear at their doorstep, and they kindly let us call the worried husband; they also offered us soup. I phoned the one person whose phone number I knew by heart to explain the situation, but I couldn't offer assurances that we were all okay, because I didn't know that for a fact. We headed back, and I drove right by the parking area in the dark; when we finally returned to the parking area, the third woman was still waiting.

By then we were truly worried. We set a time at which, if we hadn't heard from them, we'd call for help. Ten minutes shy of that time, we heard their voices. They had been seriously slowed down coming off Cornell when Frank—nearly eighty—slipped and dislocated his finger.[1] His best crampons, alas, were in the shop being repaired. The group was extra cautious after Frank got hurt, and it had already gotten dark. We gave half-hearted cheers for achieving the final winter peak and left, driving until our cell phones worked.

View toward Slide Mountain from Cornell Mountain. Photograph by Paul Misko.

We wanted to make sure that the injured man got to the hospital right away, so one woman agreed to take him. I would take her dog to her house, which was near mine. The man who'd turned around on Slide's summit had almost gotten the State Police after us, but he was able to call them off just in time. All of us were exhausted. I drove back to New Paltz with two sleeping dogs and a tired but triumphant friend. I dropped her and the other dog off, and then, when I started the car up again, my leg cramped so badly I couldn't push in the clutch. That made for an interesting ride home. By the time we got home there were two of us in the car who were dog-tired. Dog ate well that night.

Afterwards some people criticized us for splitting into two groups. Those of us on the hike felt differently, however. Both groups were large enough for safety, and the forward group was able to get out quickly and contact people. In retrospect—20/20 hindsight—I think we should not have tried to go up Cornell that day, but we were all so focused on gaining that thirty-fifth winter peak for our friend that we didn't set a contingency plan for a definite "turn around now!" time.

As a thank-you present, Addie got me a really nice headlamp. Just in case. 🚶🚶

---

[1] See "Frank's Story."

44

POSTHOLING THE BIG CATS

BEST LAID PLANS

Joe Herrod

The Plan: leave my car at Woodland Valley; Chris, Big Mully and I will drive to the Peekamoose trailhead, hike over 3,843-foot Peekamoose Mountain and 3,847-foot Table Mountain, stay at the Denning lean-to on the East Branch of the Neversink River, and meet Mike Palencar there. He would hike south on the Wittenberg-Cornell-Slide trail to the col between Cornell and Slide, bushwhack down an unmarked trail, picking up the headwaters of the East Branch, and meet us at the lean-to for the night. On Saturday we would hike over Slide, Cornell, and Wittenberg, and spend the night at the Terrace Mountain lean-to. From there it would be a short two- to three-hour hike back to Woodland Valley.

It didn't happen that way.

Low snow conditions made us decide to bring only crampons—no snowshoes. After spotting a car at Woodland Valley, we got started on the trail at 10:45 AM, starting on bare ground with occasional patches of snow. This is the south slope of Peekamoose. We stopped after half an hour to put new crampons on, which took a while. There were no problems until we got above 3,000 feet, then the snow began to get deep. A previous hiker had postholed[1] through here. At 3,200 feet we started postholing as well. We reached the open shoulder of Peekamoose, at 3,500 feet, after a hard struggle and stopped to rest on the rocks. The views were great, but we chilled quickly from our sweat-soaked clothes.

The hike up the more level, mile-long shoulder of Peekamoose was easier. After reaching the big erratic[2] that caps Peekamoose, we started down the 200-foot sag between Peekamoose and Table. Suddenly the snow became firmer and the postholing stopped. Maybe we could make it down to the lean-to before dark after all. But the snow was deeper on the north slope of Table, and we were postholing to our knees on every step. Floundering in the snow! Big Mully grazed his calf with a crampon spike and thought he had punctured it. He howled like a hit dog.

By now it was late afternoon; we weren't going to make it to the lean-to, still two and a half miles away. We were floundering along at a snail's pace, and it was painfully obvious that we'd better find a place to set up our tents, pronto! We found an area where the slope moderated, and tramped down snow to make a solid base for our tents. There was a brilliant sunset and then a sliver of a waxing moon and a sky full of stars. The temperature had dropped to 12°. We were busy melting snow for water, feeling our feet become numb. We put boiling water into water bottles later, and stuck our feet up against them to thaw our toes. It works well, but takes a while.

Condensation made the inside of the tent like a rainforest. I had a non-Gortex down sleeping bag and feared that the dampness might collapse it. I didn't relish having to sleep in a wet bag the next night. By morning the temperature had risen into the low twenties. It was heavily overcast. Big Mully went ahead, hoping to find Mike at the lean-to. We met a lone hiker with no snowshoes who was planning to bushwhack from the top of Table over to the trailless peaks; we advised against such an undertaking.

Mike was not at the lean-to. We hung out there for the rest of the day. It was threatening snow all day, with the temperature barely reaching above the freezing point in mid-afternoon. We went to bed early because we had a long hike ahead of us. We had heard from other hikers that bad weather might be coming in. There was a mouse in the lean-to, and it was last seen skittering toward Big Mully's head.

We got up at five o'clock Sunday morning. The temperature had dropped to 16°. It's amazing how long it takes to get going in the morning, especially in the winter. You have to boil what seems like gallons of water, and Big Mully even had to thaw his boots out over the open flame. Putting on gear can be a tedious and time-consuming task; it seems like you are constantly twisted around like a pretzel trying to do something you can't see to do. And you have to do it with fingers going numb.

Our choice was either to continue on for nine miles to Woodland Valley, or retrace our steps seven miles back over Table and down Peekamoose. Ahead, we didn't know what the snow conditions were like, so we chose to go back. The hike back up Table was slow and cold. Too cold to stop, and no place to sit anyway in the deep snow. We reached the erratic on top of Peekamoose before noon, and the area was sunny and sheltered; we stayed for an hour and a half melting snow and having soup.

Back at Woodland Valley, there was a note on my car from Mike. He had proceeded as planned, but floundered in the snow after leaving the trail in the col between Cornell and Slide. (He foolishly took our advice and left his snowshoes in the car.) Having gotten a late start, he was caught by nightfall while bushwhacking down the headwaters of the East Branch. He hiked for several hours in the dark, and finally had to bivouac in the snow along the stream. He had no tent. It must have been one hell of a cold and miserable bivouac. The next day he continued on to the lean-to, but decided not to wait to see if we would show up. He made the long, nine-mile hike up the Denning–Woodland Valley Trail past Lake Winnisook and back to Woodland Valley, reaching there by four o'clock. He said he then drove to a motel in Woodstock and spent the evening in a bar before driving back to West Virginia the next day.

WHAT WE LEARNED:
1. Never hike in the Catskills in winter without snowshoes.
2. Carry a lot of fuel. You may have to melt a lot of snow.
3. Don't carry food that will freeze. You end up packing it in and packing it out.
4. When planning a winter backpacking trip, set what you believe to be a reasonable distance, and then reduce that by one-third. 👫

---

[1] Breaking through a crust of snow into deep snow.

[2] A boulder that has been carried by a glacier and then deposited far from its original position when the glacier receded.

Always bring snowshoes. Photograph by David White.

45

THE OPTIMIST AND THE PESSIMIST
HIKING THE WINTER 35

"HOW MUCH TROUBLE CAN WE HAVE?"

David White #860, #310W, and Carol White #859, #311W

An Easy Hike

It's only 2-plus miles to the Halcott summit, okay for our absurdly late start at 11:45. Even at one mile an hour, we'll summit this trailless mountain and easily descend by dark. We set a turn-around time of three o'clock on this January day. Our snowshoes sink only half a foot into the soft snow as we hike up into a hemlock grove, the snow flattened by myriad deer hoofprints. Higher up, each step now sinks in more deeply; the terrain steepens and the pace slows.

"Should this be our turn-around point?" I suggest. "This snow is hard to walk in."

"Nah, give it another half hour," Dave replies. "This isn't bad."

After a while the terrain suddenly becomes much steeper and the snow is knee-deep. We stopped for a snack. "Dave, this is the turn-around place," I press him. "It's three-thirty."

"It can't be that much farther … the summit must be at the top of this rise."

The summit is not at the top of the rise. Dave tries in vain to pack down the fluffy snow with his knee where he will next place his foot. We've lost all our body heat in the slow-motion climb. Exhaustion begins to take its toll.

It is four o'clock. "Dave, please, it'll be dark soon."

"We're going to be there before long; can you pass me?" I find breaking trail almost impossible now. It takes tremendous strength to lift one leg upwards from the sunken position of the other, making progress glacial. I go as long as I can, and then he resumes. At 4:30 twilight colors the landscape.

The terrain finally levels. "Here it is!" yells Dave, lunging for the canister. It's solidly frozen shut. He whacks the latch with his fuel canister until it gives way. We sign in with frozen fingers in the dark, grab gorp and a quick drink. We're down by seven o'clock.

Marie's Dream House appears along the road. Looks expensive—but enticing tonight. With icicles hanging from his hair, Dave asks about a room. Including dinner and breakfast, it's not out of sight. We eat breads, salad, two soups, sumptuous entrees with home-style bowls of red cabbage, spaetzle, creamed spinach, and sinful desserts as if it were our last meal on earth.

Glazed Sugarloaf

Who would believe that totally different snow conditions the next morning would make this climb equally challenging? A little way up the trail, a lone man is descending. "I left my buddies up a ways; the trail is hard going," he says, easing down a steep pitch.

The snow texture changes to a hard glaze as we ascend; tracks become barely discernable on the snow surface. With only serrated crampons on our snowshoes, it's difficult to get a secure foothold; ski poles don't dent the icy surface. Two more young guys are coming down. "It's bad up there! My toes are sore trying to knock in footholds," one states. "The ledges are impassable." I turn to follow them down.

"Let's look it over—I'll make steps for you to follow," Dave encourages me.

"But if they gave up, it must be dangerous!" I argue.

"C'mon," he says nicely. "We can always turn back." Where have I heard that before? The slight track ends and I look up at a shiny, smooth, white, near-vertical rise. I look below at the hard-glazed surface steeply falling away.

"I'm not going up there! If we misstep there's no way to stop ourselves or grab anything. This is dangerous and I'm absolutely going back!" I say in my most positive voice.

"I don't think it's all that bad—see where it ends up there? I'll dig in good steps."

"It'll take time, and who knows how many more sections there are? And how do we safely get down here?" I protest.

"We've come most of the way up; remember, there's level trail on top. If we can maneuver this part safely, and we can, we can make it!" Dave insists. "And we just come down our steps backward."

I can't believe I'm going to go along with this. "I'll see whether you can make totally secure steps," I growl. "Look how far we'd slide if we lose control—we could hit a tree and be injured or killed!" This is my last, futile attempt to dissuade Dave. He kicks into an unyielding hard surface so he takes off his pack and, using his knee, gradually creates a stairway up the cliff—giving a whole new meaning to "needing" this peak! He backs down and gets his pack.

"Okay, these steps are level and deep into the snow; I'll be right here if you need my hand," he says, confidently. He's always so sweet about my squeamishness that I hate to disappoint him by turning back. Halfway up there's a vertical stretch with no trees, rock ledge or anything to grab. Dave hovers above.

"C'mon," he encourages. "It's really all right." It *is* the last bad pitch! Finally at the summit, we see that it's three o'clock—it's taken hours; we've got to get off these ledges by dark! Dave descends partway down the vertical steps backwards and holds the back of my heel as I put a foot into the first step. Very slowly and carefully, we descend.

Two days of hair-raising hiking! And the winter has just begun.

"Well, at least we've learned some lessons," I pontificate. "Don't start late no matter how easy the hike seems. Don't hike after a thaw and freeze. Bring full crampons …"

"What'll we do next weekend?" Dave enthuses.

Bailing Out

The morning is murky and cold. Tracks ascend a bank by the brook sooner than the ridge ascent of Doubletop, but we follow them anyway. The steep climb seldom relents; checking the compass, we verify that this is a return route from Graham. Icy, crumbly snow texture makes ascending many near-vertical pitches challenging and glacially slow in the higher reaches. The wind is howling with sub-zero windchill.

"What time is it getting to be?"

"Where the heck is my watch?" Dave shouts. "I hope I left it in the car—but I never leave it." The sun's position is unreadable in the fog. At the summit we squeeze inside the snow-incased door of the abandoned structure to get out of the wind for a quick lunch.

Huge rock ledges must be carefully descended for 850 feet down to the col to Doubletop. Dave finds a stuff sack with good gorp and puts it in his pack.

"We don't know what time it is," I state. "The weather is terrible—I want to bail out."

"Oh, no," Dave says, very disappointed. "We can do it. C'mon."

"For once, we're going to do what *I* want to do!"

Dave realizes we're going to bail out. "It could be worse descending from here—we've never taken this route," Dave argues, futilely trying to make me reconsider. Within one minute he sinks into the snow up to his armpits. "See what I mean?" He digs out snow, heaves up, digs and heaves and eventually wriggles out, not happy. But the remaining descent is scenic and uneventful, arriving at a cabin. Deer cross the ice on the brook.

It was another scary weekend. Why do I continue this foolishness? Winter hiking in the mountains is beautiful and great exercise, but my main inspiration is Dave's enthusiasm. After noting my split pants and boots, he jokes that my personality is also split; we both know I'm as competitive as he is, just as determined to dive into this experience full steam ahead.

Devil's Path

We set out for Jimmy Dolan Notch on the Devil's Path between Indian Head and Twin. Great, a trailed hike and relatively warm weather—probably no surprises today!

We climb Twin first so we can take the long way back over Indian Head. We indulge in a luxury rarely enjoyed on frigid summits: Dave cooks Ramen soup. Near Indian Head's summit, I remember last autumn when geese flew below us between the mountains. Over the top, I suddenly realize I'm where I don't want to be—on a narrow ledge with an enormous drop to my right. Dave has traversed the ledge.

"We've got to go back. Sorry, but I am definitely not going next to this drop!"

"Oh, come on; it's really no problem. I'll be here to grab you; it'll be just a few steps," Dave urges. "We don't want to go back," he adds.

"I do!" I counter. "I'm absolutely not going over this ledge. It's fifty feet straight down." I'm unhappy that he has to walk back over it, but at least it's slightly upwards for him.

"Carol, this is not bad. I'll come up and help you," Dave pleads.

"No way—then you'd have to back up! Dave, we're turning around."

He doesn't get impatient, just insists nicely that I come over to him. In his irresistible way, he starts joking. "Remember Navajo Knobs? Here the remains will be recognizable." Navajo Knobs in Utah's Capitol Reef National Park is a rock perch at the pinnacle of an ascending canyon walk. From there the road looks like a ribbon. We still joke about whether remains will be recognizable or not. I see that he really wants to continue, so I'm going to have to go over. Give total attention to not making a mistake.

I'm over and he hugs me; now the hike is a piece of cake! Or so we thought. We suddenly see the forgotten second plunge downward. The trail vanishes off a ledge. Dave blurts out, "Good grief! Now *I* want to go back!" But we can't go back because it would mean going up over that cliff. "Okay, let's put on our crampons," he says. *Can this really be done?* he asks himself, having the sensation of being on a much higher diving board than he wants to be on.

"I'll kick in steps." Facing the snow, he stretches his left leg onto the slide, kicking in a firm step, then another, and climbs down the cliff backward. From the high diving board, maneuvering onto the vertical snow stairway feels like starting down a children's spiral slide and not being able to see around the curve. The snow texture, luckily, is good for making steps.

"Remember, you've got crampons on; just back down on the steps," Dave yells up.

This isn't bad! There are no rocks or trees to hit at the bottom, should I lose control. "Can I just slide down?" Dave says yes. It turns out to be great fun.

Cliff-Dangling

The forecast called for strong wind and bitter cold, but we'd arranged to climb Black Dome and Thomas Cole with Wanda Davenport and Marty Cohen, and no one canceled.

The frigid wind whips across the ridge and stings our faces; it's the coldest day yet! Wanda gets frostnip on her face and a frostbitten toe. As vertical pitches steepen, we face a hard fact: we must expose fingers to put on full crampons—and lose precious body heat. Dave hunkers under a rock ledge and helps me change, insisting that I keep my hands protected.

Crampons work on the packed trail across Black Dome, but in the wide col to Thomas Cole no one can find the trail and we keep sinking to our knees in snow. We again have to expose hands and change back to snowshoes. Dave tells Marty and Wanda about the cold and wind on Graham, getting into snow up to his armpits, and finding someone's stuff sack.

"It's mine!" Marty exclaims.

"Your gorp was good!" Dave says.

A scary ledge, only one snowshoe wide next to a cliff, greets us on the descent. (I bushwhacked above this on the ascent.) I see a flat spot eight feet below that I can jump to, and a similar drop after that; better than across this ledge! The others continue across. Stretching down from a handhold, I let go. No problem to the first

Dave and Carol on Kaaterskill High Peak, February. Photograph by Wanda Davenport.

spot. Jumping off that, my gaiter string catches on a branch halfway down and I'm suddenly hanging headfirst. It's too high to reach up and free it, and the tension of the string is too strong to wiggle it free. Unhurt, I'm almost enjoying this comical position.

I yell, but they can't hear me; the trail has taken them north. Eventually they climb steeply to get to me. Marty can't pull the string off until Dave arrives and lifts me so that Marty can pry it off. Dave says I resembled a side of beef hanging in the butcher's cooler.

Like Hiking Through a Hedge Lengthwise—A Summer Adventure

We bushwhacked up Friday Mountain over much blowdown and fern-obscured, slippery rocks. Rather than descend such terrain, we got the brilliant idea of bushwhacking to Cornell and descending on an abandoned trail. The plan seemed so rational—a short bushwhack with little loss of altitude to a beautiful lookout on another range, then down an old trail—and we like hiking loops.

A misty rain began and the temperature dropped. As the forest became claustrophobically dense, we got on our hands and knees to peer through inflexible evergreen scrub to see where any passage might be. Virtually immobilized, damp, generating no body heat, we became thoroughly chilled. After a while we were descending a little—to Cornell? We were lost. We began contemplating a cold, wet night out in the woods, a scenario for hypothermia. Taking another compass reading, crawling through underbrush, Dave was suddenly eyeball-to-eyeball with a trail marker on a downed tree on the ground. The trail!

Two people, barely visible in the fog, are ascending. Bushwhacking out of nowhere in terrible weather, we meet hikers! Cornell's summit is just ahead, they say. Thanking them, we looked back and they were gone. A genuine mystery. The steep, rocky, "primitive trail" to Moon Haw Road took us to where we began, and we bumped into Mr. Shultis, a friend to the hikers who had to cross his property. He told us how stormy weather created the big slide.[1] "That day," Mr. Shultis said, "the air smelled different. I knew something had happened up in the mountains."

A Devil of a Path

Five days after a major April nor'easter hit New York State, dumping heavy, wet snow on the mountaintops, we stupidly decided to hike the new Long Path from Silver Hollow Notch up to 3,840-foot Plateau Mountain, across and down the Devil's Path. The new Long Path here is a gorgeous trail with several splendid views and nice variety. Just before the last steep pitch up to the summit, we noticed many broken beech trees. We figured we were near the top and the main trail would be okay.

We were relieved to see the red Devil's Path marker after pushing through unfinished trail, but the blowdown from the storm was so horrendous that we often could not see the trail and lost it regularly, pushing around and through huge downed evergreen on all sides. Rather than retracing, we hoped the situation would improve. We rarely found the trail again, however; the devastation was incredible. We postholed up to our knees and sometimes to our thighs in the snow, scrambling around and through this 1.7-mile lengthwise hedge. The trail meandered in and out of private property, and we tried to stay on the state-owned side of signs, but this took us onto steepening slopes with dense forest. We reached the top of a rock ledge that resembled the ledge in the middle of Plateau's summit, so we eased down the snowy ledge to find the trail. This was only one of many false landmarks. Re-climbing to the top, we would find old red markers, but quickly lose the trail again. It took us about three hours to cross the summit.

When we finally got to Orchard Point, we thought, *okay! Home free!* Wrong. We lost the trail almost immediately. We looked back and located a marker on one tiny tree, but we could not find any other markers. They were probably on the downed trees that littered the trail. Even this popular section of trail up to Orchard Point was not broken out, and we could not tell where the trail was. It was 7:30 PM and we faced a 1600-foot bushwhack descent. This mountain has incredible cliffs, ledges, and talus slopes. We could still see far enough ahead in the dwindling light to pick our way to the right or left as we reached drop-offs. After getting off the upper cliffs, the descent turned out to be the easiest part of the day, although very scary because we didn't know what lay ahead. The deep postholing eased, there was little blowdown on the rocky talus, and it wasn't too slippery in packable snow to get good footing. Still, we had to be very careful with our footing, and at the same time try to get as far down the mountain as possible while it was still light enough to see a distance ahead.

Just as we needed to put on our headlamps, Dave bumped into the trail. We were still quite far up. We finally got down at 9:00 PM, and then had a two-mile road walk. To top it off, Dave was wearing shorts on this bushwhack! We were both so scratched that it reminded Dave of one time when we were standing at an ice cream stand after an Adirondack bushwhack and a small boy said to his father, "Does that man have a cat?" 🚶🚶

---

[1] See "Something Happened in the Mountains."

46

MY LAST WINTER PEAK AND THE DAY AFTER

THE ESCARPMENT IN WINTER

Jerry Licht, #1423, #562W

As the winter of 2002–03 approached, I had only a few peaks remaining to finish the 3500 Club's list of peaks and, hiking most in winter, I'd almost finished the winter list as well. I had no way of knowing that this winter would not only be one of the hardest, most challenging winters, but also one of the most beautiful I'd ever experienced. This is still true three years later, after more than twelve years of hiking in the Catskills.

That winter started off with unusually heavy ice conditions high on the peaks, which caused extensive tree damage. The ice-laden tree branches bent towards the earth, and many became frozen to the ground or to other trees. Many trails on high ridges became impassable because of the bent branches. Often it was better to be off the trail in the woods where ice-laden branches were supported by nearby trees. In addition to the early ice, a storm left deep powder that steadily accumulated all winter, making for rough going all season.

After the first big snowfall, on December 26, I attempted Sugarloaf via the Mink Hollow trail from Elka Park Road. Breaking trail alone, I made it to Mink Hollow when I realized it was late and I was exhausted, so I abandoned the attempt. Later, in January, I climbed both Sugarloaf and Twin under similar conditions, again breaking trail over the same route. On the top of Sugarloaf, I found myself crawling under the trees to traverse the top of the mountain.

A week later I participated in a 3500 Club hike up Doubletop and Graham. The hike lasted eleven and a half hours, even though the route up Doubletop was broken out! We glissaded through three feet of snow on the descent from Doubletop, and the col offered no escape from deep powder. Climbing Graham, we couldn't see more than ten or fifteen feet of our route because of the ice-laden trees bent over and frozen like cement into the ground. During the last quarter-mile to the summit, we felt like rabbits crawling under the trees. I knew any future hiking that winter would be a challenging experience.

I had done much of my hiking alone. This was partly because of a lack of climbing partners; they were all interested in the more challenging hikes. I enjoy company, but I also enjoy solo hikes. They seem to offer a greater sense of achievement, and I find solo hikes more of a spiritual experience than group hikes. Having completed the peaks on my summer list solo, I was looking forward to a celebratory hike with friends to complete the winter list. I had decided to save Windham High Peak for my final hike since it is a beautiful, scenic hike, but moderate enough for friends to join me. I didn't plan ahead, however; as I was off for winter break on January 20, I drove up from Long Island and down Big Hollow Road to climb my last peak solo.

As I signed in I saw a lone hiker heading up the trail towards the Black Dome Range Trail. I headed up the red trail towards the Escarpment Trail and was pleased to find the trail well broken, apparently by a large group. When I topped out on the Escarpment Trail and turned west towards Windham, however, the trail was not broken. The group apparently had only come up for the view. The snow depth was at least two feet and deeper off the trail. After only a few steps I had serious doubts as to whether I'd be able to make it to Windham. I tried to walk where the trail should be, hoping that there was packed snow under the powder; this made it a little easier than the impassable conditions off the trail. After about fifty yards I started up the first slope, slowed to a crawl and again wondered if I was going to make it. One hundred yards farther on I hit the first really steep pitch, finding the snow accumulation much deeper; I often slid back a step or two for every few steps forward.

My heart raced with every step; was my attempt to reach Windham foolhardy? But I enjoy long, hard, heart-pounding climbs, and I'm accustomed to climbing without pausing, so I pushed on. On level sections I struggled with two or more feet of powder, periodically crashing through drifts up to my waist. Sometimes my snowshoes would catch on a buried stump and I'd do a face plant. More than a few of those drifts caught me by surprise. Icy snow found its way into my thin wool pants and down my legs. With every fall into a deep drift, I expended a large amount of energy as I "swam" towards the surface and stood again. Often I would leave the trail to see if the snow was more consolidated elsewhere while I struggled through the deep drifts.

Although the going was difficult and exhausting, the truth is I felt like a kid again playing in this magnificent winter wonderland glistening in the sun. The views of the woods that snowy winter were magnificent, especially in the Burnt Knob area. The terrain was pristine; all signs of previous hikers had been wiped clean by a deep white blanket of cold powder. I was alone and had this glorious place to myself. So I continued to push forward.

At last the final climb to the summit was in sight. When I topped out I was surprised to have a 360° view; the great snow depth allowed me to stand over short leafless trees for a rare view from this summit. It had taken me seven and a half hours to get there! In other seasons I've done the same hike round trip in four and a half hours. It was close to sunset and I had expended a lot of energy, but the return trip in my own steps would be far easier and I'd get back relatively quickly. I was prepared to walk out in the dark. The going was good and I made it to the descent of Burnt Knob as the light began to fade. When it got dark I put on my headlamp, but did not turn it on. It was a clear crisp night and I watched the stars come into view one at a time as I walked. At the junction of the Escarpment Trail, I turned my lamp on and headed down; the return trip only took one and a half hours! Physically exhausted, but feeling a tremendous sense of accomplishment, I headed to Kingston to get a room for the night and an ale or two.

The Day After

The next day, although I woke up extremely sore and tight from the previous day's hike, I decided to hike again as an "active rest day." I headed back to Big Hollow Road to climb Blackhead, as I am fond of the views from there. The trail would likely be broken, because it is a "required winter peak." Also, I'd seen the lone hiker heading that way the day before. I chose to go up the east side from the Escarpment, as I usually do for the views, even though it was the harder route and might not be broken. As I signed in I was happy to see that the hiker the day before had also signed in to Blackhead. Now I was confident that the trail would be broken. Sore, I slowly headed up the trail. As I climbed to the top of the Escarpment, every fiber in my legs felt each step! However, it was another very beautiful sunny day and the views were great.

At about 3,300 feet the slope got steep and the tracks stopped. The climber had turned around, leaving 600 feet of climbing and a little under half a mile of unbroken trail to the summit. There was no way I was turning back, so I continued up even more slowly than before. The last 100 feet before the summit may be the steepest pitch, a high-angled slope interrupted by small ledges. The slope formed a snow chute with powder up to my waist. Frozen tree branches hung low at about face level. For every step up I slid back, sometimes more than one step. Ball bearing-sized pieces of ice that had fallen off tree branches carpeted the trail and glistened in the sun. Every step caused the glittering "ice diamonds" to roll down the slope chiming like a "rain stick" as they went. Finally I topped out and walked across the summit through the boreal[1] forest to the west side, where I was happy to see that the trail was fully broken; I'd be out in no time. Again I experienced that great sense of accomplishment one can only feel after a difficult solo hike. My easy rest day had turned into a five-and-a-half-hour adventure.

I will never forget my last winter peak and the wonderful day after. 𓀀

[1] Forest zone between Arctic-Alpine and Northern Hardwoods.

47

SNOWSHOE GODDESSES IN THE CATSKILLS

FROM HORNED HEADDRESSES AND BELLS TO
LIGHTWEIGHT SNOWSHOES AND FLEECE

Katherine Mario, #960, #368W, Snowshoe Goddess #1

Close your eyes and picture strong snowshoe-clad women striding through the snow. They are smiling and their hair is streaming from beneath their Norsewoman helmets. The sun is sinking and the full moon is rising. These women are carrying on a centuries-old tradition of solstice worship. Imagine the surprise of normal hikers, sloshing up a trailless peak, when—suddenly, to their amazement—a dozen women appear in horned headdresses and jingling bells. They rub their eyes and wonder if they really saw what they thought they saw. Modern women who appear in the Catskill Mountains now are outfitted in lightweight snowshoes and fleece, but they are no less fierce in their determination and in their love of great winter fun.

In 1996 a group of twenty-five women from the Mohican and Long Island chapters of the Adirondack Mountain Club (ADK) gathered in Phoenicia with the purpose of bagging Catskill peaks. The most memorable of the winter hikes occurred during the actual solstice. Jane Smalley, Mohican ADK and one of the founding goddesses shares: "I particularly remember the first winter, planning the event for winter solstice with a full moon. The next day we hiked Slide, Cornell, and Wittenberg, descending in the light of a full moon so bright it cast shadows and rendered headlamps unnecessary. What an exhilarating and powerful experience knowing that I could do this classic hike in the Catskills in winter with ten-plus feet of snow, and feel wonderful coming out in the dark! I remember all of us struggling down over the back side of Slide on our crampons and, as darkness was approaching, seeing the moon appear. We knew we were going to make it out safely. I felt a strong camaraderie among everyone on this, the first Snowshoe Goddess weekend."

Fearing lawsuits by disgruntled ADK males who longed to join the solstice worship, the auspicious outing was opened to all. As the numbers of "goddesses" grew, a gala Snowshoe Goddess dinner complemented the raucous event. Richard Maemone, one of the first five men to join Snowshoe Goddesses, says, "The Snowshoe Goddess event has been a wonderful source of merriment for ADK members

Snowshoe Goddess patch. Courtesy of Kathy Mario.

for many years. The original band of wild and crazy goddesses shall be forever immortalized in the annals of the Long Island ADK!"

Awards are given each year: Most Outstanding Goddess Headdress; Bionic Goddess; Rookie Goddess of the Year. June Fait, who missed only one goddess event, reminds us that the goddess patch that she proudly displays on her "brag vest" is the object of hundreds of fun questions from admirers. If you venture into the Catskills, you will surely cross the path of someone displaying this unique patch. June misses the peak bagging atmosphere that was so much a part of the first four or five events. Goddess hair turned gray, and members completed their winter 3500 peaks, so the event morphed into one of the premier outings in the Catskills. But the spirit of goddesses is pulling together to finish the winter Catskill peaks, June says.

"Being a part of the original coterie of goddesses was one of the most fun things I've ever done," says Martha McDermott of Long Island ADK and an "original" goddess. "We formed, miraculously, into a wonderful, warm and happy group—bold and fun-loving and spirited." This tradition ended with its ten-year anniversary on or around the winter solstice of 2006. 🌂

48

FIRST WINTER CATSKILL HIKE

WONDROUS NEW OPPORTUNITIES IN THESE MOUNTAINS

Raymond Pride, #1017, #426W
from October–December 1995 *Catskill Canister*

We have had our vacation home in the Catskills for several years and have enjoyed occasional fall hikes with friends. We would arrive at the mountain just before noon, hike to the first overlook, spread out our blankets and eat a gourmet lunch. Hagen would bring the smoked meats and cheese, Nancy chose the wines, Eldine and Heide made the desserts, and Ted and Howard would start debates and regale us with off-color jokes. On a good day we would walk four miles, drink as many bottles of wine and consume twice as many calories as we expended.

Soon, we had hiked most of the accessible marked trails and had difficulty finding new hikes and flat rocks on which to lay out our spread. Then we learned about the Catskill 3500 Club. Suddenly the Catskills exploded in size! The trail maps presented wonderful new hiking possibilities. Until then we'd never considered "off trail" hiking. The club also introduced us to winter hiking.

Armed with compass, altimeter, snowshoes and warm clothes, we set out on our first winter hike, on Slide Mountain, on December 26, 1993. The previous evening had ushered in an Arctic front, accompanied by strong, gusting winds; we started out in sub-zero conditions with a foot of snow on the ground. It wasn't long before our sandwiches and the water in our canteens froze. The tops on our thermoses would not open.

We proceeded slowly and steadily under a steel-gray sky. Nearby mountains intermittently disappeared in local snow squalls. As we neared the summit, we passed beneath the cloud base. The temperature dropped farther, and a steady light snow began to fall. The scenery turned truly dramatic, with snow encrusting the blackened balsam. Near the summit it was snowing heavily, and drifts in the trail made our progress more difficult. Our stop at the peak was brief, as the snow and wind were blowing fiercely. Back in the car, we turned on the heater and warmed our hands and feet, thawed out our sandwiches and melted the ice on our thermoses. Our first "off season" hike had proved tough but satisfying; wondrous new opportunities lay ahead. 🏃

49

A NICE HIKE BECOMES AN ICE HIKE

FUN AND FEAR

George Preoteasa, #1478, #604W

I t's April 1, thick clouds but no precipitation. The snow cover is abundant for so late in the season, but in the last few days the weather has been warm and it rained quite a bit, so the snow is hard and covered with a thick glaze of ice.

I am joining a Catskill 3500 Club hike. Our target is the hard-to-find Southwest Hunter peak. The leader is experienced, knows the Catskills well and wants to make the hike interesting. So we do a shuttle, park a few cars somewhere on a little road—possibly Diamond Notch Road in Lanesville—and drive the others to the Notch Lake parking area, where we start the hike.

Going up the Devil's Path is not a problem. The snowshoe crampons provide good traction on the hard snow. At some point we begin to bushwhack. Here the snow is deep and still fluffy. After a good struggle with the balsam trees, we find the canister. Hurray! Everybody is happy. A feeling of relaxation settles in. All we have to do now is follow the ridge that will take us to the cars on the "little road." We follow the gently descending ridge. The leader leaves the leading to whoever will take it.

The snow is again hard and covered with ice. Someone ahead of me falls and continues to slide until she reaches some small trees that stop her. A few minutes later it's my turn. Losing your concentration for just a moment is all it takes to fall and then, despite the gentleness of the slope, you cannot stop. The sides of the Tubbs snowshoes are a smooth aluminum tube. You cannot reach the snow with the snowshoe crampons, and even if you did, it would be very dangerous—you could twist a joint badly. The poles are useless when you are close to the horizontal. As I am slowly picking up speed, finally I soft-land on a tree, feet first. I realize that falling is easy, but on this slope I don't feel any fear. It is fun.

We continue on the ridge for a while. At some point, however, we start wondering why the ridge is getting narrower and the side slopes are getting steeper. According to the map, the ridge should flatten. There are also streams on both sides that were not supposed to be there. Could we be on the wrong ridge? Yes, indeed.

The leader makes the decision to go down the steep slope. The stream at the bottom is some 200 to 300 feet below us. There is little vegetation on the icy slope (where are the bushes when you need them?) A fall on that slope would mean picking up speed fast with no possibility of arrest. I can also see a significant rocky drop-off at the edge of the stream. Not a pleasant way to end a slide. Suddenly, it's not fun anymore.

I think everyone realizes this is dangerous; still, we proceed. I don't feel comfortable. I am already on the steep slope looking for a place to switch to crampons. There is no convenient spot, nothing flat. I find a log and manage to take off one snowshoe. The bare boot slides like it was on sheer ice. Very scary. I do not find enough support to take the crampons out of the backpack, so I have no choice but to put back on the snowshoe. Looks like I will have to continue like this.

In the meantime, other members of the group have made significant progress toward the stream. They shout at me to climb down backwards. It certainly feels safer. So I continue, very concentrated on not making a mistake, one move at a time—one leg, opposite pole down, the other leg, opposite pole down. Always have three points of support, and always make sure that the snowshoe or the pole just moved is firmly planted in the snow. It's a long descent. I cannot take off my gloves, but I am sure my knuckles are very white.

The feeling of elation is great as I take the last steps. The others have been waiting patiently. We have to hurry—it's getting dark. We see some houses, probably trespass on private property and find a road. But that's not where we left our cars, obviously, so we hitchhike. A couple of young locals driving old pickup trucks kindly take us, but there is no room in the cabin, so I jump in the back on a pile of melting snow that must have been accumulating over the winter. My clothes are quickly getting wet, but who cares, we are off the mountain and alive. What an adventure we've had; it does not get much better than that!

Epilogue

I've had my own ice axe for a few winters now. I carried it two or three times in all, although I never even came close to needing it. I decided to learn self-arrest. I went to an Appalachian Mountain Club class (it was fun), and I bought the axe afterwards. I'm kind of sorry I haven't had a chance to use it. But who knows, maybe one day ...

In the meantime, it's a nice piece of aluminum, very decorative. I'm sure some people admire it, but I have to be careful not to impale myself. 𖤐

50

WALT GREGORY'S CRAMPONS

SOLO BUSHWHACKING: A METAPHOR

Bill W. Collier, #297, #95W

On a hot Sunday afternoon in the middle of August in the late 1970s, I was repairing the wood rot in the kitchen floor stemming from a long-term leak in the clothes washer. As I worked, I recalled the woman I'd broken up with eight months before—how she had complained that I never did anything. I had vowed to climb the Catskills that summer to prove her wrong. Then I realized it was August and obviously way past time to get started. I put down my tools, dug out my maps and compass, hopped in the VW, and drove up to bag Vly and Bearpen.

Over the next several months I bagged all the rest of the peaks. It was the perfect exercise for that period in my life, requiring a lot of energy, a lot of time, and not much thinking. In December I bagged the four winter peaks necessary to qualify for the 3500 summer badge. I knew Larry Futrell (#296) was also closing in on his summer badge, so when I came down from my final peak, I did not mail my climb record to Bill (#1) and Elinore (#2) Leavitt. Instead, I drove over to Hudson and hand-delivered it, hoping to get a lower number than Larry. The Leavitts were gracious. While Elinore was looking up what number I would get, she said that it was unusual to have two climb lists arrive in one day—she had just gotten a letter in the mail that morning from a guy named Larry Futrell. Justice was served, and I was spared a lifetime of being reminded that I had been one-upped by a competitive spirit overstepping all rational and decent bounds.

One thing I realized, as I finished up the summer badge and contemplated pursuing a winter badge, was that I loved bushwhacking. Bushwhacking was full of adventure, solitude, and uncertainty. Trail hiking was deadening, like driving on a super highway. Another analogy may be less easily appreciated: parallel computer programming versus ordinary programming. Trail hiking was like ordinary programming. Bushwhacking was like parallel programming; at every step there was a chance for error.

One day in January I set out to conquer Blackhead, Black Dome, and Thomas Cole. There had been an icy rain the day before, and then a couple of inches of fresh snow overnight. I had snowshoes, but no crampons. I realized very shortly that this was not going to be an easy hike. I could see the tracks of two people ahead of me, however, and I said to myself that if they could do it, so could I; five minutes later I met them. I learned later that their names were Walt Gregory (#18, 8W) and Betty McMahon. They had turned back and said the going was too tough. When Walt saw that I had no crampons, he told me that I would never make it; the trail was just too icy. But, he added, he made crampons as a hobby, out of angle-aluminum, and he had some back in the car he would sell me for $10, his normal price. I hesitated; I didn't want to hike back to the cars and start all over. Betty saw my hesitation and offered me the crampons she had on her snowshoes.

It was very, very cold. Gloves had to be removed, bolts had to be loosened, cold metal had to be transferred from her snowshoes to mine. Ten dollars had to be transferred in the other direction. Walt and Betty headed back to their car, and I headed uphill. My new crampons made the impossible achievable. I went up Black Dome and then over to Thomas Cole. I was not sure exactly where the summit was, so I descended a bit to the west. I returned to the col between Black Dome and Blackhead. I was tired, but wanted to bag this peak and finish this area of the Catskills, so I slogged up Blackhead and back down to the road.

I was surprised to see Walt and Betty beside my car. Betty explained that the crampons they had sold me were the first that Walt had made, and she was sentimentally attached to them. Would I exchange them for a brand new pair? I agreed, of course, and we removed the crampons from my snowshoes. Walt asked me what I'd climbed. I said all three. Did Walt look askance at me? If so, I put it down to the contempt "real" hikers have for mere peak baggers, which I knew I was.

I used the crampons a lot during the next few weeks, but I began to think that I would not finish the winter peaks. Then, in early March, there was a freak warm spell. Salley Decker (#629) came back from the mountains and reported that there was a very hard crust on the snow, even at the summits, so snowshoes were not needed. I reacted to this news by taking eight days of vacation from work and bagging the remaining nineteen peaks to qualify for my winter badge, all but one of the nineteen solo. Solo winter bushwhacking—what a thrill!

At the annual banquet, after I got my badges, Betty McMahon told me that when I'd said that I had climbed all three peaks that day, Walt had not believed me. He had thought it impossible to do that in the time that had elapsed. So he had gone back the next day and, instead of climbing Blackhead (which had been his original intent), he had climbed Black Dome and Thomas Cole. It had not snowed in the interim. There were only my tracks in the snow, and from Black Dome he could see my tracks all the way up Blackhead. So he had had to conclude that, though I might be merely a peak bagger, I was a truthful one.

A couple of months after the annual banquet, I walked into my kitchen and something in the corner caught my eye. It was the pile of tools I had been using the previous August to repair the hole in the floor. And not just the tools—the hole was also still there. I managed to ignore it for a while longer, but eventually did finish the job.

I wondered what to do next. I thought of running a marathon or climbing the Adirondacks. Then I remembered a problem I had been working on in parallel processing, namely, how to represent the rules that programmers believe a computer obeys. Almost twenty years later this effort resulted in a book, *Reasoning about Parallel Architectures*. There were times in writing the book that felt like solo bushwhacking—being completely alone and in grave danger of failing, but with the conviction that if I could just keep taking one step at a time, eventually I would succeed. The fear and exhilaration were the same in both situations, and I like to think that the one endeavor helped me prepare for the other. 🏃

Black Dome summit scramble. Photograph by Carol White.

51

THE DAY I USED IT ALL

Lots of Lightweight Equipment Weighs a Ton

Marty Cohen, #728, #330W

Every time I finish reading an article about the possible dangers of winter hiking in the mountains, my pack gets a bit heavier. Even though I have never spent a full, unplanned night in the woods, I try always to carry enough to survive such an event; in the winter that means a lot of extra clothes, a bivy[1] sack, headlamp, and more. Since I have learned by sad experience that it isn't possible to predict with accuracy the conditions to be found at an elevation until one gets there, I lean towards also carrying extra equipment for climbing in snow and ice. When a small group of us climbed Indian Head from the east one January, in addition to my extra clothes, first aid, repair kit, etc., I wore snowshoes and also carried an ice axe, crampons, rope, carabiner, and ski poles. To be sure that my feet were warm, I wore Sorel Dominators, good to –20°, it is claimed.

We snowshoed along the Devil's Path on a beautiful winter day ascending the east slope of Indian Head, which seemed steeper than I remembered, most likely owing to the weight of the gear I was carrying, my antiquity, or both. As we neared the summit ridge we found that the steep wall—a couloir[2]—leading to the east face's prominent ledge, was filled with snow. The snowshoes couldn't broach the ascent; they kept slipping back in the steep powder. Time to switch to crampons. Also, since my pack weighed a ton, I convinced others to line some of the heavier packs up the ledge, thereby making that near-vertical step less daunting. Such lining was facilitated by the rope and carabiner I was carrying. The crampons worked quite well in the couloir, although getting them on was time consuming, as only one person at a time could fit on the only flat place available on the couloir approach. In fact, in attempting to maneuver around, one of the party lost his footing and slid down the steep packed snow below the couloir until he collided with another of the party who, in turn, joined the slide until they both slid in to me, the three of us completing the farce. Fortunately, none of us nor our clothing was impaled by a crampon point.

Once the entire party was up the prominent ledge, we changed back into our snowshoes. This was premature, there being at least two more ledges that, though small, were difficult to ascend under the snow conditions. On these I used my ice axe to great advantage, as handholds were unreliable under the slippery conditions. Eventually we achieved the summit, weary but elated at having completed an arduous climb. Although the sun was a bit too close to the horizon to suit my tired body, we made it down Jimmy Dolan Notch and back to Prediger Road without having to don our headlamps.

Despite the title of this vignette, I actually didn't use everything I carried, but I used a lot more of the complement than usual, which raises the question: at what point does the added weight of the contingency equipment become more of a safety hazard than a help? Had I carried less, I would have had less difficulty in both the ascent and the descent, thus reducing the chance of a mishap caused by fatigue and the likelihood of spending some dark hours on the mountain. ᛘ

---

[1] A cocoon-like device that folds up to a small size, for an emergency in the woods.

[2] A steep mountainside gorge.

52

FIRST DAY OF THE THIRD MILLENNIUM

A Winter Ramble

Constantine Dean Gletsos #1128, #444W

Halcott Mountain, as most Catskill Mountain hikers know, is a relatively small (3,520 feet), easy-to-hike summit, yet it is one of the required trailless Catskill Mountain 3500 peaks. I had hiked Halcott, along with a group that included one of my sons, for the first time one November when there were three inches of snow on the ground. It was fun and easy. After I finished climbing all thirty-five Catskill peaks over 3,500 feet, I decided I should climb them also in winter. On January 1, 2000, the first day of the new millennium, I decided to climb Halcott alone. I wanted to be the first on top of this mountain in the new millennium, so I left home early to beat anybody else who might have the same idea.

New York State owns Halcott Mountain Wild Forest all the way east to Route 42. It is possible to approach Halcott from the south or west, but these approaches involve crossing private lands, and permission from the landowners must be obtained. I decided to hike in via the easiest way, from the regular hikers' parking area on Route 42. From there it is only a four- to five-mile hike round trip. It was still dark at 7:30 AM when I left home. Thanks to a recent thaw, most of the snow had melted at the lower elevations, leaving behind a mixture of mud and dead leaves. My car was the only car in the parking area. *Great*, I thought, *I beat the crowd!* There were icy spots around the partially frozen and beautifully cascading waterfalls from Bushnellville Creek and its tributaries, so I put on my instep crampons for better stability. The day was partially sunny, breezy, and 35°.

I went south, first, to meet the main Bushnellville Creek and followed it to reach the summit, making sure to stay on the ridge between the main creek and its northern tributary. My instep crampons were a must as I encountered more snow and ice. I passed dry stone walls from old farms, orchards and homestead foundations from another era. It was so beautiful and quiet, with gentle wind gusts and the soothing sound of the rushing creeks flowing below. The sun was reflected on the icy parts of the trail, an exquisite sight that I tried to capture with my camera. At the summit the snow was up to six inches deep. I found the canister at eleven

Canister on Halcott Mountain. Photograph by Scott Lane.

o'clock and was the first person to sign in on this mountain on the first day of the third millennium. Mission accomplished!

I hung my backpack on a tree branch, cleaned a place on a boulder and sat down for lunch. When I finished, it was too early to descend the way I had come. There were no views on that route, and I remembered reading that there were nice views south of the Halcott summit at about 3,000 feet. *Let's explore this*, I said to myself, setting my compass in a southern direction and bushwhacking through black cherry and hardwood forest. Staying on the mountain ridge, I did reach a high point over boulders that offered very nice views to the southeast—forest and mountains as far as one could see, with no sign of human presence. It was peaceful and magnificent.

It was early in the afternoon and I still didn't want to descend; the occasional appearance of the sun encouraged me to do more exploration. At a low point between the mountains, I met an old lumber road going east-west, crossed it and soon was heading uphill again. My map said I was heading for Rose Mountain, which is just off the Catskill Park boundary divide that separates the Delaware River Basin (west) from the Hudson River Basin (east). I had entered deep into private land, but I didn't see "No Trespassing" signs. I wanted to push on to another mountain that perhaps I would never do again, if I had to find and obtain permission from the landowners. The Rubicon had been crossed already; it was too late. I was on my own.

In a half hour I was on another summit without views. At two o'clock the sun was already behind the trees to the west. Night comes very quickly that time of the year; I had to get out of there soon! Bushwhacking downhill was rather easy, through a typical Catskill forest with occasional bushes and scenic rock ledges to bypass. After descending below the snow-covered heights to the snow/mud/leaves mess, I lost one of my instep crampons, but I didn't discover this loss until I was "back in civilization" and saw farms and houses on Route 42. I loved those insteps because they were part of my Adirondack mountain adventures, but I decided not to go back and look for it with such slight expectations of finding it. It was like losing an old, good friend. Those insteps were easy to pack and just right for most hiking conditions. But the sun was almost gone, and I was at least two miles south of my car. House lights were on already.

The sun was long gone when I reached my car. It had been a full, adventurous day and I had achieved my goal of being on the summit of Halcott on the first day of the third millennium. I still lament the loss of my beloved instep, but that hike of Halcott Mountain was a day to remember. 🥾

53

FIRST HIKE

HIKING FROM SPRING INTO WINTER

Kathleen Balthazar Heitzmann, #520, #230W

In 1984 my former husband, the late Antonio Vega, was visiting from Spain. I decided to show him our beautiful Greene County, so took him on a camping trip. It was early May. The village of Catskill was awash with the pinks, yellows, and whites of spring. After setting up camp at the lean-to, I took a hike to Windham High Peak. Tony figured he was not in good enough shape, so he stayed at the campsite collecting firewood.

Off on my first high-peak hike—I was surprised to see bare trees and snow. I had entered into another world. The deciduous trees were barely starting to bud, giving the mountain a barren, dead look. The weather was cool with intermittent sprinkles and an overcast sky. It was more like March, instead of May, without the prettiness of winter. I passed a creek, later realizing it was the Batavia Kill. It is amazing to me how much I have learned about these mountains after more than twenty years of hiking. I noted beautiful yellow birch in my journal and ate an icicle. Near the top there were small, pale, purple flowers with five petals. The petals have darker purple lines with a yellow stamen.

When I peaked, I could see Point Lookout Restaurant off to my left and the Blackhead Range massif on my right. After enjoying the view I headed back. As I neared the lean-to, the snow along the rocky ledge looked like water frozen in space, the crystals like a white kaleidoscope. The snow must have melted and frozen again. There was a family of white birch. It was eerie the way the trees squeaked in the wind. At the top it was eerie as well—I felt as if I were at the end of the earth. 𝍫

LOST IN
THE WILDERNESS

*The terrain was rough, the footing treacherous; we
exchanged snowshoes for crampons. … We had to
make our way down rock faces. Whenever we hit
level ground, we speeded up as much as we could
until we started tumbling down the next rock face.
There's no doubt in my mind that it was by the grace
of God alone that neither of us sprained or broke
an ankle.*

Ken Krabbenhoft

Photograph by Larry Gambon.

54

WHEN THE CHIPS ARE DOWN

THE PARADOX OF MISADVENTURE

Ken Krabbenhoft, #1338, #595W

It was –4° on the morning of January 11, 2004, when we left the car at the end of Moon Haw Road with a note for Buzz Friedel on the dashboard. The sky was clear, the air was still, and the snow was fresh—a beautiful day. My hiking pal, Dan Saks (#758, winter #341), had climbed Friday and Balsam Cap many years earlier for his winter patch. If we reached them today, I would be within five peaks of mine.

We bare-booted to around 2,200 feet, where there were clear views of the Ashokan Reservoir. The snowshoes went on shortly after. Soon we were at the base of Friday, where we made our first error of judgment—or maybe it was just bad luck. It was my idea to go right (northeast), thinking we could outflank the cliffs, instead of left to the col. We ended up negotiating steep rock faces in deep snow, using the snowshoes for crampons and our hiking poles for ice axes. It was harder than the usual route from the col, but more thrilling, with the bright sun on the untouched drifts, depths of air below us, and Cornell and Wittenberg close enough to touch. It was winter bushwhacking at its most spectacular.

The sky had grown overcast and the temperature had climbed to a calm 8° by the time we reached the canister on Friday, and when we left for Balsam Cap around noon, there seemed no reason why we wouldn't be back at the car by dusk. Following a reading of 200°, we plunged into the Balsam Cap thickets. A view appeared of what seemed to be the summit ridge, uphill to the left, with Rocky in the distance on the right, but back in the thickets we started to veer unknowingly to the north. At two o'clock we happily stormed a lightly forested hill that we assumed was Balsam Cap, but it turned out that we were on Rocky instead. It fell to me to open the canister and see my own signature in the book: I'd been there ten days earlier with Rocky Walberg on a club hike! Not only had we overshot our goal, we'd gone way out of our way and didn't think there was enough time to go back to Balsam Cap and get out in daylight.

That was our second error in judgment. The direct route back to Moon Haw Road, in fact, led straight over Balsam Cap, but all Dan and I could see on the map was a route down and off the mountain. We were cold, the sun was already beginning to fade, and we didn't want to take any chances, so we took a compass reading east that angled back toward Friedel's property, and started breaking trail through thickets and down rock faces. Some of this was rough going, with the constant danger of spruce traps. At one point a branch cut a gash on the bridge of my nose and, although I didn't feel a thing because of the cold, Dan got a scare when he saw my face covered in blood. The light was going fast, but we both agreed on our compass headings. We were headed east, and at some point we would start losing altitude.

At 4:30 we were still at 3,000 feet and had to admit we didn't know where we were. We were on relatively level ground that shelved gradually downhill with no prospect of sudden progress toward any road. It was clear that we were going to have to bushwhack in the dark. So there it was: the moment one always dreads, the thing that always happens to the other guy—getting lost on a mountain at nightfall and maybe having to spend the night. The brush with fear. What would our wives Ferris and Beth think? Could we ever again persuade them not to worry when we went winter hiking? And what about the loss of face? Should we make a pact to keep it a secret? What would it be like to spend the night up here? The wind had picked up and the temperature had actually risen to about 15°. Dan had an emergency blanket. If we shared it and kept moving, there was no danger of freezing to death. But it would be a long, cold, hungry, thirsty, exhausting, and entirely miserable night, and we would be all too aware of our wives' worry.

I was very glad that I wasn't alone, and not just because I didn't have any emergency equipment (ever since, I carry two foil blankets and two headlamps with extra batteries whenever I go out). To have Dan there, to hear him say that at the worst we'd have an uncomfortable night and that Beth and Ferris would call the ranger—that turned disaster into something approaching adventure. We would make it and have stories to tell. But we were still determined not to spend the night.

That led to our third error in judgment: the decision to alternate going straight downhill with following our original compass heading. That way (we thought) we could make headway while there was still some light to see by, zigzagging toward our point of departure and reducing the amount of time we would have to find our way in true darkness. There was no moon that night. Reconstructing our actual route the next day, we found that our zigzag had not been bold enough. It was more like a wavering line that led us, in effect, southeast, increasingly farther away from the car.

As night fell around five o'clock, we figured we were about halfway between Rocky and Moon Haw Road. I paid the price of not packing a headlamp by having to walk behind Dan and having to figure out where to put my feet in the dark by remembering what I had seen in the light from his lamp. The terrain was rough, the footing treacherous; we exchanged snowshoes for crampons. At one point I stepped on one of Dan's poles and snapped it in two. We had to make our way down rock faces. Whenever we hit level ground, we speeded up as much as we could until we started tumbling down the next rock face. There's no doubt in my mind that it was by the grace of God alone that neither of us sprained or broke an ankle.

At seven o'clock, after two hours of bushwhacking in the dark, we were still lost. It didn't make any sense to us that we should have come so far without having lost any altitude to speak of. Whatever anxiety I had felt was replaced by irritation. It was one of a handful of times that I have actually been angry at a mountain itself, as if it had a personal grudge against me! Just as our nerves were beginning to fray, we made out lights in the distance. We were so lost that we thought we were seeing Boiceville, when in fact it was West Shokan—we'd put a ridge of unnamed peaks between us and Moon Haw Road. But they could have been the lights of Baghdad, for all we cared—that small sign of human habitation picked up our spirits and infused us with new energy. We speeded up, descending what we still hoped was Maltby Hollow, while ahead of us rose what we thought was Samuels Point.

Ken Krabbenhoft (left) and Dan Saks. Photograph by Ferris Cook.

The sky cleared and bright stars took the place of house lights in the distance. We came to a good-sized brook with a path next to it and fresh footprints in the snow. We followed them to the end of a logging road and found a dirt track that led to a paved road. Our wavering path down Rocky had led us miles off course; we were in Mine Hollow, not Maltby Hollow. What we had assumed was Samuels Point was in fact Hanover Mountain. We had arrived at Peekamoose Road, two and a half miles from Maltby Hollow and the car.

There was something almost theatrical about the relief we felt when the first house came into view—a house with lights on and an SUV in the driveway. It was eight o'clock. We took a moment to slip off our crampons and packs and tuck in our shirts. I had already washed the blood off my face, but we figured Dan looked more presentable, so he gingerly knocked at the door. We didn't want to startle our prospective rescuers. They turned out to be a couple with a young son, and when they'd gotten over their surprise they gave us a friendly welcome, inviting us in to warm up and have something to drink. They let us call Beth and Ferris, and the wife drove us back to our car. Later, we tried to think of what we could do to express our gratitude, and we decided that the best thing was to do nothing. Their hospitality had been freely given and, as mountain hikers and hunters themselves, they understood what we'd been through and how grateful we were to have found them.

Dan and I have often shared the sense of accomplishment and relief that comes when you open the car door and turn on the ignition at the end of a hike. How much greater the relief that night after being lost, despite the disappoint- ment of missing Balsam Cap! On the way home that night, with the roads clear and the fan blasting heat, we were already laughing about what had happened and how narrowly we had avoided the scenario of spending a night lost in the Catskills in the depths of January. We had the survivor's gratitude for having been spared, along with an absurd touch of pride for having bushwhacked off a mountain in the dark. The two didn't seem to be in contradiction.

If all had gone according to plan—if we had found Balsam Cap instead of Rocky, retraced our steps back to the base of Friday and walked straight back to Buzz Friedel's parking lot—it would have been just another successful hike. But because we'd found ourselves in a situation that had tested our physical strength and our spirit, that made us draw on our experience of the mountains and on the reservoir of our friendship, it was the most important, the most meaningful, and the most memorable of all the hikes we've ever done together.

When the chips are down, you learn what it's really all about. 🏃

55

LESSONS LEARNED IN THE WILD

HARD-WON WILDERNESS WISDOM

John Lounsbury, #1257, #524W

In May 1999 my son Richard, age thirty-one, and I decided to make our first foray into the Catskill high peaks. We had spent a long weekend the previous August climbing our first five Adirondack high peaks with Richard's two sons, ages seven and nine. Our ignorant thought was, "If we could get two small children up and down Adirondack peaks, how hard could the 'little' Catskills be?"

We had selected 3,843-foot Peekamoose and 3,847-foot Table for our first climbs. We left the trailhead on Peekamoose Road at 8:00 AM and rambled to the top of Peekamoose[1] and then over to Table by 10:15. Lone Mountain appeared very close, so we decided to add that to our day's itinerary. We dropped into the col from Table and found the trek to be an easy stroll to the summit of Lone, with only a slight detour around ledges near the top. It was just after eleven o'clock.

We made an early lunch and, feeling contented with food in our stomachs and confident with the ease of progress so far, we decided to continue to Rocky Mountain. Rocky appeared to be a shorter jaunt from Lone than Lone had been from Table. We dropped to the southeast to avoid steep ledges straight ahead, and after a 200–300-foot loss in elevation, we veered left, attempting a 90° heading. Very dense growth and undergrowth required zigzagging in what we felt was the direction we desired. By 12:30 it seemed we must have gone at least a mile, and maybe two. Rich got out his GPS for the first time and we found that our forward progress in one hour and fifteen minutes was a little less than one-half mile!

The terrain was very flat and densely forested. Even the view from climbing ten feet up the largest tree yielded nothing but vegetation. We forced our way in as nearly a straight line as possible, keeping a constant eye on the compass. After another half hour we were relieved to be climbing uphill. We forced our way uphill for another thirty minutes until we reached the Rocky summit canister.

It was 1:40 and we decided we could reach Balsam Cap Mountain, less than one mile distant, in the next hour if we continued our successful strategy of "straight ahead no matter what." Our confidence was buoyed because the east slope of Rocky appeared less densely vegetated, and the descent into the broad col was as easy as it looked from the summit. But as we progressed across the col, the growth became just as dense and now had frequent blowdown obstructing our path. We climbed over, crawled under, and made large loops to circumvent fallen trees.

Things only got worse when we started up toward the summit ridge. In places the blowdown seemed more than three dimensions, it was so entangled! Enmeshed tree trunks were interwoven with the most vicious, razor-like undergrowth we had yet encountered. Blood oozed from scratches on our faces and arms, even though we were wearing long-sleeved shirts.

When we finally reached the summit ridge, our estimated hour had ballooned to a little more than three hours. No canister was obvious here, but we circled for ten minutes and finally found it. It was now five o'clock; we had three hours of good daylight remaining. Examining the map, we determined that the only way not to spend the night in the woods was to drop east off Balsam Cap to Moon Haw Road—much less distance and all downhill.

We headed downslope as rapidly as we could, directly away from the summit canister and fighting through the increasingly dense undergrowth. After twenty minutes we came to a brief clearing; I noted a familiar skyline at eight o'clock to the direction we were heading. I was looking at Peekamoose and Table—we were headed north-northwest straight toward Slide Mountain! We had wanted to go east! The day was heavily overcast with no sun to help us with our bearings; absent the sun, it had been extremely unwise of us to leave the summit without taking a compass heading.

I was contemplating a night in the woods. We each had an extra fleece jacket, foil thermal blankets, at least a liter of water, and packets of gorp. I thought about a business appointment I had at 10:00 AM the next morning. We retraced our way back to the canister and took a careful compass heading. We headed south along the ridge for thirty minutes until we found a spot to drop safely through the ledges. The steep slope was covered with unstable scree[2]; uncertain footing made progress very slow.

At about seven o'clock Rich shouted—he was pointing at a bear scrambling obliquely down the slope away from us. In all the hiking I've done since in the Northeast, that remains my only bear sighting. At eight o'clock we reached a trickle of a stream that we followed downhill to an old woods road, which involved some road/streambed scrambles. Just as nightfall was nearly complete, we were finally on a continuous roadbed. It would have been very difficult to negotiate the dangerous terrain higher on the mountain in the dark.

We started the ten- or eleven-mile road walk at 9:00 PM. A car coming down Moon Haw Road stopped, and the driver asked us if we needed help. The driver was Susan Shultis (her maiden name), a legendary name to lovers of the Catskills,

I later learned. I was very thankful that a woman on a dark mountain road would give a ride to two men who happened to be there because of very poor judgment.

My first hike in the Catskills held several very important lessons: (1) Always set a turnaround time with a safety margin. The safety margin should include allowances for differences in terrain and conditions for the rest of the day, and allowances for the tiring factor. (2) Refer to your compass continuously. If you take too few readings, very serious complications can arise. (3) When hiking in unfamiliar terrain, be conservative. (4) Never start a day in the woods without gear you would need if you had to spend the night. (5) Don't start a hike without a plan. Don't change the plan without considering contingencies if the unexpected were to arise.

My younger son, Tom, then age twenty-seven, was full of derisive comments about the "out-of-shape" old men. That set the stage for my second Catskills hike two weeks later. I took Tom out to repeat the adventure Rich and I had had. We spotted a car on Moon Haw Road at 6:20 AM and were on the trail by 6:45. Before we summited Peekamoose, at 8:30, it had started to rain. Tom said he was still game if I was.

This time I followed the advice in the guidebook and dropped off the north side of Lone. From the map, we expected the slope to lessen after dropping 300 to 400 vertical feet. The rain had become moderately heavy and the clouds had dropped even lower. I completely lost track of the elevation change. Suddenly we emerged below the cloud level, and 100 feet below us was a small river with the backdrop of a rapidly rising slope. We had dropped 1,000 feet from Lone and were looking at the East Branch of the Neversink River!

I'd been looking for a flattening of the slope of Lone as a signal to turn more east toward Rocky. The compass heading I'd taken from Lone had been 0° (due north), and that resulted in a uniform slope all the way to the Neversink. A heading of 10° to 20° was needed to get the flattening of slope below 3,500 feet.

We headed east until we reached two small streams close together. We took a compass heading of 120° for the summit of Rocky and scrambled 750 vertical feet to the summit. The thickets near the top were less formidable than those we encountered two weeks earlier. It was now about noon, and we spent less than five minutes eating; inactivity was chilling in fifty-degree rain. We proceeded on a heading slightly closer to due east, because previously the summit ridge had been reached north of the canister—and today we arrived fifty feet from it. Tom got to experience the blowdown and thicket tortures his brother had endured.

We left Balsam Cap at three and arrived at our car a little before five. In subsequent climbs of Balsam Cap, I discovered a vertical cut through the ledges very near the canister that shows signs of frequent use and leads to a very stable old woods road within thirty minutes of leaving the summit on an east-southeast heading. This road permits rapid, leisurely walking so that Moon Haw Road is scarcely more than an hour from the summit. The woods road featured piped spring water with a tin cup hanging on a tree nearby.

Tom suffered from as much hobbling discomfort as Rich and I had, and he never again had any deprecating comments about his father's or brother's hiking stamina. He also had a lot of questions about exactly what would be involved whenever I invited him to go hiking after that.

Additional lessons learned: (1) Be very exact when taking a compass heading. An error of as little as 10° can lead one to entirely miss a target as close as two-tenths of a mile distant. (2) Be observant of your surroundings. Explore topographic features carefully before choosing any particular option. 🏃

---

[1] A 2,600-foot ascent, the greatest ascent in the Catskill high peaks.

[2] An accumulation of loose stones or rocky debris lying on a slope or at the base of a hill or cliff: talus.

56

LOST ON WINDHAM HIGH PEAK

TWO NIGHTS IN THE WILDERNESS

Robert Quinn
Originally published in October–November 1983 *Adirondac,*
the magazine of the Adirondack Mountain Club, Inc.

Almost every lost hiker seems to start his story with "the weather seemed fine." A few paragraphs later, "the weather took a turn for the worse." And so it was for Rhoda Brown along the Escarpment Trail in the Catskills.

The Adirondack Mountain Club (ADK) spring outings have a long tradition, one that has included plenty of good weather. May 14 was a beautiful Saturday with five hikes planned; twenty-five folks signed up for a trip over Windham High Peak. A few cars were left at the Elm Ridge trailhead on Peck Road, and the others traveled to the red-marked Acra Point/Burnt Knob trail at the end of Big Hollow Road. The hike leader didn't know that five late hikers had arrived at Elm Ridge, including myself. Once a National Park Service ranger in Alaska, I have led many hikes. We went on to the end, signed in, and took off after the main group that we thought was just ahead. We didn't realize that the main group was heading toward us from Elm Ridge.

Half an hour later we reached the Escarpment Trail, took a short break, then headed west toward Burnt Knob. At the first steep slope, two others and I got ahead of Rhoda and Joe Dawson, a hiker of many years. Rhoda became ill and told Joe she would head back to the parking lot. She refused his offer to go with her or hike slower—she didn't want to ruin anyone's day.

The heavy blowdown on the trail made it difficult to follow at times, to the point that Rhoda immediately thought she was off the trail and bushwhacking down the south slope toward the red trail. She was not. Instead, she was bushwhacking down the trailless north slope toward NY Route 23, some distance away. She would not get there for two days.

When Joe met the rest of us, he told us about Rhoda's leaving the hike. Given the perfect weather, early hour, and head start back she had, no one felt a need to head back to accompany her. An hour later our group met the main party, hiking the circuit in the opposite direction, and they were told about Rhoda. Car keys were exchanged so that all groups could head back to where we were staying, and everyone arrived at about 5:00 PM. After dinner, one of Rhoda's roommates noted she hadn't seen Rhoda. Darkness had set in. A search of the resort was started and a call made to the police. By 10:00 PM, Forest Ranger Dennis Martin was called and efforts began to get a state helicopter, but clearance for its use could not be obtained. A search party was organized for first light. Most of the search volunteers did not sleep that night; they heard the wind and rain start at 2:00 AM.

As Rhoda had headed downslope Saturday afternoon, she soon encountered yellow blazes on trees, marking the state land boundary. More familiar with Harriman State Park, Rhoda assumed this was a trail, but it was merely the blazed northern boundary of the forest preserve. She followed it in one direction, and it began to go uphill. Following it in the opposite direction, she again decided that could not be right. She then followed a small, unmarked path, but it faded as it descended. She returned to the security of the yellow blazes.

Despite her unfamiliarity with bushwhacking, the terrain, or map and compass use, her resourcefulness saved her life through a day and a half of cold rain—perfect hypothermia weather. She had left her wool shirt and poncho behind for the first time in years, but she did have matches. She started a fire the first night and kept it going until daylight. She rationed her trail lunch over two days. She found an old plastic tarp that provided protection from the rain.

It was not until Monday morning that Rhoda felt her plight desperate enough to try that unmarked path again. This time she followed it farther, and it widened. Soon she was down to Route 23. When Rhoda arrived by police car at the Hensonville Town Hall an hour later, she looked better than many of her searchers.

After her rescue Rhoda spent the rest of the day with my wife and me. An emergency medical technician, I made sure Rhoda went through a gradual but thorough warming. She wasn't aware of the massive search that was in full swing on Sunday and growing on Monday until her appearance on Route 23. The Hensonville Hose Company rescue team had joined in, as well as local police, DEC forest rangers, ADKers, Catskill 3500 Club volunteers, State Police and others.

Since then, New York hiking groups have been reviewing their outing guidelines and educational efforts. It's a tough way to learn, but this time the outcome was happy. ⚉

57

MY FIRST COMPASS HIKE

SETTING A COMPASS COURSE AND
PUTTING IT IN YOUR POCKET

Anne Bartash, #423
from Summer 1984 *Catskill Canister*

On the many enjoyable hikes for my Catskill 3500 Club patch, I practiced compass skills I had begun to learn in an orienteering class. I look back now with mild chagrin on my initial experience. Being new to the Catskills area, I was introduced to an array of folks, including Richard and John. By way of introduction, Richard told me that John had climbed the wrong mountain the previous weekend.

We three set out early one Saturday to climb trailless Fir Mountain, with John's wrong mountain ("Fake Fir") nearby. We followed the Big Indian Trail for a bit, then a streambed, and then bushwhacked. I was impressed by the abundance of undergrowth that gave the woods a bright green tone compared to the northern New England woods with which I was more familiar. A pleasant warm hike to the summit, and we indeed found the Fir register. Traipsing around the summit, we were unable to find a view. (A fair view is found ten to fifteen minutes straight north from the canister.)

We began the descent, realizing we were slightly east of our planned route. Richard, with his long stride, kept a fast pace. John and I followed down the steep slope, grabbing tree trunks to steady ourselves. I had a penchant for grabbing dead trees, which would fall over. John and Richard began to refer to me as the firewood gatherer. We came to a stream and followed it down. "I remember that rock, or that waterfall," we would say. "This stream must join the other one, then." An hour later: "What does the compass say, anyway?" "We're going northeast." "But we're supposed to be headed southwest!" "Maybe the stream takes a sharp turn soon."

Then, people ahead—nude sunbathers, in fact. Richard bounded out and boldly asked, "Could you tell us where we are?" They advised us to go back from whence we had come, as it was five miles farther to the road in the direction we were headed. We decided it was not a day to follow the advice of nude sunbathers, continued in the same direction, and within a short distance came within sight of buildings. A climb up another stream bank put us in a pasture belonging to a large and mean-looking horse. A scramble out of the pasture put us next to some surprised-looking vacationers relaxing by a pool. Again we inquired as to our whereabouts and were informed that we were about ten miles from our car.

Moral of the story: check your compass frequently! 𝕏

Snowshoe hare. Photograph by Tom Rankin.

58

FIR TO DOUBLETOP

LOST ON A SOLO BUSHWHACK

Robert Silver, #539
from Summer 1987 *Catskill Canister*

I started climbing mountains in the Catskills as a way of getting out of New York City on gloriously sunny summer weekends. After topping about fifteen of the Catskill peaks, I took out my newly acquired compass and headed off Graham Mountain on a 200° bearing to bushwhack down the mountain to the Beaver Kill River and back to the Quaker Clearing trailhead. I had freed myself from the trail (or obvious path).

Having tested my wings on a descent, I was now ambitious to do away with trails altogether and trust myself to maps and compass. I laid out the following route to Doubletop Mountain. Starting at the southern trailhead of the Pine Hill-West Branch Trail, I would hike north to the Biscuit Brook lean-to. From the shelter I would strike a 42° bearing up Fir Mountain, and from there a 298° bearing would take me across to Big Indian Mountain. Continuing west of Big Indian, I would find the Pine Hill Trail again, which I would follow south to the point where the trail turns sharply east. There, I would strike off on a 270° bearing that would take me to Doubletop. A bearing of 170° would take me down to Pigeon Brook and out to the highway about one mile south of my car. I would camp whenever I felt like it.

On a bright, clear Saturday morning, I arrived at the Biscuit Brook lean-to to find four campers who had stayed overnight. The number of empties and the crew's collective hangover indicated that hiking was not on their day's agenda. The embankment there is about ten feet above the brook, and one of the campers had fallen over it the night before. He had been disabled and feared that his foot was broken. I looked at the foot, and it was terribly swollen. He could move his toes a bit, and when I gently wiggled them, he experienced no sharp pains. I concluded that nothing was broken, that the ankle was badly sprained and that, with a little help from his friends, he should be able to make it to the trailhead—after soaking his foot in cold water.

The 42° bearing from the lean-to carried me straight up Fir in a direct ascent. In what seemed no time at all, I was there; it had been a breeze. I had not missed using a trail at all. In fact, it had been easier than using a trail—I never had to check for markers. More surprising than the ease of the ascent, however, was my discovery on the summit of a metal canister nailed to a tree with a plaque: Catskill 3500 Club. Never having heard of the club, I nevertheless registered and, fighting off swarms of black flies, rested myself with an apple.

There is a saddle between Fir and Big Indian. It humps up towards the north, much like a horseshoe, with its open end to the south. I had two choices. I could bear 320°, which would take me on an angle northwest to the saddle's notch, where I would turn west onto 288° for the climb up Big Indian's east ridge. This route approximately followed the horseshoe shape. My second choice was to cut straight across the horseshoe on a direct bearing from one peak to the other, but this would entail descending 250 feet into the Biscuit Brook gorge. I didn't know much about the topography or have much faith in my ability to read the land, but I had no desire to surrender and then recapture that 250 feet with my full pack! I chose the horseshoe.

As I set off on 320°, angling down from Fir with the mountain sloping up on my right and down on my left, I reasoned that I'd know I had reached the saddle when the terrain to my left leveled off, and I would know I'd crested it and was too far north if the terrain sloped up on my left. In either case, I needed only to turn left onto my second bearing of 288° and I would be climbing up Big Indian. Unfortunately, I had not considered the rate at which I was losing altitude, and as I slowly circled down around the inside bowl of the horseshoe of Biscuit Brook gorge, the saddle at 3,500 feet slipped by above me on my right. Before I knew it, I had totally disoriented myself.

When I finally stopped, I was on the west side of the gorge facing south, while thinking I was on the east side of the gorge facing north! I'd been hiking for almost an hour and could not understand how I could still be angling off the side of Fir Mountain. Where was that damn saddle? Checking my compass at last, I not only discovered that I was no longer on my bearing, but that 320° led straight into the slope to my right.

Once in a while I have come up from the New York subway and been surprised to find myself completely turned around. This was much worse—I was on a trailless mountain, facing the wrong way, and the right way was leading straight into a mountainside that should have been about 135° to my right!

I didn't know which way to go, so I sat down to figure it out. It was a hot day, and I was getting awfully tense checking and rechecking that compass. Each time I hoped to find it changed, and each time the compass pressed me to admit that I was the one who had erred, and not it. As I struggled with that idea, the answer finally came to me: the only way I could be facing the wrong way was if I had hiked down and around the horseshoe, missing the saddle completely. I was now on the far side of the gorge, sitting on the east side of Big Indian, south of the saddle; all I had to do was turn to my right and start to climb. I would not know if I was correct until I hit the Pine Hill Trail on the far side of what I now assumed to be Big Indian, and at the moment I was all too aware of how fallible my assumptions could be. It was with a lot of concern that I started to climb.

An hour's anxious hiking brought me over the mountain. Much to my relief, I intersected the trail. Locating an appropriate site, I immediately set up camp. It had been a long day and I had been drained by its events. After midnight it began to rain. I was roused to run a line between two trees and drape my oversized tarp over it. Staking the tarp down to form an inverted "V" and throwing my poncho over my pack, I moved my ground cloth and sleeping bag into the improvised tent and dozed off to the increasing patter of rain.

The morning dawned clear. At my departure point off the Pine Hill Trail, I headed off at 270° toward Doubletop. I was alone, without a trail and, in my fantasy, hiking where perhaps no man had before. It was an experience that brought me as close to those pathfinders who'd hiked these hills 300 years ago as it did to those who hiked it yesterday, a perspective I've come to enjoy as one of the great pleasures of bushwhacking.

The crossing between Big Indian and Doubletop is broad and open as it drops down a gentle 300 feet before the steep ascent to Doubletop. As I casually strolled alone, heedless of my surroundings, a fawn broke cover not more than six steps ahead of me. It bounded off into the woods and was gone before I knew it. I was surprised by the suddenness and intimacy of this encounter, and as my heart regained its normal beat, I marveled at my luck.

The climb up Doubletop was strenuous. As I struggled up its east face, I thought about a friend's suggestion that I set up a base camp and day-hike the peaks. It was an idea I'd dismissed as unworthy of serious backpacking, but this bushwhack was giving me cause to reconsider his suggestion. It was very hot, and the pack was very heavy. Reaching the southern peak, I dropped in my tracks, thoroughly exhausted. The black flies were terrible and the weather was starting to turn quite nasty. Had I known that a register lay on the north peak, I would have gone for it. Hearing thunder, however, I thought it best to get off the mountaintop.

A path descends from the south peak of Doubletop, and I gratefully accepted its winding ways. Light rains followed me down the more or less discernible trail until it opened up into a series of logging roads that led down to Camp Wawayanda.

It had been a hike of many firsts for me: the first aid, the bushwhacking, the canister, getting lost, camping in the rain, and the fawn. 🐾

59

LOST

THE GORDIAN KNOT

Will Nixon, #1070, #420W
originally published in *Half Moon Review*, an online literary journal

Ⅰ desperately wanted goals in my life. Here was one: finish climbing the Catskill 3500 peaks in winter. After moving from Manhattan into my log cabin, I'd hiked the thirty-five summits over 3,500 feet during the course of six months, an experience that made me feel like a genuine resident of these mountains. I'd learned to identify bear claw marks on beech trees, pileated woodpecker holes as large as my face, wild turkey tracks in the snow. And I'd fallen in love with snowshoeing. In some ways, winter was my favorite season both at home with a wood stove and in the field amid the quiet solitude and stark black-and-white beauty. Under bare forests, the mountains seemed more rugged and monumental, exposing their cliffs like stone ribs. By now, my third year in the Catskills, I needed only five more peaks to earn my Catskill 3500 Club winter patch. But I also had only three weekends until spring.

On Sunday morning I woke early and kissed my girlfriend good-bye in bed. Still drowsy from her headache medicine, she weakly hugged me and wished me luck. Neither of us wanted to replay the fight we'd had about my leaving her for the day. We wouldn't see each other again until the following weekend. I pulled on my winter hiking clothes: polypropylene briefs and long johns, Gortex pants, and a wool shirt. From experience, I dressed lightly for snowshoeing, letting the exercise generate most of my warmth. The only drawback was stopping for lunch. The cold didn't take long to sneak up my spine. I knotted my boots and strapped on my gaiters. My canteen filled with warm water that would cool soon, I squeezed the side pockets of my green daypack to make sure they were stuffed with mittens and hat. The back pocket held my map and compass.

It was the last day of February. Winter already looked beaten. The snow pack had receded up into the hills. This old farmland lay bare, with dull green lawn grass and nearby fields of blond plant stalks. Hanging mist revealed the valley but smothered the ridges. As soon as I stepped off the porch, my glasses smeared with droplets. The radio weather forecasted drizzle all day—a miserable day for hiking, but I wasn't going back.

At the end of Spruceton Road, I parked, hoisted my gear, and took heavily foot-printed trails 1.5 miles up to Diamond Notch, where the bushwhack began. Two years earlier I had learned this route on a Catskill 3500 Club hike led by a petite veteran who had found the canister three times in three attempts, a remarkable perfect record. She told us not to march straight up the prow of the mountain ridge. If we did, we would spend lots of time bashing through the dense summit forest of spruce and fir trees, which felt like car wash brushes made of snappy dead branches that poked and whipped you around the eyes and every place else. Bushwhackers joked about hiking the spruce fir zone as a form of self-flagellation, but nobody enjoyed it. Instead, our club leader took a precise compass bearing that skirted the prow and crept directly up on the summit from the side of the ridge.

I took my own bearing: 132° east. In my snowshoes, with hiking poles for balance, I began kicking my way up the steep slope of the lower notch, finding the snow good and solid. I didn't need to grab the scattered shrub trees for handholds or worry about sliding. Soon I broke a sweat, but my jitters subsided. For the first time, I felt glad to be taking this hike. The snow carpet under the bare trees above me looked clean and untouched, still a virgin winter, unlike the ragged remnants down in the valleys. I had this mountain all to myself. Behind me the mist curtain hid all but the foot of the mountain right across the notch. I would spend my day in the belly of the clouds.

Above the lower notch, the slope grew easier. After checking my bearing to avoid the ridge prow, I lined up three trees ahead of me in the proper direction and headed upwards. I was in my groove. Softly, I sang one of my favorite hiking songs, U2's "Who's Gonna Ride Your Wild Horses." To counter my sweating, I unzipped the slats under my rain jacket's armpits. I appreciated the cold mist on my face. Sooner than expected, I saw to my right the jumbled rocky escarpment below the summit plateau. Not wanting to fight the spruce fir too soon, I paralleled this final rise for quite a distance before my bearing insisted I ascend. I climbed a gap in the rocks and crawled up into the prickly branch skirt of the first spruce tree.

After wiggling through this barrier, I discovered the summit forest to be more open, more forgiving than I remembered. It was easy to dodge between the trees. The problem was determining which way the forest floor sloped uphill. It didn't— at least, not for very long in any one direction. And the herd paths worn by previous hikers wound among the trees like figure eight's or worse. After stepping across the same fat log for the third time, I abandoned the ground approach and studied the gaps in the tree canopy. In the distance stood a tall spruce tree, a sentinel. It must be growing on the summit mound. But after walking that way, I couldn't tell tree trunks apart to identify this tree from below. Anyway, none of them wore the orange canister. I tried another sentinel. Then a third. Then I stopped for a canteen break. I picked out the twigs and needles that had fallen down my neck. According to my watch, I'd just spent twenty minutes on this goose chase. My snowshoe prints diagrammed a Gordian knot in the snow.

In fact, I already stood on the top of Southwest Hunter Mountain, didn't I? This summit was a plateau, not a peak. What difference did the canister make? This sport wasn't an Easter egg hunt. Besides, the Catskill 3500 Club didn't check their summit registers before admitting members. They took your word for it. Surely I wouldn't be the first hiker to check off Southwest Hunter without actually scribbling my name in the little canister notebook. Did they really expect me to spend my entire afternoon wandering around these stupid trees?

From here, I still needed to bushwhack across the saddle, intercept the Devil's Path trail, and hike up Hunter Mountain to the fire tower. If I wanted to finish before dark, I couldn't dawdle. But the hard part of the hike was over. I laid my map flat on the snow, oriented for magnetic north, and took my bearing across the saddle: 80° east.

Sometimes nothing succeeds like quitting. Ten minutes later I encountered a new herd path with frozen boot tracks that took me right up the summit hump, which seemed larger than I remembered. Bold as a traffic cone, the orange canister was nailed six feet up a mature spruce tree in a small clearing worn by hikers. After lifting up the lid, I pulled out the ziplock bag with the registration book and proudly printed my name with the stubby pencil. This hike had turned into a satisfying triumph. I'd found the Holy Grail all by myself! How many others could say that? And, thank goodness, I hadn't cheated. I'd merely stopped too soon to hunt for the canister.

From this crowd of trees, I followed the tracks eastward. The saddle would take about half an hour to cross. After a gradual descent, the summit stand of uniform conifers gave way to a roomier forest with scattered birches standing over smaller spruce. By paralleling the saddle crest a few hundred feet down along the northern side, I seemed to pass through more clearings and made great time. Wading through a wide patch of baby spruce, like a Bonsai Christmas tree farm, I lost the old boot tracks in the snow, but hardly cared. After all, how could I be sure that hiker had known where he was going? When bushwhacking, I always favored my bearings over herd paths and footprints. Besides, it was more adventurous to blaze my own trail than to follow somebody else's.

I wondered why these white birches at higher elevations had salmon-pink bark. It was one of those nature mysteries I'd long meant to investigate but had always forgotten by the time I took my hot shower, sipped a hot chocolate, and checked my messages at home. This time I would try to remember. It would be fun to learn something new about the woods.

Then I glanced down at my compass, although I hardly needed to. The topography was guiding me right across the saddle. The crest had been easy to parallel. To my left, clusters of spruce trees guarded the rim of the plunging valley filled with grainy mist. No one could miss that. And by now, I had snowshoed for more than half an hour, putting the Devil's Path somewhere nearby. In the shifting mist above the splayed birch branches, I sensed the massive sweep of Hunter Mountain just ahead, like a photograph about to emerge in developing fluid.

But my bearing was backwards. The red needle lining up in my directional arrow pointed right, not left. I was walking 180° in the wrong direction. That couldn't be. The topography didn't match. The valley to my left, the saddle to my right. And I'd walked straight through an open forest. If I'd climbed through rock crevices or ducked through dense trees, I might have gotten turned around. But I had a great sense of direction. My ex-wife said so. My girlfriend said so. I knew so. I could emerge from Manhattan subway stops and know which way to walk on the busy streets. I could explore rural roads for hours and finish where I wanted to be. I'd led friends bushwhacking up Catskill mountains they'd found as confusing as foreign cities.

I shook my compass. Perhaps it had stopped, like a dead watch. But the red needle was alive and jiggling. It just wouldn't point the right way. I opened my map on the snow. I oriented, took another bearing, and studied the pale brown contour lines. The lima bean shape of Southwest Hunter was so small on the map. But nothing changed. Except now when I looked up at the birches, the forest had never appeared so huge, so indifferent. The pink trunks had their own unique twists and sways. To bears or woodpeckers, they must be as recognizable as street signs. But I couldn't tell them apart for more than a moment. They wouldn't yield one clue about where I might be. They didn't care. They presided over life and death every day.

What stood beyond the next cluster of trees? What if I was only a hundred feet from the intersecting trail? Certainly, I had walked far enough on the saddle. Bushwhacking, you often didn't see a trail until you were ten feet away. In minutes I could be standing on the well-trampled Devil's Path, chuckling about this silly panic. And the Devil's Acre lean-to would be nearby. It stank from fireplace smoke, and the outhouse was wrapped in chicken wire for protection against the porcupines.

Last fall I'd spent a wonderful hour there with my friends Terry and Bob from the city. Nearly a decade older than I, in their early fifties, they were brotherly mentors. Taking a break from their wives and kids and their work, they'd joined me on a hike up Hunter Mountain with the jovial spirit of a Boy Scout Old Timers' Day.

The temperature had fallen twenty degrees that afternoon. The white sky looked ready to shed the first snowflakes of the season. The ferns had shriveled and turned brown. A wild apple tree held blackening fruit.

More birches. I stopped and peed for a second time. God, did I want to find that lean-to! Hey, I should give Terry a call. Maybe he was Hollywood rich by now. He sure wasn't standing here in the cold drizzle staring at the cruelty of birch trees. This was the worst possible winter weather. If it snowed, I would stay dry, but everything was getting soaked, endangering my body heat. People suffered hypothermia at 40°. This was 20°. So long as I kept moving, I'd stay warm, but where was I going? And what if I had to spend the night? Some day-hikers carried emergency supplies: a sleeping bag, a bivouac sack, a fistful of Power Bars. An excellent idea. I hadn't even bothered to pack a second sandwich.

What an idiot.

In the next clearing I spotted a pink ribbon of survey tape tied onto a spruce branch. Thank God! Someone had been here. Maybe they'd marked their own trail from Devil's Path up to Southwest Hunter, an unethical if not illegal act in this official wilderness, but a savior for me. I ran ahead, lumbering on my snowshoes, my daypack bouncing on my back. I felt ridiculously lucky. Then the ribbons ended after fifty feet. It couldn't be. Nobody left ribbons in the middle of nowhere. Now I needed to be systematic. At the last ribbon, walk fifty feet in each direction. A hundred feet. Two hundred feet.

The color pink couldn't hide.

Now I couldn't even find the ribbons again. Every one of these small clearings looked the same. I threw my daypack on the snow.

All alone.

Maybe I deserved it.

Who cared anyway? My father? He hadn't called in a month. My girlfriend? She just wanted to get married.

How I hated this shifting mist, always about to reveal something it never did.

I needed to stay warm. In my daypack were an extra sweater and mittens, my sandwich, and a canteen three-quarters full. In the bottom was an emergency first-aid kit I hadn't checked in three years. Surely it had matches. Maybe a space blanket. Probably medicines that were expired.

I didn't even want to think about getting injured. Not here. Not now. Not me. Not my foot turned sideways like the time I was a tackling dummy in eighth-grade football practice. On the hospital bed before surgery, I rolled my knee back and forth and watched my numb, rubbery foot lie motionless against a triangular white prop. No connection. My mother almost fainted when she walked into the room. But she was dead. And I was lost.

"Hello!" I shouted. "Anybody?"

I thought I heard something. I waited. And waited. The dead silence of winter. The occasional pattering of wet snow slipping off the trees. Had I only heard an echo?

"F**k you!"

Stop it! I thought. *You're panicking.* I opened my map on the snow.

Maybe the plunging valley wasn't such a bad idea. It was guaranteed to lead down to a stream that was guaranteed to flow down to a road. The Catskills weren't so big that you couldn't reach humanity within a day. By nightfall I'd be soggy and sore, but I'd be knocking on somebody's door, sheepishly asking for a ride around the mountain back to my car.

At the top of the rock bluff, the spruce grew thick as a hedge. I barged into the swarm of rough branches, then settled on my butt and slid off the edge seven feet down into a snow embankment. Standing up from my sloppy landing, I shook the snow out of my sleeves and brushed it off the folds in my rain jacket. The first step was always a doozy. Hadn't somebody said that on the moon? I readjusted my daypack, which had nearly gotten snagged up in the trees. I checked that my compass still hung from its cord around my neck.

On the bluff behind me I noticed a green band of frosted moss. And a streak of dirt. Around me the snow was much thinner, even bare in places. A fallen tree trunk lay glistening wet, not sleeved with snow. I was standing in a southern exposure. And yet I had just dropped off the northern rim of the saddle. I looked at my compass. The red needle pointed uphill. North. Downhill was south. The melted snow told me the same. The compass was right. It was my instincts that were trying to kill me.

I felt so relieved. I didn't need to understand this tricky topography, or figure out how I had made a U-turn while walking straight ahead, or even know exactly where I was on this hideous mountain. All I needed to do was orient the map and take a bearing. And I didn't care about the lean-to, or Hunter Mountain, or anyplace else. I would head back to Diamond Notch where I started.

Rock climbing in snowshoes may be a clumsy art, but I managed to hoist myself back up into the hedge of spruce, then crawl through the snappy twigs to the small clearing. I almost smiled at what I saw: a yellow pee hole and my snowshoe prints pacing in all directions as if an entire patrol had argued here. The record of my fear. I laid my map on the snow. 290° west. I started walking. This time, I raised my compass every few moments like a prayer book. I knew better than to trust my line of sight.

For an hour I didn't recognize any of the trees or topography, but I remained confident of my course along the northern side of Southwest Hunter Mountain. High to my left ran the balcony of jumbled cliff rocks and dense conifers that bordered the ridge plateau. Down here the snow lay soft and deep, harder for snow-shoeing. Walking felt like shoveling with my feet. But I was glad to trade this labor in return for knowing where I was.

At a flattop boulder I stopped for lunch. During my half hour of fear, I hadn't even sipped from my canteen. After shoving snow off the rock, I hoisted up my butt and slung off my daypack. The nylon had grown a stiff icy skin in the freezing drizzle. After shaking some looseness back into the pack, I tried the zipper. It, too, had frozen solid! I couldn't even reach my food! Then the zipper gave. I took a deep breath. And a second. I wasn't lost anymore. I had to believe that.

The water was delicious. But I gave up on the sandwich after three bites. It tasted fine, but I had no appetite. And the boulder under my butt was very cold. I hopped off and started marching, 290° west, each and every step, until I spotted my morning snowshoe tracks ascending at a steep angle up the steeper hillside. I started bounding down between the scattered trees, my churning feet trampolin-ing through the deep powder on my springy snowshoes. I was nearly skiing, sort of running, almost tumbling. I was laughing and loving this crazy descent through this merciful snow, my private playground in the wild. ⚐

60

LAST PEAK: A MEMORABLE EXPERIENCE

LOST IN THE NEVERSINK

Tom Farre, #1296, #482W

The last peak you climb for 3500 Club membership should be memorable. Some aspirants plan it carefully, leaving a scenic or accessible peak for last and celebrating it with friends. Others, like me, do the easy ones first, which means finishing on one of the tougher hikes. I finished on Rocky and Lone, a hike I'll never forget because the leader left me and two other hikers behind.

It was late May of 2000 and I had signed up for a 3500 Club hike of these two remote, trailless peaks that rise above the Neversink Valley in the southern Catskills. Rocky, guarded by thick stands of spruce and balsam, is the farthest from any road. Hikers usually climb nearby Lone on the same hike. When approached from the Denning trailhead, the trail is blocked by the Neversink River—no bridge, just a downed tree to maneuver across.

I arrived at Denning to find the leader (who shall remain nameless) and five other hikers ready to go. I knew one of them, Pat, a thirty-something guy from Long Island who was just starting his peaks. After introductions, the leader opened the map and explained our route: We'd take the Peekamoose-Table Trail across the river, then veer off-trail on a fishermen's path and follow that 2.7 miles until a fork in the river, where the bushwhack up Rocky would start. From there we'd head to Lone and back to the trail.

Also at the trailhead was a strong-looking hiker with a big pack and long hair like a mountain man. He was embarking on one of those heroic excursions—Table, Peekamoose, Lone, Rocky, Balsam Cap, Friday and who knows what else, all in the same day. We started together, which may have contributed to our difficulty. Our leader, an amiable sort, was setting a fast pace with the mountain man, chatting as they went. This caused our group to spread out behind them. No problem when we were on the trail and crossing the river, which was low that day, but when we reached the fishermen's path, it wasn't clear which way to go. Soon Pat, Arnie, a trim, sixtyish retiree from New Jersey, and I found ourselves at the river's edge with no sign of our leader or the rest of the group.

We yelled, blew our whistles, wondered what the heck had happened, and cursed our luck. No reply. In this state of anxiety, I had a brainstorm that was totally illogical. Some distance back, I had heard a garbled shout from behind. Maybe someone on the trail had twisted an ankle or worse, and our leader went back to minister to the injury (I thought this even though he was ahead of us). In a kind of group brainlock, we rushed back the way we had come looking for our companions. After about a mile of fruitless search, we had to decide: should we head out again toward Rocky, hoping to find the group, or turn back? Rocky and Lone being my last two peaks, I wanted to go on, as did Arnie, who had only a few peaks left. Pat, more cautious and concerned because he had forgotten his lunch, decided to go back. Arnie and I retraced our steps, soon finding a path that the group must have taken. We quickened our pace until we came to the fork in the river that the leader had described. We again mightily blew our whistles hoping for a response, but none came.

Arnie and I had planned to passively follow the leader, but we both had maps, compasses and some experience, so we decided to continue the bushwhack together. With a knot in my stomach (Arnie probably had one, too), we headed upcountry on a compass bearing that would take us to Rocky, if we were in the right spot. And we were. Picking our way around boulders, over small cliffs and through blowdown and balsam, soon we approached a peak that had to be Rocky. We made it to the top, signing in at the canister with some elation over the bushwhacking skills that we hadn't planned on using. Just above our signatures were those of our leader and the two others with him.

Nice thing about Rocky—on a clear day you can see Lone from the top, so it wasn't hard to reach the second peak of the day. Down we went, then up and up until we heard voices. We yelled and blew our whistles, they yelled and blew, and we rejoined our group on the summit of Lone. What a reunion! The leader, feeling guilty about losing three hikers, was ecstatic to find us again, and we were happy to be back. He explained that when he realized the group had split, he and his group waited and shouted and blew for quite a while at the fork in the river. With no sign of us, they continued on. When I mentioned that this was my final peak for 3500 Club membership, we celebrated again.

I next saw Arnie at the 3500 Club dinner in April of 2001, where we both received our patches. We had a few laughs recalling the day when, after going the wrong way and being left by our leader, we bushwhacked Lone and Rocky together.

Lessons learned: When the distance is more than a few dozen yards, don't expect much from a whistle. If you get lost, take time to reason things out; if you can retrace your steps carefully, you may find where you went wrong. Leaders should brief hikers about the route and trails to take—and work hard to keep everyone together, especially on a bushwhack. And, like the Boy Scouts, every hiker should be prepared. 🏃

61

A LESSON IN ORIENTEERING

The Nervous One and the Brave One

Kathleen Balthazar Heitzmann, #520, #230W
from Summer 1986 *Catskill Canister*

When a friend and I decided to bush-whack North Dome and Sherrill, I was still fairly new at orienteering. Each trip into untrailed woods had taught me a little bit more about how to start at two thousand feet below a mountaintop and then find a canister hidden somewhere among a grove of balsam. We left for North Dome from Camp Timberlake at 9:00 AM in overcast conditions. The trail looked as though it had been blazed by escapees from the graffiti team of the New York City subway system; there were reds, whites, yellows, and bright oranges, and designs that included dots, dashes, swizzles, circles, zigs and zags, but it followed the ridge I'd planned to use. *Since this trail is so well marked*, I thought to myself, *we should have no difficulty in spotting it on the way back*. My plan was to circle North Dome on the return trip to avoid reclimbing it, thereby saving both time and energy.

At about 3,300 feet the trail veered to the right to a lookout, so I struck a magnetic north course. Until then the forest had been deciduous, beech being the primary tree. We saw our first black cherry, and soon after entered a cloud layer. With the high humidity, the atmosphere was saturated and we could actually see water droplets in the air. At 3,400 feet we were on a flat meadow and walked into a large stand of thirty-foot balsam; we both caught a glimpse of a snowshoe rabbit, white with still a little brown left from its summer coat.

The water droplets were a little larger now—not rain, but a very heavy mist. Nearing the top always has a special feeling. Things look and feel different; there is a stillness and peacefulness, as well as a change of vegetation. When all sides started going downhill, we relied on the landscape and continually headed for the highest mound of land. Ten minutes later Vic spotted the canister. After signing in and reading some humorous entries, we started out for Sherrill Mountain.

It began to rain, and visibility was very low. I took a direction of 288° and started walking off the north side instead of the west. First lesson in orienteering: a look at the map would have shown me a gentle exit off to the west, rather than the abrupt drop we experienced. In order to keep my 288° reading, we were circling

PART VI: LOST IN THE WILDERNESS

left at the 3,400-foot level to reach the col, while our senses told us to go down. I checked the map and still did not know what had gone wrong, but I knew that I didn't want to go north. I was in a quandary: I didn't want to cause Vic to panic, but I also did not want to go back the way we'd come. Even if we decided to skip Sherrill, it would still be easier to skirt around and get back to the southeast side of the mountain—so I insisted on pressing on.

By the time we continued around with some descents to avoid boulders and hobblebush, we were at about 2,800 feet. Now below the clouds and with visibility regained, I realized what the situation was: descending to the north and then heading west, we had missed the col and were now below it. We could see Sherrill ahead. We were wet and a little cold. Vic had lost faith in my outdoor skills and had wanted to turn back for the last half hour, but once I saw Sherrill, we were going for it! A short lunch break kept hypothermia at bay! (Don't stop for long, but do get some nourishment.) At 1:10 we spotted the canister. After signing in, we headed out without delay. This time I read the land first and then set my compass at 110°. We were at the col by two o'clock.

With regained confidence, I decided to go ahead with my plan: ascend to 3,300 feet and stay at that elevation all the way around to the southeast side of North Dome and back to the trail. After one and a half hours of contour-hiking southeast, Vic was getting nervous again. I said, "Look, it took us two hours to go from peak to peak, so let's give this a little longer." Just then he looked over my shoulder to see the trail. Hallelujah! By 3:50 we were back to the car, very wet, very tired, but very happy to have learned valuable orienteering skills. I wound up marrying Vic. (He is still the nervous one, and I am still the brave one.)

Analysis (by telephone):

Franklin Clark: There are two common reasons for hikers to get off course. One is subtracting instead of adding 13° for declination, giving an error of 26°. Does your compass have a built-in adjustment for declination?

KBH: No, I have to make the allowance.

Clark: I have checked your bearings with the map, and they were correct for your compass. The other reason to get off course is that the compass bearer does not look at the compass often enough.

KBH: That's the lesson we learned. We started off North Dome and did not look at the compass until later.

Clark: It has happened before. Four of the best hikers in the club, going fast from Wittenberg to Peekamoose, found the Friday canister twice, because they had made a U-turn on the ridge. One of them told me, "Someone set a fine compass course and then put the compass in his pocket." ⚄

62

CLIMBING LONE TWICE

A Stubborn Compass and a Stubborn Hiker

Marty Cohen, #728, #330W

The trailless peak, Lone Mountain, is often last on the list of summits climbed by 3500 Club members, not because they are saving the best for last, but because they have difficulty finding it. Well, one day my wife and I managed not only to find it twice, but to climb it twice! While the summit of Lone is not completely protected by a thick moat of balsam, as is its companion, Rocky, it does have its share of chummy evergreens and not much of a summit view, which raises the question "Why climb it twice in one day?"

Here's the story. One day of a Memorial Day weekend on which we were camped on Peekamoose, we decided for our daily excursion to climb Lone and Rocky, which are quite accessible from Peekamoose. We had little difficulty navigating to Lone, descending into the col between it and Rocky, and then climbing up Rocky. For our return route I took a compass bearing that would skirt Lone along its left side on the way back to Peekamoose. We descended Rocky to the appropriate elevation and then began our traverse to the left of Lone. As we progressed, I frequently checked both compass and altimeter to assure that we followed our planned azimuth and elevation as we crossed the thickly wooded flank of Lone.

After a while my wife, Wanda, said: "My compass bearing seems to be shifting." I checked mine and observed the same thing, but remarked in a confident tone, "It's only a local variation. It will shift back to the proper heading shortly." To hasten losing this local anomaly (and to attempt to out-distance the hordes of black flies that were feeding on us), I picked up the pace and resisted checking my compass often, as that recalcitrant device wasn't confirming what I knew was right. Some time later, after considerable and arduous bushwhacking, I could refrain no longer from checking my compass (possibly because Wanda was now expressing doubt about her husband's vaunted navigational skills). The compass, in its stubborn ignorance, yielded a bearing that indicated that we were traversing Lone not to its left, but to its right, which I knew was wrong. So, asserting my manly pride, I insisted we continue on our course.

Finally we reached a point where the woods had thinned enough so that despite the rivulets of sweat dripping into our eyes and the need to continually swat black flies, we could discern through the trees the unmistakable profile of Table, which somehow had relocated itself to the left of Lone, rather than to its right. At this point I decided, finally, to calmly review the evidence and think, instead of just plodding along the "correct" route. The evidence pointed to only one conclusion: my original bearing intending to traverse Lone on the left had been a tiny bit off, and we had drifted to a course taking us to the right of Lone. Since we had gone halfway around that mountain of no small girth, we decided that, rather than retrace our route or continue circumnavigating Lone, we would instead opt for a straight-line route to Peekamoose, which, obviously, would take us back up and over the summit of Lone a second time. Tiring though that was on a hot day, it did get us back to our campsite before dark. 🥾

Reconnoiter Rock on Peekamoose Mountain. Photograph by Larry Gambon.

Part VII:

NAVIGATING IN
THE WILDERNESS

*The forest and I stir awake with birdsong begin-
ning to fall from the canopy. In the dawn's half-
light I lounge in my bed for a delicious moment and
tell myself: This is good. Right now, indeed for each
moment of this endeavor, I am a rich man.*

Bob "Grey Dog" McElroy

Photograph by Andrew Moroz.

63

THE HARD WAY TO PEEKAMOOSE MOUNTAIN

THE FOREST PRIMEVAL

Bob "Grey Dog" McElroy, #797
originally published in December 2002 *Appalachia,* a publication
of the Appalachian Mountain Club, Inc. (AMC)

Late March 1999. The trail along Kanape Brook leads me uphill through hemlock and hardwood to the blueberry meadow on top of Ashokan High Point. To the northwest, mist still hangs lightly over the Bush Kill. Rising from the valley's far side, a wall of forested peaks fills the horizon—the headlands of the Slide Mountain–Panther Mountain Wilderness, one of the largest wilderness areas east of the Mississippi. Its expanse includes much of New York State's little-known treasure: the ninety-five square miles of Catskill virgin forest. I stand in the meadow and stare for long minutes, enthralled by the line of dusky gray summits and their resemblance to a passing fleet of enormous ships.

Several weeks later, with my multitalented friend and fellow mountaineer Chris Adams (classically trained musician, blues band leader and composer, building contractor, furniture maker, boat builder, sailor), I start before dawn to climb to the top of the imposing wall. There is a gentle breeze blowing when we reach the crest of the Wittenberg[1] and look out over a sea of ridges and sharply defined gorges.

The sight of the contorted landforms, thrown into high relief by the low-angle light, checks our conversation. I break the silence by wondering if it would be possible to hike directly south from Romer Mountain to the Rondout Creek's Gulph Hollow. A tough trek, involving probably three days of travel through the remote eastern third of this wilderness. It would be the longest bushwhack in the Catskills without crossing a road or footpath. From our vantage point, we can survey part of the route.

"It's an interesting notion," Chris says. "But the odds are against it. You'd be fighting every ridge and canyon at right angles to their flow." He turns toward me and hesitates, "With all due respect, Bob, you're no spring chicken, and that's not a landscape—it's an obstacle course."

Chris is a bright guy and his brief is compelling, but I'm not entirely disheartened. For much of the journey, an explorer would be deep into forest primeval, ancient growth never subdued by logging, thanks to its daunting terrain, and one of the rare places where one can see the country as it was before Europeans came. The thought of trying to walk all the way across this truly wild world excites me.

An Odyssey Ahead

Three more weeks pass. Although April is almost over, winter hangs on along the high ridges among naked, wind-tortured trees and in snowdrifts in the shadows under balsam and spruce. Below the mountaintops, clear sight lines before the leaves open make this my favorite time to roam the high country. And now the idea of attempting the longest bushwhack has become irresistible.

Where the Esopus Creek carves a deep notch through the highlands, Romer Mountain forms the gap's southern buttress. An old friend and local townsman who goes by the handle "Blue Dog" has agreed to drop me off at the mountain's base and now watches as I vanish from sight, swallowed by the forest. If I'm not delayed by rough country or injury, we will meet in seventy-two hours at Gulph Hollow.

Almost three days of lonely route finding lie ahead of me. For fun, I will try to find my way without looking at a compass and, unless I encounter poor vis-ibility in rain or fog, I will steer a course in the manner of travelers before the invention of the magnetic needle. I enjoy a quirk that puzzles a lot of my hiking friends: I would rather visit places that people rarely see than follow trails. Many of the trackless summits to the south have felt the crunch of my boots, but on those climbs I ascended the main ridges. This trip, though, will take me through the seldom-visited forests that lie between the ridges. I'm feeling so drawn to these lonely parts that I selfishly refuse Chris's last-minute petition to come along. His good company would be a distraction, and I want to drink deeply of, and savor, each moment of the adventure.

So here I am, plunging into a questionable odyssey, but with joyful intensity and so energized that I can't restrain my pace until, eventually, a low cliff band tempers my headlong ascent. Higher up, as I close in on the summit of this first of the eleven mountains along my route, I remember Thoreau's "We need the tonic of wilderness . . ." and my pulse beats even faster at the promise of solace and fulfill-ment in the old-growth forests ahead.

From Mount Pleasant to Cross Mountain

By late afternoon, I'm on the natural causeway that links Mount Pleasant to Cross Mountain; two down, nine mountains to go. Overhanging rim rock trims the edge of the 1,100-foot falloff into Traver Hollow on my left. Ahead I catch glimpses through the trees of a towering citadel. Dark green, boreal Canadian forest caps its summit; it has to be the Wittenberg, the first and most massive of the eight Catskill high peaks along my route. Almost 1,500 feet higher than their neighbors, their summits are in another, colder world.

The landscape grows wilder as I move deeper into the mountains, and the forest's mood turns mean, with quickening gusts rattling the branches. Soon a harsh wind is wailing through the trees as an anemic, amber-colored sun fades below the shoulder of Cross Mountain. I snug my shell's zipper a little tighter and note that the grade ahead is climbing steeply among snow-covered ledges. Rather than risk being caught by darkness on treacherous ground, I drop my pack and spread foam pad, bivy sack, and sleeping bag in a shallow scoop between the roots of a yellow birch.

Night falls, and moonlight bright enough to travel by casts a shadow fretwork across the forest floor. Soon the gale is punching through the trees in measured pulses, each surge howling its approach. I wonder if this curious effect, which I've endured before at night in these mountains, might be waves in the rushing air, just as water configures itself in an ocean storm. But nestled snugly in GoreTex and goose down, the tempest loud overhead, I fall asleep with a smile, as wind song becomes a lullaby.

Farther into the Wild

At dawn, somewhere off in the trees, a great horned owl sounds its melancholic dirge. I open my eyes to see the eastern sky glowing purplish red as the last stars dim. The forest and I stir awake with birdsong beginning to fall from the canopy. In the dawn's half-light I lounge in my bed for a delicious moment and tell myself: *This is good*. Right now, indeed for each moment of this endeavor, I am a rich man.

A half-frozen energy bar stills my hunger as I hurry to pack the sleeping gear and move out, careful to leave no sign of my visit. Working my way past the problem ledges, I kick steps up the north-facing snow slope. The grade eases into sunlight; the snow pack thins, then fades away. Minutes later I'm standing on the summit of Cross Mountain. Ahead of me, the Wittenberg's east face rears skyward as her conjoining twin, Cornell, peeks out from behind. To the south, Friday and Balsam Cap, the northern outliers[2] of the trailless "Bushwhack Range," that punisher of peak baggers, stand striking and bold in the morning light.

I follow the rim of a rock ledge downhill, through hardwoods stunted by exposure and shallow soil, to a crossing beneath the Wittenberg's soaring mass. Here, finally, I enter the realm of big timber. The stately trees are growing robustly in the shelter of the high mountain, and I'm cheered to recognize the woodland community that can only be virgin forest: red and sugar maple, black cherry, yellow birch, and ash gray American beech—the signature trees that, when unmixed with other species, certify deciduous first-growth in the Catskills. Aged, toppled carcasses lying amid the mounds and stump craters of earlier fallen and long-since-rotted timber are further signs that humans have never disturbed these ancient woods.

An Increasing Challenge

My straightforward navigation along mountaintop hogbacks ends at this point and the larger challenge begins. From here on I will be scrambling up the sides of the massive lateral ridges and climbing in and out of the canyons that slash the eastern flanks of the remaining eight high peaks. A vigorous workout is assured, but the allure of new terrain and my light pack should ease the effort. Not counting food and water, because their weight isn't constant, but with snowshoes and camera, my pack weighs less than ten pounds. Nothing safety-critical has been left behind, and both my balance (so important when bushwhacking) and comfort are enhanced. This super-light, basic style (carrying only the essentials, carefully chosen for function and ultra-lightness), long practiced by a few hard-core backpackers, is lately being embraced by many of North America's most experienced alpinists and mountain guides.

A quarter-mile farther south, tested by my first unstable talus slope, I'm reminded of historian Alf Evers' admonishment by an old-timer: that these Catskills "begin where one finds two stones for every dirt." For twenty minutes I pick my way across a mountainside of loose sandstone and shale, frost-wedged from the Wittenberg's crags almost a thousand feet above. I'm on a moving glacier of rock, nudged downhill a fraction of an inch farther with each freeze-thaw cycle. In a few weeks, a dense cover of ferns here will shroud any traveler's foot placement, rendering this traverse even more venturesome.

The faint, two-pitched song of a mountain stream—a sort of white noise, thin and static-like above a muffled, rumbling under sound—gladdens my ear as I drop over the south side of Cornell's east ridge. At the bottom of the gorge, my senses are further caressed as I enter a haven of wild beauty. Brimming with snowmelt from the heights, rivulets spilling into the green wetness of a mountain cove are assembling one of the headwaters of Wittenberg Brook.

A long, steep climb delivers me atop Friday Mountain's east ridge, and I am immediately startled by a brace of ruffed grouse exploding underfoot and fleeing recklessly through the branches. I turn toward the evergreen-cloaked summit and continue upward, past a series of formidable ledges that step up the ridge crest *en echelon.*[3] Scaling an easy inside corner gains me a stance atop the uppermost ledge. Squatting at the brink, I pause to review my progress. Ahead, to the south, the brooding prow of Balsam Cap is emerging out of blowing mist and cloud tatters. To the east and north, prominent spurs and valleys of tangled forest fall away to the distant edge of the Ashokan Reservoir. I look down on an ocean of treetops. From this height I see each tree as a plump, green dot, ten thousand dots dressing the mountain's contours, bringing to mind the pointillism texture of a Seurat canvas. But as much as this worthy setting invites it, the hour is too early to make camp, and I press on toward Balsam Cap, shouldering into the bracing fragrance of the balsam fir jungle.

The Beauty of the Night

I clamber over storm-downed conifers, and dense undergrowth rasps against my body as I follow the cliff rim. At last the bush releases me into a small clearing, invitingly tucked among red spruce and paper birch. A cliff-side window in the foliage frames a panorama to the east, and I gaze out upon a subdued tableau of mountains and foothills all washed in the soft colors of the evening. Unwilling to pass up another perfect bivouac site, I stop for the night.

The sky has cleared. Back to the north, Friday's east ridge palisade blushes golden in the sunset's alpenglow. When dark arrives it rides a cold northwester, and I'm forced to don every piece of clothing I carry. I seldom burn an evening fire, preferring the silent beauty of the constellations. Weather permitting, I sleep under open sky instead of shutting myself inside a tent, cut off from the mountain's nightlife. In tonight's clear air, galaxies glitter through my cliff-rim window, and later, just before sleep comes, I watch a rising moon dim the stars and turn the Ashokan Reservoir into a shimmering, silver mirror.

View from Peekamoose Mountain. Photograph by Larry Gambon.

I'm taken by surprise in the middle of the night when a lone coyote shows up close under my aerie to bark vigorous disapproval of my presence. I have never heard a coyote bark before (wild canines rarely do), or make sounds other than mournful howls or high-pitched yips. Marveling at the wild dog's chutzpah but enjoying the novel circumstance, I fall back to sleep when the protest is finished. Later, as the wind's increasing force bends and buffets the spruce trees, the earth beneath my sleeping pad moves up and down with each flexure of their shallow roots.

Isolation Supreme

I break camp at dawn, and my snowshoes carry me over knee-deep drifts in the Friday-Balsam Cap col. Beyond Balsam Cap begin the most remote forests of the trip, a region of silence and mystery blanketing the east slopes of the final four mountains: Rocky, Lone, Table, and Peekamoose.

Excitement spurs me through the pass separating Balsam Cap and Rocky. In less than a mile, down under Rocky's summit, I come upon an impressive escarpment. Broad and towering, it's a rock climber's fantasy, and so hidden that I'm confident its sheer face remains unchallenged. For the next hour I follow wide mountain benches laced with diamond-clear streamlets and flaunting their extravagant moss nurseries among the ledges and boulders. Striking specimens of black cherry and yellow birch inspire my admiration. Miles farther south in the afternoon, high on the side of Peekamoose, my eyes widen with awe when I wander into a grove of huge sugar maples, the biggest I have ever seen. But I can't linger among them; difficult miles remain before my hoped-for rendezvous. I push on.

In spite of each day's generous elevation gain and loss, Chris's envisioned obstacle course never materializes. When I'm below the spruce and balsam fir thickets and into open, climax hardwoods, I enjoy relatively easy passage.

Finding the Soul

During these last hours on Peekamoose Mountain, I descend from the heights and leave the primeval Catskills behind. In the woods below 2,000 feet, the land's earlier role as a source of human sustenance is suggested by the occasional toppling rock wall or squat, thick-boled oak or white ash of a shape only formed in an earlier, open meadow. My hiking pole helps me balance across a weir of mossy stones spanning Buttermilk Falls Brook, the final stream, tumbling toward its namesake cascade. Around me, shafts of sunlight filter through the tracery of new leaves, dappling lichen-draped ledges. Trudging down the last, long grade, I approach the far foot of Peekamoose, wincing inwardly each time my boots disturb one of the delicate carpets of emerging ferns and trout lilies.

I'm tired and wondering if I've missed my ride, yet sorry to end this journey. I have traversed the length of the dusky gray wall and have tasted the soul of the place—an illusive quality I can't put into words. But as I depart, I feel something akin to a deep love. In the future, when I view this wild terrane[4] from a distant mountain, it will be with a fresh perspective—mystery now traded for comfortable, knowing intimacy. And I marvel that so much virgin wilderness exists almost unnoticed, virtually on the edge of suburban sprawl, a sanctuary, vast and lavish, through which one may travel for days, as I just have, without encountering a soul or seeing any sign of human passage. For me, the seeker of solitude and lover of lonely places, the experience has been not only a small miracle, but as much fun as I have ever had in the woods.

Now, deep in the hemlock-lined ravine at the bottom of the last mountain, I'm greeted by a comforting sight. Parked alongside the narrow road that traces Rondout Creek, Blue Dog and his pickup are waiting. 🏃

---

[1] Often referred to simply as Wittenberg, the Wittenberg is now the only Catskill peak to have the distinction of having a definite article in its name.

[2] Parts of the formation separated by erosion from the main outcrop.

[3] Roughly, in offset series. Mountaineers often use the term to describe glacier travel, when roped climbers walk offset from front to back to prevent more than one person from falling into a hidden crevasse running parallel to the direction of travel.

[4] An area or surface over which a particular rock or sediment, or group of rocks or sediments, is prevalent.

64

THE MOUNTAINS BECKON

THE REWARDS OF BUSHWHACKING

James D. Malumphy, #890, #337W

My love affair with the summits and hollows of the Catskill Mountains began many years ago as an eager participant in my hometown's youth wilderness program. As part of the program's activities, we would pack up and hit the road on a regular basis, hiking and camping in various areas, including the Catskills. Those long-ago trips still trigger fond memories. Our intrepid group stuck to the trails on our typical weekend backpacking trips, but nonetheless I was struck by the beauty and infatuated with the spirit of the mountains. My youthful adventures eventually led to membership in the Catskill 3500 Club, used as a means to climb all of the 3,500-foot peaks safely in winter with the support of other experienced hikers. I then became a qualified hike leader for the club, and subsequently have led trips to all thirty-five 3,500-foot summits. Along the way, I was inspired more and more to explore off the beaten path.

Traveling along a trodden trail to any mountain summit is no doubt enjoyable, but bushwhacking—traveling off trail through the forest—presents a most intriguing and challenging aspect of outdoor travel. The Catskill Forest Preserve offers an unbelievable 300,000 acres of state land ripe for exploration. The Catskill forests are generally quite open, making off-trail exploration that much more inviting. There are exceptions to this rule, however. Anyone who has donned raingear on a sunny day to keep from being ripped to shreds by impenetrable spruce growth, struggled through hobblebush, or encountered those swear word-inducing waist-high nettle fields, knows what I am talking about.

Don't get me wrong: the rewards of bushwhacking are many, and far outweigh any obstacles encountered along the way. The thrill and anticipation of a new discovery is most appealing to me. I always have the feeling—whether or not it's true—that I am the first visitor to walk through a secluded patch of forest. Potential finds awaiting the traveler off trail are many. They include majestic waterfalls, old-growth trees, old ruins, elusive views and a diversity of flora and fauna. Some people set up goals as a means to explore, such as multi-summit traverses or locating cultural ruins found throughout the mountains. Good route-finding skills can open up a whole new world of discovery no matter what your intended goals or ambitions may be.

I am a firm believer that good navigation consists of a mixture of skill, common sense, intuition, timing, and luck, more or less in that order. But most important of all, off-trail travel necessitates a solid background in map and compass skills. These fundamentals of wilderness travel can be acquired through outdoor workshops, club clinics, or through your local orienteering club, such as the Hudson Valley Orienteering Club. These resources are invaluable and will give you practical hands-on experience taking bearings, contouring, figuring declination, reading topographic maps and all that other important stuff. Back in the mid-1980s, I entered my first competitive orienteering event and have been hooked ever since. The learning curve can be harsh, but once the fundamentals have been mastered, a whole new world opens up. I have since traveled all over New England and New York participating in this "thinking sport" while continually honing my map and compass skills. The same skills are easily transferable to a conventional USGS map of your favorite Catskills haunt.

New technologies such as the GPS are changing the way we navigate through the woods. More and more, people are relying on these devices to aid their progress to the trailless peaks. A GPS can produce remarkable results, but should not be solely relied on for route finding; map and compass skills should not be dismissed. One of these days I will step into the twenty-first century and acquire one of these electronic gizmos for my own. For now, however, I will stick to doing things the old-fashioned way.

One of my favorite off-trail trips in the Catskills is to climb the Blackhead Range from Colgate Lake. In the summer months, hikers are rewarded with a refreshing swim after the hike. Another adventure involved leading a 3500 Club hike to explore the vast Panther Mountain wilderness. Leaving some cars at the state parking area on Route 28 in Big Indian, we shuttled around and entered the woods from County Route 47 at Giant Ledge. Upon reaching the height of land below the summit, we proceeded to encircle the mountain en route back to Big Indian. After about nine miles of ups and downs, a metallic glimmer was spotted. What a great feeling to catch a glimpse of our cars through the trees and arrive precisely back at the parking lot!

On another, non-club hike one winter, some friends and I decided to attempt Evergreen, Spruce and Fir with heavy snow cover. In one of the strangest experiences I've encountered in the outdoors, we made our way through snow-covered evergreens in a freezing fog. It became difficult to tell what was up or down, as any depth perception was stripped away by a three-dimensional covering of white. With some perseverance and patience, we were able to complete our snowshoe hike successfully, albeit victims of vicious spruce traps en route.

Yet another journey I am particularly proud of is bagging Lone, Rocky, Balsam Cap and Friday all on one day. And, at some point, I plan on traversing from Phoenicia to the Rondout Creek's Gulph Hollow, said to be the longest bushwhack in the Catskills without crossing so much as one trail. I can't wait.[1]

I believe my bushwhacking skills have become pretty good over time. I have been quite fortunate over the years, having never really been lost, though several times "mislocated." However, I try not to take anything for granted and always try to err on the side of caution. Bushwhacking does include a certain amount of inherent personal risk. Safety is paramount, and one should go out alone only after very serious and careful consideration. At minimum, a precise itinerary and expected time for your return should be left with a trustworthy soul. In addition, one should always be prepared to spend the night out, in case one is beset by some unforeseen circumstance. As always, carry a good-quality compass and accurate, up-to-date maps.

From a hike leader's perspective, there is always a certain amount of pressure felt when leading a group. Not only is it your responsibility to ensure the safety and well-being of your participants, but those participants likely arrive counting on you to lead an unwavering, efficient route to a chosen mountain summit. There is always a chance that things will not go as smoothly as planned, but those are the risks one assumes when attempting off-trail travel; participants on a group hike should anticipate those possibilities and assume their share of the risk as well. In my own experience I have found that hike participants are grateful for the efforts put forth by the leader and realize that if the route wanders or wavers somewhat, it usually is not a real cause for concern. If one has reservations about the route-finding progress, those reservations should be voiced to the hike leader in a tactful manner.

If time runs out, or you simply fail to locate your objective, take heart. Experience, conditioning, weather, snow conditions and the like can all affect the outcome. Getting "skunked" is always a real possibility when bushwhacking. Remember, you are out there to have fun and to explore the unknown. John Burroughs, famous Catskills naturalist and author once said, "I go to nature to be soothed and healed, and to have my senses put in order." The mountains beckon. Grab your pack and get out there and explore. You never know what you'll find. ᚛

---

[1] See "The Hard Way to Peekamoose Mountain."

65

IN PRAISE OF TRAILLESS MOUNTAINS

THE TRAILLESS FOREST IS A MAGNET

Bob McElroy, #797
from October–December 1997 *Catskill Canister*

West of the Ashokan Reservoir lies a wild, remote area. From Gulph Hollow on Peekamoose Road near Bear Hole Brook, a bushwhacker can trace a course over high ridges and into remote valleys for more than twenty-six miles north to the village of Phoenicia. Crossing only two dim herd paths, his route will traverse eight of the range's highest mountains and visit rare stands of ancient hardwoods, denied to the logger's saw by their isolation.

Many years have passed since I first came to the Catskills with my partner, Annamaria, and climbed Table Mountain. We sat on the edge of a long-since overgrown viewpoint and looked north over a wild and trackless region. Lone Mountain and her sisters—Rocky, Balsam Cap, and Friday—seemed mysterious and inaccessible. It would have surprised me to know that decades later I would be on intimate terms with each of them.

The trailless forest is a magnet for me. I often wander this refuge by myself, sometimes for days, and the rewards are rich. The enjoyment that companions provide is relinquished, but the trade-off is significant. When I'm alone, every aspect of the natural world is felt with heightened intensity.

The region's allure can be as intangible as the chemistry between good friends. But most of my memories are vivid—like the thrill of entering a primeval grove and realizing the pillar-like trunks are silent remnants of a virgin forest. I feel favored to be in the presence of such noble trees and I envy future generations who will see old-growth timber covering these slopes again. I look for secret places. Lovely, hidden spots perhaps known only to me, where I can hang my hammock and relax for an hour or even a day, enjoying a special tranquility while absorbing the sensory gifts the forest offers.

Catskill route finding holds many surprises. In other mountains one sees consistent patterns of vegetation and soon determines how the flora distributes itself. One learns not to get trapped in the alder thickets in secondary canyon bottoms in the Sierra and the North Cascades; that travel is easiest in the redwoods or oaks on north-facing slopes in the California-Oregon Coast Ranges, yet may be impossible in the dense chaparral on south slopes. But in the Catskills, the explorer takes nothing for granted. One ridge may be open and afford easy passage; the next may be a traveler's nightmare. On one mountain a hiker may drop out of the barely penetrable summit bush into open trees, and on the adjacent one find the balsam and spruce descending another 400 vertical feet on a seemingly identical west slope. It is this portent of the unknown that adds adventure when a new route is undertaken.

Mountaineering friends who have explored and climbed with me in the higher ranges of North America wonder why I hold these hills so special. The richness of the landscape includes a bounty of individual treasures. Among them are the falls and deep pools of Bear Hole Brook and the upper Rondout; the unusual rock window giving access through the final cliff band on the eastern approach to Rocky's crest; the lofty treasury of springs that are the source of the Rondout; perhaps the tracks in the snow of an elusive fisher on the Friday-Balsam Cap saddle. This corner of the Catskills offers an abundance of small wonders.

Tucked under the west side of Balsam Cap's false summit, fountainheads of emerging streams bring to mind a phrase from the late writer and wilderness defender, Wallace Stegner: "The sudden poetry of springs." On another mountain, appearing through a lattice of beech and hemlock, a fern-draped cliff may loom. If it bars my route, the challenge is welcome. Will I search for a ramp, find a safe line for a direct ascent, or try to skirt it? As I climb higher and distance myself from human enterprise, cares fade, purged by the mountain's bold and reassuring presence. The trees part to reveal a distant view. Absorbed with the spectacle, I pause and listen to the wind threading through the balsam needles.

Nights spent on the mountain are even more stimulating. The stars can be brilliant in a black sky. Coyotes may draw near for a spine-tingling concert. Yet sleep comes easily. In warm months I awake to birdsong, sunlight filtering through the leaves. Winter mornings begin with intense cold and perfect white beauty. I marvel at the snow-muffled silence. And in any season, far from the nearest trail, peace and solitude are my reward.

Romer Mountain, Mount Pleasant, Cross Mountain, Samuels Point, the east slopes of the The Wittenberg and Cornell; Friday, Balsam Cap, Rocky, Lone and parts of Table and Peekamoose are the dominant heights. Below the summits spirited rills tumble excitedly through deep ravines. As I wander this exhilarating arena, I can visualize my predecessors, the Esopus and Maquasis tribes, the backwoodsmen and the first homesteaders, all walking the same ground I walk now. These mountains, each with its unique personality, are my intimate companions—sometimes moody, sometimes robust, always sublime. 🚶

66

MY FIRST SOLO BUSHWHACK

THE TYPE-A HIKER

Tom Farre, #1296, #482W

To the avid hiker, "bushwhacking" means climbing trailless peaks—those lacking formally marked and maintained trails. This is important to 3500 Club "aspirants," who seek membership by hiking the thirty-five Catskill peaks over 3,500 feet in elevation. Because sixteen of these peaks are trailless or nearly so, aspirants have to find their way via map and compass, topographic study, local knowledge, or by following a seasoned leader.

Some trailless peaks have PVC canisters nailed to trees at the highest point. Each contains a logbook that hikers sign and record the date, their thoughts, and often their 3500 Club numbers. In years past, canisters were day-glo orange—easy to spot when hunting for the top—but today most are painted a less intrusive gray.

A few trailless summits are easy to find. Old woods roads may lead to the top, or you can follow "herd-paths," rough trails carved by hikers and animals such as deer. Other times you just burst up the mountain through virgin terrain. In the Catskills this terrain ranges from inviting meadows and spongy turf to rocky fields, steep cliffs, thick balsam fir and endless patches of stinging nettles. With snow on the ground, you often hike above the brush and downed trees, though key landmarks and cairns may be obscured.

The easy bushwhacks include Graham, where an old road takes you to the summit—one of the three on private property. In winter this part of the southwestern Catskills always seems blanketed by deep snow, causing some hikers to miss the turnoff from the Dry Brook Ridge Trail. The old Twilight Park Trail marked in faint blue leads steeply to the top of Kaaterskill High Peak, off a snowmobile trail. A hunters' road passes about 700 feet below the top of Vly, and Bearpen is scarred by a patchwork of old roads from a long-abandoned ski resort.

Most of the other trailless peaks require map and compass work, if only for a short way. To reach the anticlimactic, 3,700-foot summit of Big Indian, you bushwhack a quarter-mile east after hiking 4.5 miles up the Pine Hill–West Branch Trail from Biscuit Brook. The turnoff point is easily found, marked by a 3,500-foot elevation sign. My first solo bushwhack and a peak I've now climbed six times, Big Indian seems easier today than it did at first.

Solo bushwhacking, a slightly daft endeavor, suggests a dichotomy in the personalities of 3500 Club aspirants. Like the yin and yang of Chinese philosophy or the A and B types of modern psychology, aspirants fall into two main groups. The laid-back, uncompetitive B-types hike for fresh air, for exercise, for the views, for the pure joy of living. If you ask where they are in their 3500 Club quest, they seem to barely understand the question. "Oh, I don't know, I'm not counting," they say. "I'm not a peak bagger." Of course, at some point, and in some hidden recess of their files or psyches, they do keep a list of high peaks they have climbed. Eventually, realizing how close they are to 3500 Club membership, they may, almost without knowing or caring why, complete the series and apply for membership.

I am, or was, the other kind, a type-A hiker: competitive, goal-oriented, obsessed with achieving milestones and bagging peaks. Though Zen meditation has helped, it's not easy letting go of a grasping nature that always wants more, such as fast membership in the 3500 Club (after all, who wants a really high number?) Some A-types have given the 3500 Club a bad name when, intent on a summit, they abandoned slower companions or compromised group safety.

That didn't happen on my winter bushwhack of Big Indian, because I was alone. In February of 2000 I had tried to register for a 3500 Club hike of Lone and Rocky—one of the toughest bushwhacks of two remote peaks—led by Harry Rampe, but the hike was full. With typical type-A enthusiasm, I asked if I could just tag along, unofficially, like Gollum dogging the ring party in *The Lord of the Rings*. I don't recall what Harry said exactly, but I took it for a yes.

The group was to meet at 8:30 AM on Saturday at the isolated Denning trailhead. The forecast called for freezing rain and snow, so I left my home in Melville, Long Island, early the night before—around 3:00 AM. The forecast was correct. After a harrowing ride through rain, snow, poor visibility and slick roads—especially heading south on County Route 47 from Route 28—I pulled into Denning at 10:00 AM in a white-knuckled but happy state, happy because I was going to bag two peaks. But the trailhead was deserted. The hike had been canceled, and I, an unofficial participant, hadn't been notified.

Much as I wanted Lone and Rocky, I realized that hiking these distant, difficult peaks without preparation wasn't smart. It was early; there was still time to hike. Consulting my ADK *Guide to Catskill Trails*, I saw that the trailhead to Big Indian was near. With only a quarter-mile off-trail, it was perfect for a solo bushwhack. I arrived at the trailhead at 10:30 AM, ample time for the 9.5-mile hike, nine of them on trail, but I resolved to start back no later than 1:30 PM—everyone knows the danger of lingering too long on the summit.

Gearing up with gaiters and snowshoes, pulling on my pack and fixing my poles, I set out in a feverish state of nervous anticipation—very common for type-A hikers. The day was cold but sunny, the ground covered with heavy snow about sixteen inches deep that had fallen the night before, and Biscuit Brook was scenic as always. After a steep start, the first three miles are easy-going across gently rolling hills, especially when, as on that day, others have broken the trail. I glided rhythmically across the packed snow, following blue markers at a good pace until I reached the lean-to, where the snowshoe tracks ended.

I didn't relish having to break trail the rest of the way, but I pushed on slowly, tiring as the pitch steepened. *Why does everyone think that snowshoes keep you above the snow?* I wondered, as I sank a foot deep with each step. Around noon I remembered something Rich Niegocki, an excellent hiker and leader, had said on one of my first winter hikes: "You don't hike on your muscles; you hike on your food." Time for a snack, starting a routine I would always follow when winter hiking: divide the food into four units; eat one an hour before lunch, one at lunchtime, one an hour later, and one as a snack on the way back. It always works for me.

Energized a bit, I soon came to a giant fallen hardwood whose broken and twisted branches had obliterated the trail markers. I went left and couldn't find a marker, then to the right. Tried left again and then right again—still nothing. Flustered and sweaty, I sat in the snow to rest and reason it out. If I backtracked, maybe I would have a better view of the trail beyond the tree. It worked. Some 100 feet ahead, I saw a blue blaze I hadn't seen earlier. I kept climbing, wondering how long it would take to reach the top.

Funny thing about winter hiking alone. Usually you feel energized by the beauty, the brisk air, the exercise, but sometimes a stab of fear creeps in. What if something happens—a slip or a health problem? You're far from help, you're cold, the cell phone's dead—wonder how long you would last? Best to be prepared and focus on the moment. Just this step, just this breath. But the farther into the unknown you hike, the more such thoughts reverberate.

Deep in my reverie, I noticed the trail getting steeper—must be near the ridge—so I started looking for the 3,500-foot elevation sign marking the spot to turn off-trail. It was close to 1:00 PM, I should be starting down soon, must be around here somewhere. What's this—big yellow blazes painted on the trees, aiming in an easterly direction? Maybe the sign was gone and some helpful person blazed a trail to guide aspirants to the canister. That must be it—I'll follow these blazes.

Off I went through thin woods, following blazes that I now know marked a parcel of private land that adjoined the trail. When the blazes started leading down the side of the mountain, I realized my error and backtracked to the trail. Tired, but not ready to quit, I continued until I came to the 3,500-foot sign and headed back into the woods. I hiked east, glancing at the compass to sight trees and heading toward them, then sighting again. I scratched my face running into branches, and fell a few times after getting tangled in brush, but the land seemed to be rising, the summit must be near. How could I be sure? Through deep snow my hiking speed is about one mile per hour, and the canister was a quarter-mile away, so fifteen minutes out I would begin a serious hunt.

The time was 1:30 PM, my turn-back time, but still nothing. I hiked toward the highest point nearby, thinking it positive that the land was rising. In the distance, over a hill, I saw what looked like another hiker, wearing a bright red jacket. Funny, I didn't see anyone come up … no, wait, that's the canister! I ran toward it, fast as possible weighed down by snowshoes and a full pack, cracked it open and signed the logbook. (I wonder if anyone ever checks these when you submit your 3500 Club application?) No matter, even if I die on the way back, at least I got Big Indian. I hardly remember the rest of the day, except that I was in my car by 3:30 PM, tired but elated after my first solo bushwhack.

Now, where will I hike tomorrow? 🚶

67

A CIVILIZED WILDERNESS EXPERIENCE

LIGHT NOTES ABOUT A HEAVY BUSHWHACK

Nancy Wolff, #364
from Autumn 1986 *Catskill Canister*

There are two schools of thought about peak bagging: those who enjoy the practice, and those who deplore it for ecological or other reasons. Then there are the rest of us—we agree with saving wild places, but we have followed enough hike leaders through the years that we have been to the tops of most of the mountains where anyone regularly hikes. People frequently state that they think the untrailed peaks should be left alone, "but I just happen to have climbed all but seven of the 3500's in the Catskills (or the New England 4000-footers), and I couldn't just ignore the rest when I was that close. Finishing them gave me a great goal for this year."

Well, here we are, forty-seven strong, enjoying a wonderful wilderness experience at a civilized lodge in the Catskills—two or three in a room, sleeping on real beds instead of being stacked like flapjacks in a bunkroom. No snores of dorm mates from every corner; no agonizing bumps and grinds of those who just cannot get comfortable on the bunks or cots; no thuds of unfortunates falling out of upper bunks at three in the morning; no pitter-patter of size thirteens sneaking off to the bathroom at 4:00 AM; no creaking and rustling and crackling of people organizing their gear into plastic bags at 5:00 AM. Hot running water for a shower after a hot running hike, not the cold stream dip. Instead of a few hardy souls enduring the rigors of the wilderness, forty-seven motley humanoids cheerfully queue up for breakfast—real food, not freeze-dried chicken chips.

Well, civilization has its price. Pondering the thought of four-dozen pairs of Vibram soles trudging up a hitherto untrailed mountain brings a shudder to my frame. Surely the once untrammeled shoulders of my final Catskill peak would be ruined forever by such a multitude. It is with relief that I hear the trip leader announce several alternative hikes on this day, leaving us with only two-dozen soles to brave the unknown. Having done some bushwhacking in Harriman Park, they feel a spirit of adventure and glee at the opportunity to celebrate a friend's achievement.

Resting on the trail, butterfly-style. Photograph by Larry Gambon.

Our leader is a veteran of many trips. A member of the Catskill 3500 Club, he has led and followed on many untrailed peaks, and has experience with map and compass. Not for me, the leadership position on a Catskills bushwhack. Let others work their way through the spider webs, force their way through the car-wash-brush barriers of evergreen trees, slog up cliffs to find impasses and slog down to try another route. I know: you say there should be two kinds of peak bagging memberships, one for leaders and one for followers. I do not gainsay your opinion; I just tell the story.

It is a very hot, sunny day. We drive to the beginning of the hike and start up a logging road. Then we plunge into the woods, following a line on the compass set by our leader. After half an hour, two of our people turn back. "Too hot," they say. Fearlessly, we sweat up the steep angle. Logging has taken the shade trees, and the sun beats fiercely on us. Unsightly bulldozer scars erase my guilty feelings about having induced all those Vibrams up the hill. The paths they made were not even going our way. The ultimate insult!

Up we crawl, scramble, curse. One of us becomes ill. A quick conference: two people who have previously climbed this mountain will accompany her back down. She argues that she could wait for us to come back—but who knows where we'll come down? The heat persists. We persist. Up a rock slide with a teasing trickle of water underneath. Agonizing question: "Is the water potable?" Even on a trailless peak the question calls for some discussion among the experienced hikers.

The famous and infamous cliffs of the typical Catskill mountain emerge, the false summit, the evergreens that block your way and threaten your eyes. Just keep telling yourself, "I'm having a good time." Well, yes. The cry of "rock!" and a thud ten feet below, landing at the foot of an astonished hiker—fortunately with no contact. The leader goes one way, some followers go their own way. Frequent census stops assure us that nobody has become lost. One young man behind me urges me to follow the leader so he will not have to make any decisions. Nobody wants to start a search party. Up and up! It seems as if we have been hiking for weeks. Ah, the summit—or is it another shoulder?

It seems that we must be at the top, for we see sky all around us. And yet, no canister. The leader plunges into the underbrush. "Egad! I don't want to go in there. Where's he going?" A shout. The canister! We plunge in to meet the leader and sign in. Hugs and kisses all around, congratulations to all, the champagne flows. We eat lunch, discussing four excellent answers to the question, "Why do we climb these mountains?" We take pictures to commemorate the occasion. We intentionally spill a few drops of champagne to placate the wilderness gods who are unhappy with the revelry.

After resting a few moments, we descend. Just as on the ascent, there's the danger on the descent that someone will relax his or her vigil and stray from the flock. Care is taken to avoid twisting an ankle or a knee when we fall through the mossy covering of the rocks and logs. Oops! There goes someone into a hole! Pull her out before we lose her! We trip over unseen obstacles. We slither over the slithy rocks. Downhill is a different ball of wax, but it's as much work in this heat as uphill. The chattering that accompanied our entry into the woods has faded into a concentration bent on placing our feet steadily as we move down. One contingent mutinies and insists on going its own route. Our leader escorts us out of the woods exactly at the cars. That's class! 🏃

68

CATSKILL MOUNTAIN HIGHS

STEEP PLEASURES

Edward Ripley-Duggan, #1389, #548W

For twenty years I have lived in the Catskills, close to the Ashokan Reservoir. Down the road, at the beginning of the dividing weir, is a superb view—the long ridgeline of Ashokan High Point to the south, and Overlook Mountain and the peaks of the Devil's Path in the middle distance to the north. But these are not what seize the eye and awe the imagination. Directly ahead is a great glacially scooped bowl in the mountains, a true cwm,[1] the eastern face of the Burroughs Range and the peaks adjacent. Wittenberg, Cornell, Friday, and Balsam Cap stand as a serried rank. Behind, the cap of great Slide Mountain is visible, frequently trailing pennants of cloud. The mountains climb more than three thousand feet above the reservoir. A ridge, starting broad at the base, but often narrowing to a steep knife-edge, rises to the summit of each.

The woods cover them all, with little visual evidence of human impact. Still, the lower slopes were logged and farmed, and are crisscrossed with woods roads, where lumber and bark were brought down to the valleys. There are the remains of great charcoal kilns on Hanover Mountain, a small peak below Friday Mountain. But the summits are indeed inviolate, covered with first-growth spruce and fir. Below them, deep moss covers the rock, its growth fueled by the moisture of the clouds that often roll over and obscure the summit view.

Watch these hills for an hour or two in summer, and the light changes constantly with the play of sun and cloud. In winter, snowstorms sometimes swirl around the peaks, even while it is still—even sunny—elsewhere. Occasionally, fierce winds roll down the slopes and out over the waters of the reservoir, which then has whitecaps (on rare occasions, even waterspouts have been seen). On other days, the waters are flat and mirror the sky.

Each of these ridges has a local name, most not reflected on any map. The ridge to the north is Blackberry; that to Cornell is Petey; Friday's ridge is sensibly named Middle; and Gibbon Ridge rises to Balsam Cap. Blackberry and Middle are easy enough, but who were Petey and Gibbon? Or Samuel of Samuel's Point, whose winding ridge extends to Wittenberg? Lost names, lost farms. Those versed in local lore remember individuals like Old Billy, who farmed the ridge called Little Sam.

Most of this activity was in the nineteenth century, the era of John Burroughs, who saw much of these slopes bare in the aftermath of the bark and lumber industries. What a different vista that must have been!

A place like this fires the imagination of one who loves mountains, as I have since I was a child. I grew up in rural Hertfordshire in England, a pretty place, but not one known for its peaks. Early memories are of battling up some seemingly impossibly steep slope, likely in reality to have been a fifty-foot earthen bank. When I went to North Wales as a teenager, I saw Tryffan and climbed Snowdon. It was love at first sight. I've never been an athlete, so real climbs—the great peaks of Europe or Asia, or even the gritstone climbs of England—never occurred to me as possibilities. I think that failure of imagination haunts me and is one of the things that impels me to climb the peaks of the Catskills.

There's also the fact that all mountains are magic places to me. I can easily understand the desire to build chortens[2] and hang prayer flags. All this explains why, for me, the quintessence of pleasure is working my way up one of those ridges, climbing ledges and trying to avoid being skewered by the odd branch. I have had more fun on the peaks of the Bushwhack Range—Lone, Rocky, Balsam Cap and Friday—and the Burroughs Range—Wittenberg, Cornell, Slide—than any reasonable person should have; but I make no claim to reasonableness. I'm a little obsessed by these mountains.

Wittenberg's ridge begins at Samuel's Point. The first time I walked this in its entirety was with a friend who was a minister, one who shortly after quit his church in a crisis of politics and faith. This was not, I think, cause and effect. We climbed Little Mountain (on private property; permission should be asked to use this route) and Little Sam first. Little Mountain has a lovely dwarf oak summit with an understory of blueberry and crisp, reindeer lichen. An old woods road from there enters fine forest, some sadly cut in the past couple of years. The views from Little Mountain are always a pleasure, a vision of rurality—the Ashokan Reservoir, fields, houses and roads. I've sat there on a Sunday and heard hymns drifting up from the church below, touching even for one who is a nonbeliever.

The morning that my friend and I walked up was sunny and still cool, a perfect day for hiking. Little Sam, the next high point on the ridge, was almost as pleasing. Then we scrambled up the earthen banks and ledges of Samuel's Point itself. Though tall enough, at 2,885 feet, atop it is an old fence. Perhaps Old Billy kept sheep or goats up here. Beyond, after a brief push through spruce, we descended along the ridge, passing a collapsed tin shack that looked out of place in this wild country. Below was the area of Brown's farm. It's hard to see how anyone could make a living this deep into the hills, but they managed somehow, a hard-working, independent people, like most of the hardscrabble farmers of the Catskills.

The ridge ends at the foot of Wittenberg (or, "The Wittenberg," now the only Catskill peak to have the odd distinction of possessing a definite article before its name). We scrambled ledge to ledge for 800-plus feet. It was grueling work, but eventually we had the satisfaction of summiting right at the great overlook, a huge ledge that provides one of the most noble of Catskills vistas. Looking over what we had traversed, this route felt like an accomplishment. We descended to Woodland Valley, where we had left a car.

The ridge to the peak of nearby Cornell rises between the junction of two streams, the Wittenberg and an unnamed brook that descends from the col between Friday and Balsam Cap. It is a relatively gentle ascent up to 2,500 feet, but becomes progressively steeper as the summit is approached. In winter these sections are sufficiently exposed that this climb can demand technical skill, rope, ice ax and crampons. Even in the summer, some of the ledges present serious scrambling, and a fall would be distinctly inadvisable! Climbed on a beautiful day, it is an exhilarating trek, scary enough at times to heighten the adrenaline, but not so dangerous as to be truly foolhardy. My only injury the first time I climbed it was when, on a level ledge, I stumbled and was stabbed in the arm by a peg of spruce, leaving a mark I still bear. The views were spectacular. The steepest portion was exhausting, and the summit path, when reached, was welcome.

That day, my hiking partner and I traversed the section of the Burroughs Trail called the Bruin's Causeway, and descended the rather vertiginous Dutchman's

View of Wittenberg and Cornell (background center right) from the Ashokan Reservoir. Photograph by Ted Shemella.

Path that drops back down to the end of Moon Haw Road. This rather strange name is apparently derived from the Munsee Indian language. The route emerges on the road by the still-standing chimney of an old house where the path's maker was once caretaker. Also called the Van Benschoten Path, the Dutchman was probably as American as they come, as this is an old Ulster County name.

From Moon Haw Road one climbs Friday Mountain and Balsam Cap; a property line with state land is reached at about 2,200 feet on the ridge of Friday. There's usually a strong herd path up the middle of this ridge, but the most traveled route veers off to the col with Balsam Cap, avoiding the ledge-girt summit of Friday itself. That's a shame, because this is a pleasant scramble, although near the summit a huge cliff band looks imposing and impassable. Careful search will reveal a detour, a series of steep chutes that lead to the summit proper. In spring the ledges have the densest growth of painted trilliums that I have ever seen in the Catskills.

In the drainage between Friday and Balsam Cap, a tragedy is concealed. This is not a place to idly wander—it is steep and, in places, dangerous. There's a glint of metal between the trees. Follow this, and there sit the remains of a WWII-era B-25J Mitchell bomber, the fuselage largely intact, but with other wreckage scattered all over this section of the mountain. From beneath the site comes the sound of running water, the drainage for the creek that runs into Wittenberg Brook in the valley. The plane, piloted by Richard B. Willis, crashed at the end of March 1948, killing the three occupants. The Catskills are littered with plane wrecks, but this is one of the most evocative.

Exploring the ridge of Balsam Cap is another steep pleasure. The top is awkward, particularly when descending, where at one point there seems no possible way down. With a slither here and there, however, the trickier portions are surmounted. The ascent is easier for reasons psychological rather than practical. This is not a ridge from which to stray—as with much of this cliff-girt country, there are serious dangers for the unwary.

These are some of the more challenging bushwhacks that the Catskills have to offer. The rewards are the extraordinary views, the satisfaction of surmounting some truly awkward terrain, and the sheer pleasure of exploring steep and wild country that often is within a couple of miles of roads and stores. The Catskills have given me many pleasures, but few to match those found on these ridges and peaks. 🏃

---

[1] Geological term: a deep, steep-walled recess in a mountain caused by glacial erosion.

[2] Tibetan: a shrine or monument.

69

A SOLO WINTER BUSHWHACK

BEARINGS AND BEARS

Andrew M. Moroz, #1218, #452W

February 26 and 27, 1999

"These are the hardest of the 3,500-foot peaks to reach," the ADK's *Catskill Trails* guidebook states, referring to Friday, Balsam Cap, Rocky, and Lone mountains. Of the thirty I had reached thus far, yes, these were the hardest. Extreme bushwhacking is required to reach these four remote summits. I was closed in by seemingly impenetrable fir stands, encountered hidden cliffs, repeatedly crossed fresh bear tracks, signs and dens, but a bright blue sky and plenty of sunlight kept me optimistic. My pants were ripped to shreds, pack straps and drawstrings were frayed, my watch hung from a torn wristband, my face and hands were scratched—and I still found it to be an enjoyable couple of days in the woods. The Catskills are the southernmost Northern Forest, and the spruce-fir summits hold a strong attraction for me. Climbing through the damp maple-beech-birch forest on the way to the spruce-fir zone conjures up a Jack-in-the-Beanstalk feeling of having climbed beyond the known world.

Motoring north from my home in Philadelphia on a previously untried back road, I scattered a dozen wild turkeys and found the trailhead deserted. I was walking by 1:30 PM, figuring I'd follow the valley of the East Branch of the Neversink, get as close to Friday Mountain as possible, camp, summit in the morning, and return via the ridgeline that connects Friday, Balsam Cap, Rocky, and Lone.

Preoccupied in anticipating the difficult log-bridge crossing of the Deer Shanty Brook, I slipped and fell hard on an icy patch on the 1.2-mile Phoenicia–East Branch trail; ever since my first crossing there in the rain on the way to Table Mountain, that "bridge" has had the psychological advantage over me. I've never fallen into the Deer Shanty, but it has always taken extreme concentration, and the position of the log spanning the dizzying torrent always seems to change. Today two completely dry logs spanned the brook, a delightful bit of luck. Crossing the braided Neversink was easy. Usually it requires wading across a shallow section or two, but the polished stones of the riverbed were dry today. I turned east on a bearing of 95°, found the faint red blazes of "the Fishermen's Path" and headed up the valley.

The many tributaries and diversions of the Neversink require crossing and recrossing the river several times, testing the ice all the way. Just past Donovan Brook, the south bank is steep, so the footpath crosses over to the north. Here I tried an ice bridge that gave way, leaving me calf-deep in cold water. Instantly I was out—my foot still dry, saved by the gaiter. The top of the south bank seemed to offer a fairly clear route, so I climbed forty to fifty feet above the river to avoid crossing again later, and that proved to be the clearest path of travel. The tail-dragging tracks I followed told me that this was the route of choice of somebody very familiar with the territory— like the endorsement that trucks give a roadside diner. The critter knew innately of the easy travel and clear view from this bluff. A panoramic view of the East Branch valley opened up, including an unusual view of Slide Mountain that showed the steepness of the shoulder dipping toward Cornell, the one John Burroughs compared to a horse with its head bowed at the watering trough.

Eventually the terrain flattened and the valley turned northeast, signifying the place to head uphill to Friday Mountain. I left the river on a bearing of 75° to 80°, intending to arrive on the ridge south of the summit. Soon after leaving the Neversink, one enters the conifers and then encounters cliff bands on Friday's little-described west side. The cliffs are hidden in the balsam firs, looking no less like a wall of trees than the rock walls they turned out to be. The cliffs could be flanked or their margins climbed, but getting through the firs took patience: squat down and look for a patch of sunlight, preferably on or about your intended bearing, and shove your way to it, much as you would make your way through the crowd in Times Square on New Year's Eve. While moving from little clearing to little clearing, narrow slices of sunlight between the trees defend bravely against creeping attacks of claustrophobia. I was making good progress and feeling strong. Drawn forward by sunlight shooting directly up the western aspect of the East Branch valley and right into the slope I was climbing, summit fever took me and I surged to the summit canister, racing the sun, causing a harrowing climb through the thick balsam fir trees.

In the thickest balsams on the southwest slope, a patch of sunlight in which I emerged turned out to be a bear's den! With a shudder, my darting eyes and stunned brain put together the signs: a fresh scat pile, a bright yellow pee hole, something that looked like a bird's nest on a mammoth scale, ringed by oddly human-looking footprints with long claws on the toes. Yikes! This looked recently occupied—the only thing missing was a teapot puffing away on a stove. Reflexively I spun around and crashed into whatever was behind me, my mind racing with what I saw and what it meant: I was in the neighborhood of an active *ursus americanus* in a thick forest. There was no favorable outcome to any scenario involving a nose-to-nose encounter with a bear in this environment. We would be upon each other before we—or at least, I—would know it, with nowhere to go very fast. I crossed and recrossed fresh and old bear tracks and found a second den with more scat. The bear and I must be about the same size, since I noticed by its tracks we found the same spaces to squeeze through the trees. (I thought of my aviator Uncle Paul, who once asked if I'd "ever been in the woods with a bear behind?")

There was nothing I could do but give fair warning to the timid bruin—as I've been led to believe they are—by making a lot of human-sounding noises. I decided English speech would be a good human sound. "I don't care to see a bear!" I chanted in rhythm as I shoved balsam trunks from side to side. The last few hundred feet of ascent were thus marched in a direttissima[1] to the summit. I took a close-up photo of the canister, and when the auto camera flash went off I realized dusk had risen out of the forest. The remaining light was a soothing pink cast, reflected off the soft, undulating clouds. After a deep breath of satisfaction, off I went on a new bearing ("bearing" taking on a new meaning for me) off the ridge to find a place to sleep. At 6:30 I entered a small clearing at 3,400 feet, and a brief excursion into the next dark tangle of firs told me I could get no farther. I happily set up the tent, brewed a thermos of tea and had dinner at 7:30 by candle-lantern light. Tired, I relaxed while compelled to sing and make metallic noises, my way of bear-proofing my camp. After drifting off in the middle of "Ridin' down the Canyon" I slept soundly, waking once to cinch up the sleeping bag hood against the cold.

In soft light my eyes creaked open at 6:40 AM. Sitting in my bag while cooking in the tent vestibule, I made a breakfast of coffee and pancakes and a thermos of hot chocolate to carry. I left at 8:30 and again crossed and recrossed fresh and aged bear tracks. It became apparent that I should deviate from my direct compass bearing and drop down out of the dense firs to the hardwoods for easier traveling. Now I was where I could see my objective and a feasible route. Returning to the firs on Balsam Cap, there were again more haunting bear tracks, but no fresh ones. After a brief "bend and bash" session, I reached the Balsam Cap summit canister at 9:30, with both pants legs ripped open. Looking at the long tears, I could hear Constance, my ridgeline-hike-loving sister-in-law flatly state, "I hate bushwhacking," and I chuckled, thinking that now I'm spoiled and will have trouble staying on the trails. Despite glimpses east to the Ashokan Reservoir, I headed west off the ridgeline to the col on a new bearing, feeling like I was adapting smartly to the circumstances; the hardwoods brought relief. I reached a cliff, headed east to find an easier route, and a scramble up several manageable ledges brought me to the summit plateau, where there were human tracks instead of bear tracks.

I arrived at the canister at 11:00, after coming upon curious spiny scraps that I deduced to have been a porcupine. I couldn't tell how it entered life eternal, but its earthly remains were certainly consumed by large birds, their tracks circling the

Andrew Moroz on Rocky Mountain. Photograph by Andrew Moroz.

remaining chunks of quills and hide. There were no bones, feet, or head. It looked like there had been competition for the tastiest morsels, since several pairs of three-toed talons paralleled bits of hide. This wildness was startling to come upon. The mountains had been drawing me into increasingly more primeval scenes and sobering reflections—recalling my fear of the Deer Shanty crossing, my pride in finding the route of the tail-dragging tracks, my humility restored by thick conifers, my nervousness at bear signs, the reality of my torn pants, this harsh display of the unsentimental wild world, and now my acutely felt isolation.

On I plunged, appropriately, to Lone Mountain thinking *three down and one to go*, and then regretting that thought which drove the feeling of wildness out of my consciousness. I descended my route up Rocky to avoid ducking and bashing a new route. After swinging around 270° to the east, north, and then west to the beautiful open western slope below the col, I headed for a knob on the northeast ridge of Lone. I followed the ridge to the summit, again circling around east-northeast to the uppermost cone, and shortly found the can, an army ammo box bolted to a tree. The day was fairly warm and sunny, and I was feeling extremely satisfied. This time I set up a self-timer photo of myself at the can, displaying my torn pants.

The balsams and I reached some mutual respect, I hope. They left more of an impression on me than the summits. While giving me quite a beating, they also anointed me with the aromatic "Balm of Gilead." Seeing human footprints cast away my bear hyper-consciousness.

Finding the homeward west-southwest ridge of Lone was easy—it was a white carpet spotted with birch trees, very open and almost level. A bare flat rock at about 3,500 feet said "lunch," and I sat down, more fatigued than I'd realized. I found a bagel and cheese, and melted a quart of water from snow with my stove for soup, after which I could only recline on my backpack and doze.

I bounded down the spine of the ridge, occasionally crossing old footsteps, listening for the sound of the Neversink. I arrived at the spot where I'd climbed to the terrace above the river, and edged my way down on frozen crust. I slipped and fell and slid some twenty feet, caught myself, then resigned to slide the rest of the way down to the riverbank. I zoomed to the bottom much faster than I'd anticipated, tossed out by a mountain range that would tolerate my hubris no longer. After bashing through the balsams, I accepted this as their quid pro quo as I exited.

I quickly retraced my footprints—prints that turned into bear tracks and back to bootprints in my mind—and reached the trailhead in a little more than an hour; it took a couple of contrasting days at work to return fully to my world. 🐾

[1] A mountaineer's term for a direct route to the summit.

70

WHEN A TRAIL HIKE BECOMES A BUSHWHACK

OFF THE BEATEN TRACK

Ted Shemella, #1550

Moon Haw is one of my favorite parts of the Slide Mountain Wilderness. It is almost a secret; it's overlooked for some reason I haven't figured out yet. It still has some nice stands of beech that haven't succumbed to disease, and there are huge sugar maples and ancient-looking gray birch. It's also a shortcut to Wittenberg Mountain. When I was standing on Wittenberg's summit today, I couldn't believe my GPS said I was less than two miles from my car.

I drove to Moon Haw Road early this morning. I've finished my peak bagging, so I decided to pay less attention to time and to even allow flexibility in my route if I lost my way. Along with my new *laissez-faire* attitude, it seems my hike planning went out the window as well. I took my GPS along, but without a single waypoint prepared for the route. There is a trail, so I would simply take some marks along the way to assure a safe return.

To my surprise the road was closed except to local traffic. Let me be clear about this: Moon Haw Road dead-ends into a hollow that faces a 2,800-foot elevation to the col between Cornell and Wittenberg mountains. The only possible traffic on Moon Haw Road *is* local. It's Labor Day, so there's no construction going on; there doesn't seem to be any reason for the road to be closed unless they intend to keep out hikers. A little farther along is the state-land parking, and all the signs are gone—not just the trailhead parking sign, but also the state-land signs that used to be on alternate trees. Now I'm thinking conspiracy. This secret place has just gotten even more secret.

Moon Haw Road ends in private property that used to be a hunting lodge. The start of the hike is an elaborate walk around the private land with double crossings of Maltby Hollow Brook. I know this trail, but I can't seem to find any markings. Some "Private Property, Strictly Enforced" signs assure me that I'm making the proper circumvention as I follow an old logging road that has been washed out so many times that I'm walking on river stones one moment and deep mud the next. By the time I've covered enough distance to mark my first waypoint, I see a single, faded, red splotch on an old maple. Following this trail isn't rocket science:

you walk along the brook until it peters out, and then you climb up cliffs until you intersect the Cornell-Wittenberg trail, but I'm surprised that the trail has deteriorated so much. I descended this trail after a Friday-Cornell hike not long ago, but maybe it's been years since I've hiked up it. With the wisdom I now have from my recent trip down, I realize where I took a right fork in the trail without even seeing the left one; I have a GPS coordinate of that fork tucked away for future use.

Soon I get to an old rotten wooden bridge that I never knew existed. I've always had trouble staying on the "official" trail here, so I'm confused as to whether I'm lost or whether I've *never* been on the right track before and have finally found it. I cross and recross the old bridge until I head out on the wrong path with complete confidence that I'm right. All these trails are old logging roads, so my situation looks good until the road is completely washed out and I'm walking on river stones or, a little later, river boulders. I'm not sure when I realize I'm not even close to being on a trail but, as I said, this isn't rocket science.

Dutchman's Path route to Cornell-Wittenberg col. Photograph by Ted Shemella.

The brook has dwindled to almost nothing, but in front of me is a nice-sized pool with a small fish swimming in it. Nature is amazing. I've now ascended over a thousand feet from "civilization," and there's what I believe to be a brook trout making its habitation here in the middle of nowhere. The critter must have been born here, but how did its forebears get here? It hides from me under a rocky overhang and I don't see it again.

Without a trail to follow, I alternate walking on the riverbank and stone-hopping the almost dry creek bed. I've covered half the distance, but most of the elevation is saved for the end. Nettles are closing in on me, driving me from the bank to go stone-hopping in the creek bed. Experienced hikers have taught me not to wear cotton or denim, but I'm getting nettle stings through my nylon zipoffs. There's a dead-end ahead—a huge tree trunk stretching from one bank to the other. I'm able to slide underneath, but the nettles will have me in the end. I break away from the ever-diminishing creek bed and look for the fewest stings as I head for higher ground. The plan works. Without the river water the nettles look sickly and soon disappear. I make a mental note of the time it takes for the pain from the stings to subside; it isn't that long. I'll be more aggressive with them on the way down.

I mark a waypoint when I see the first large beech tree. It's a good healthy one, but I see diseased ones as well. How long will they be able to hang on? Soon I'm seeing the ancient-looking gray birch trees, some living, some dead. I suspect I must be getting close when a spruce tree pops into view. I mark my seventh waypoint when I reach the first cliff. I'm a little concerned now because without the "official" trail, I'm not sure I can find a safe way to the Cornell-Wittenberg trail. I'm a coward when it comes to scaling cliffs, and I'm particularly scared of getting in a can't-go-up-can't-go-down situation, which is highly possible with the thick spruce cover that is developing. I remember that the "official" route is fairly safe, but I don't have confidence in my memory. So I use my Catskill cliff strategy: keep circling at the base of a cliff until you can see a safe way up, and turn around and go the other way before the ground below gets too steep. I also decide that I don't have to summit. This would still be a great hike even if I had to turn around in defeat.

As I circle, the cliffs above get steeper. I've been circling to the right toward Wittenberg and almost expect to see the dangling feet of Labor Day hikers resting on the summit above. I call up, but hear no replies. My intuition tells me that I haven't nearly made it that far right, and as I continue, I think I see a way up. I make it up about fifty feet, but need to circle some more at that level. I can see the view and know it will be breathtaking today on the summit. I see the path up the next tier, and with a little scrambling I'm at the top! The trail is really close here, wherever "here" is, and I congratulate myself on a safe ascent. To assure a safe descent, I'm considering descending the trail to Woodland Valley and bumming a ride back to Moon Haw.

I'm still not sure where on the trail I am. It seems logical that I'd be between Cornell and Wittenberg, but I wasn't even sure of that. Before I go 100 feet, I see a pair of hikers. They don't look old enough to drive, so they are probably doing a one-way hike with their mom doing shuttle service. I confuse them by asking which way Wittenberg is; they go one way, confused, and I go the other, now clear. At the summit the view *is* breathtaking. Devil's Path peaks stand out so clearly in the distance with the Blackhead Range behind; Ashokan High Peak dominates the view in the other direction, and the Ashokan Reservoir is spread out below. There's a "seam" running down the dead center of the reservoir, and I try to figure out what it is. My guess is that the wind blows straight down from the mountains on either side and forms a disturbance where the waves meet in the middle. A single wispy cloud hovers low over the dividing weir; it must be from the effect of the still-warm water and the crisp September air above it.

I'm looking forward to talking to other hikers here, but it's still not eleven o'clock. I slowly eat my sandwich and drink most of my water. Despite my dawdling, not another soul appears. I'm surprised that I've got this spectacular place to myself on a holiday weekend. 👣

71

HIKING POLE IN A HAYSTACK

GPS GAME

Bill Drapkin, #1291, #458W

Being both a summer and winter 35er, I've hiked the Catskill Mountains many times. Even after finishing all the peaks, I've continued to go back to the Catskills simply for the pure enjoyment of hiking those mountains. I feel they provide a unique challenge and reward. A friend and I have been helping a number of other people complete their quests, not only to be helpful, but to give ourselves "an excuse" to go there as often as we can.

During January and February of 2004, we went with several friends to attempt 3,520-foot Halcott Mountain, a trailless peak. One of them needed Halcott as one of the final two peaks for the completion of her winter hikes. Snowshoes on, we headed up the mountain. The weather was cold, the snow was deep, and the going was very, very slow. We started at about nine o'clock in the morning. Two of us had GPS receivers and we tracked our progress as we made our way. Although we are all strong hikers, we trudged and labored in the extremely tough conditions. Progress was so difficult that we stopped to set a turnaround time, determining upon 12:30 for safety. The distance to the summit is relatively short in miles, but all too quickly our turnaround time was upon us. We stopped, had a quick lunch, and started down the mountain.

Retracing our steps was somewhat easier than going up, because we were no longer breaking trail. But, as anyone with hiking experience knows, going downhill can be far more difficult than going up, particularly in snow-covered, icy conditions. Several of us were slipping and falling, and on one steep spot I went down and slid about fifteen feet. One of my hiking poles slipped from my hand, and when I stopped, I looked around for it. Hard as it might be to believe, I couldn't find it after ten minutes of searching. More as a lark than anything else, I set a waypoint on my GPS receiver and announced that it might be fun to come back in the spring and see if we could find the pole. We laughed and agreed it was a great idea. Small as our own chances of finding the pole in trailless woods would be, the likelihood of anyone else coming by this exact location and finding and taking the pole were near zero.

Spring arrived, and that hiking pole in a haystack called to us. It was May, and the black flies had not yet paid us their annual visit; it was a very nice time to be out hiking. We started up the mountain, GPS in hand. The going was, of course, "day and night" easier. Up we went toward the waypoint I had marked on the GPS, zeroing in on the coordinates, and when we arrived at virtually the exact place on the GPS, there it was! The hiking pole was lying on the ground waiting for us. We continued up the mountain, laughing and enjoying this new variation on the pleasures of hiking. 🥾

Fawn in the Catskills. Photograph by Larry Gambon.

72

SEARCHING FOR SPENCER'S LEDGE

ELUSIVE BEAUTY

Peter Ford, #755, #293W
from October–December 1999 *Catskill Canister*

With not enough snow to ski, I contented myself with hiking. I usually pick a spot where I don't expect to see any other hikers for most of the day. That often means hiking off trail, which I enjoy. One day, accompanied by my dog, Puma, I headed south from Peekamoose Road on the Long Path towards Bangle Hill. The first part was very steep and followed a creek cut deeply into the mountain. After about 800 feet of climbing, the trail started to level off before reaching the ridgeline at about 2,500 feet. In winter you can see across the road through the trees to the more popular mountains of Table and Peekamoose. From the ridge the trail descends the other side of Bangle Hill. But Puma and I left the trail and cut east, following a compass bearing and the blurry image of a summit to the top of Samson Mountain, at 2,850 feet. Samson's summit is so covered with trees that it has no view, even in winter.

We continued east down Samson to a long ridge that ended at Spencer's Ledge, our destination. Staying towards the southern side of this long ridge, we were treated to many decent views through the trees, but there was one clean rock ledge with unobstructed 180° views to the south. On another winter hike I followed a different route and turned around before finding it. This time, I was determined. Whenever a stand of hemlocks looked familiar, I thought the ledge would be just beyond. As the minutes ticked by and I passed many stands of hemlocks, I began wondering if I'd ever find Spencer's Ledge. Luckily, Puma didn't question me and didn't seem the least concerned about getting back to the car before dark.

Then I recognized a stand of hemlocks and the remnants of an old logging road—a definite sign the ledge was near. Almost as if I remembered exactly, I headed to the right and straight through the trees to the ledge. The sun had reappeared, and the view was glorious. We sat down—Puma with her biscuit, me with my thermos—and took it all in. Eventually, I noted that it was 3:20 PM and knew we needed to start down to avoid crossing the Rondout Creek in the dark.

My plan had been to follow a rectangular path: I'd reached my goal by heading south and east; I would then turn north down the mountain, ford the creek and walk west on the road. To minimize road walking, however, I decided to veer northwest—a longer route through the woods. That meant that I might have to cross the creek in the dark, so I rushed down too hastily, stumbling through leaf litter and sinking into a crevice up to my knee. Fortunately my knee didn't bang too hard into the surrounding rock, but the incident shook me and woke up my Zen consciousness. Imagining myself a monk, I walked purposefully down the hill with a greater awareness of my surroundings. I now descended north to the road. Coming to a large cut in the mountain that would have been pointless to cross, I followed it down and was treated to a route through majestic hemlocks and frozen waterfalls.

The creek appeared sooner than I expected; the weather had changed and thrown off my altimeter. The creek was some twenty-five feet across; I had to find a spot to cross without getting too wet. It was 4:30 PM and just beginning to get dark. I walked west looking for a downed tree that spanned the creek or enough rocks to hop to the other bank, but always the rocks would go only halfway before a gap of a few steps. The water was deep enough to go over my Gortex boots, so I kept walking, and at times I had to cut back up the steep bank. I saw a waterfall across the road that was more than two miles from where I parked; I'd never make it by dark. I reached a place where, again, I'd have to climb up the bank to continue, and it was now dark. There were a number of large and small rocks that I could step on out to the middle of the creek. This was it.

The first rocks were easy; the next rock was icy, so I simply stepped into the fast-flowing water. It seeped over the tops of my boots, but surprisingly it didn't feel cold. I waded all the way across and realized that my fear of getting my feet soaked was unfounded. Thanks to two layers of synthetic socks, my feet remained warm. Puma and I scrambled up the bank to a fine road walk in the dark. 🐾

73

MAINTAINING THE CANISTERS ON

THE TRAILLESS PEAKS

MAP, COMPASS, AND EXPERIENCE
WILL NOT ALWAYS GET THE SUMMIT

Scott Lane, #1161, #431W

Editors' Note: The Trailless Peaks of the Catskills are: Balsam Cap, Fir, Lone, Rusk, Vly, Big Indian, Friday, North Dome, Sherrill, Doubletop, Halcott, Rocky, and Southwest Hunter. Three requirements for hiking to the trailless peaks are a good compass, good maps and, most important, experience. Yet, as the club's current canister maintainer, Scott Lane, writes, these aids will not always help you! Scott hikes the trailless peaks on a regular basis, replaces missing canisters, exchanges notebooks each year, and files a report with the DEC about usage from six of the logbooks when they are replaced each year. This is one of the club's important jobs, and below he describes the variety of conditions he faces on the peaks.

Fog on Halcott

At the summit there was little visibility, but with warm winds blowing, it was kind of exciting. After lunch it was very foggy and raining steadily. I decided to jaunt over to Northeast Halcott and then down to Deep Notch on Route 42. In thick fog everything is different. We came upon a road and decided to follow it. It's funny how fast you can get to Delaware County from here! I saw an old cabin with smoke coming from the chimney, swallowed my pride and knocked on the door. Inside was an old-timer swilling Budweiser on a Sunday afternoon. He got a good laugh about our day and said we weren't the first folks to arrive at his place. As we trekked back to Route 42 via Gooding Road in Pine Hill and back to the parking area, we thought that when you start your hike in Greene County, then go into Delaware County, hike back through Ulster County and finally into Greene County, you may not have taken the best way off the mountain. May I add that this was the first time our friend ever used his new GPS!

Snow on Sherrill

My favorite way to the mountain is from Peck Hollow Road. At the summit the snow really set in on us, so we did not include North Dome that day. We set the compass to south to ride the ridge out and east to the valley. The compass was act-ing up, so it was downhill from there. Suddenly we were looking at a green school bus on the side of the mountain. From the can to the bus had been a workout, with three to four feet of snow on the ground. We made it out just as dusk appeared. We went back in the summer to that area, but couldn't find that bus again.

Frozen on Fir

As we pass by a lifetime buddy's house, we always give him a toot on the horn. He'd looked at the temperature when we passed en route to Fir and Big Indian moun-tains, and it was −11° at 7:00 AM. He crawled back under his covers! At Fir's summit can for lunch, our bananas were frozen and the hot cocoa in our thermos was cold. It was windy, and to stay more than five minutes was unbearable. We went to set the compass to the divide over to Big Indian, but the needle wasn't moving—the liquid in my old trusty compass was frozen! We trekked right back down to Biscuit Brook and to the parking area.

Bus to mountaineering class on Mt. Sherrill. Photograph by Lisa Weismiller.

Snow-Swimming Southwest Hunter's Spruce Traps

With the snowdrifts, trail markers were no longer visible as we headed up from the Spruceton trailhead. Past Geiger Point, an overhang with excellent views to Southwest Hunter and the valley, I ended up off the trail and somehow crossed the old railroad bed. We came to an open spot where I fell through a spruce trap five feet into the snow—the whole area was one huge spruce trap! I removed my pack, dug my way down to remove my snowshoes, and sort of swam my way out of the trap.

Rocky Mountain in Four Feet of Snow

With every step along the Fisherman's Path knee-deep in snow, we knew it was going to be a long day. In the upper reaches it started to get tougher, with thick balsam fir packed in four feet of snow and glued together with rime ice. We did a lot of going around, over and under to get to the summit canister six feet up on a tree—which was below knee level. We weren't going to Lone today! Nine hours later, we finally reached the parking area with a story to tell. 🚶

74

BUSHWHACKING WITH BLACK FLIES

CONDITIONS REQUIRING HUMOR

David M. Galvin, #1201, #461W

Ted Duggan, Sera Galvin (honorable #1 daughter) and I climbed two and a half mountains in fair, breezy weather from the southern terminus of the Mink Hollow Trail. It had been twenty-plus years since I had been on this end of Mink Hollow. Not much had changed, although there seemed to be even more cutesy Woodstock-style houses along the road. The trail appeared to be extensively rerouted. Nonetheless, much of it was under several inches of water. There was a healthy crop of black flies that year and we were a moveable feast for the little darklings all day. The hike was about the most miserable adventure I'd had since I last went hiking with Duggan.

I'm getting ahead of myself. We turned off the trail right after the last private inholding and last cutesy house. We headed west on a promising herd path that soon petered out to nothing, followed an old woods road intermittently, and found ourselves climbing the eastern face of Olderbark. The going was steep but not difficult. Ted thought we were on a ridge, but I would hardly call the shallow bumps on that side of the mountain a ridge.

After topping out on the surprisingly open summit, Duggan suggested we "pop over" to Little Rocky, which he assumed would be an easy ramble. Sera and I were too busy swatting flies—not to mention choking on flies, chewing on flies, digging flies out of our eyes, ears, noses—to object. An exhausting, hobblebush- and fly-filled hour later, we stumbled onto the viewless bald that is the top of this putative "mountain." Actually, it's an eighty-foot-high lump on the western ridge of Olderbark, and if some idiot hadn't once given it a name, Duggan would have never come up with the bright idea of going there. We stopped on the summit to eat lunch—and more flies—before pushing back up Olderbark.

It was on this return that we made our first discovery—an extensive crop of elaborate, if shallow, talus caves or rock shelters. The most pleasant thing about the structures was that the black flies wouldn't come into them. They were also cool and dark. One was large enough inside to either stand up or lie down. We squandered an hour exploring the area; I suspect there are more caves there to be discovered. The center of the complex seems to be at: N 42°06'45.6" W074°11'36.4".

A short climb above the caves found us on top of Olderbark once again. We pushed north and east along the ridge, through open areas and dense balsam stands. At one point, frustrated with Duggan's repeated stops to check our bearings, I took the lead. Within twenty minutes I had us heading south through a horrible patch of brush that we had just struggled through going north—the right direction. Some day I will find a way to blame this on Duggan, or my daughter. For now I will not admit anything. Eventually we climbed the last steep bit of ridge to the summit plateau of Plateau, where we found a rock shelter fitted out with a steel-drum woodstove and a window frame (no glass remaining). Ted suggested that this might have been a hermit's digs or a bear-hunting camp. I thought it would be a good place to hide a body after a murder. I eyed Duggan's throat thoughtfully before realizing I had left my knife in the car. You can visit the hermit's hovel here: N42°08'06.5" W074°10'27.9". Maybe you can find an easier way to get there than we did.

We finished the bushwhack by struggling through the densest spruce/fir hell this side of the Cornell-Friday col. It took a full hour to cover a little more than a quarter-mile between the hermitage and the Devil's Path. Purely by accident, we came out only a few feet from the summit of Plateau. The black flies were relatively rare up there, but most of them were on me, so it hardly mattered.

The rest of the trip back down Mink Hollow on the flooded trail to our cars was uneventful, except that both Sera and Ted were always walking too fast or too slow, talking too much or too little, and altogether being totally annoying. Fortunately, by this point the black flies had all but ex-sanguinated me, so I didn't have the energy or inclination to be the rude and nasty individual that, in my bloodless heart, I really am. 🥾

Entangled. Photograph by Larry Gambon.

Part VIII:
REMINISCENCES

When I was a teenager, my dad, Bill Leavitt, #1 of the Catskill 3500 Club members, and I used to sit on the floor on a Friday night and study topo maps. We would look for places where the contour lines were very close together, and then we would plan a trip to those places. We saw some amazingly beautiful country in the Catskills that way. We would search our way up through the cliffs and delight in the adventure.

Ann Clapper

Photograph by Larry Gambon.

75

THE GOOD OLD DAYS

CATSKILL ACCOMMODATIONS IN 1922

Henry L. Young, #59
from Autumn 1982 *Catskill Canister*

The family of a youthful playmate of mine spent every summer in Palenville. My friend talked often about the inclined railway to the Catskill Mountain House and nearby Haines Falls. So, in 1922, when the plant where I was working shut down for a long Fourth of July holiday, I took a West Shore train to Catskill and then a Stanley Steamer stage to Palenville. After lunch I started walking up to Haines Falls and points west. It was a dusty road, but the country was green and nice. Near Hunter I went south toward Phoenicia, enjoying the mountains in the distance. I came to a farmhouse that looked like a possible place to stay, and knocked. In those days it was not difficult to find a farmhouse or a boardinghouse where they would "put you up for the night."

I was lucky, for it was the home of the Becker family. Mr. Becker and his younger son worked the farm; the older son was the firewatcher on Hunter Mountain. He would walk to work by the trail named after his family and that went straight up to the summit fire tower. The mother had died, and now the daughter kept house. They were very nice people and I stayed there several times, climbing 4,040-foot Hunter on my second trip, my first 4,000-footer of the Northeast 111 (now 115).

On Labor Day I went back to the Catskills and climbed Slide Mountain. There was a nice farmhouse in Woodland Valley where we usually stayed, but we pushed our luck too far several times. Once, my brother and I got into the backcountry and asked a farmer in the field about a place to stay. He said there wasn't any, but he talked to his wife and said we could stay with them. We had bacon and eggs for dinner and the same for breakfast, which didn't bother us at all. But the bedroom was up a ladder and just big enough for the bed and two feet of space at the top of the ladder. It was hot from the sun on the roof, so I rolled over to open the window and found several sturdy nails holding it in place.

Another time, in the Denning area, a man told us that he had sold out to a fish-and-game club and could not take anyone in. We had no camping equipment, nor food, and it was late in the day. He was not allowed to sell us food, but he said there was a lean-to a mile up the road, and he gave us bacon and eggs, a half loaf of bread and an old tin pan. At the lean-to we found a rusty axe. While I was trying to use it in the dark, a piece of wood flew up and hit me in the eye. I spent the night with a cold, wet handkerchief on it. We headed for home at daybreak, with no permanent damage to my eye. After that experience we took to packing tents and staying at established campsites.

Of all the region's hotels, my old geology professor liked the West Kill hotel best. "They give you real cream in your coffee," he said. So, one time I climbed over Hunter to stay there. They did have a good kitchen, but the place was also well known for the painting over the fireplace—a life-sized nude. The hotel burned down, and no one seems to know which fireman rescued the painting. 𝕴

The Catskill Mountain House site. Photograph by David White.

76

A YANKEE IN THE CATSKILLS

CATSKILL HOSPITALITY: EXPLORING IN THE OLD DAYS

A. T. Shorey
from Spring 1973 *Catskill Canister;* originally published in *Adirondac,*
the magazine of the Adirondack Mountain Club, Inc.
(ADK, www.adk.org)

Before the innermost reaches of the Catskills became the summer playground for the millions from the metropolitan area, in August of 1912 the writer with two friends took a walk through this charming land. Adventure followed adventure. Our objective was to cross the Catskills, using trails and old roads, with United States Geological Survey (USGS) maps as guide. We carried light packs, blankets, and shelter halves, and a few staples such as salt, pepper, sugar, two pots and a fry pan.

A shower delayed us that first afternoon, but about 5:30 we topped the ridge and came around the bend in the road under Skytop Tower. The setting sun was breaking through the storm clouds and we halted, spellbound, until the colors of the fantastic sunset sky faded. We snapped out of our spell and began looking for a place to camp. An employee of the hotel said, "Follow me!" We did—right into the kitchen of his cottage. What a meal that stranger set before us! Afterward we spread our blankets behind his house in a hayfield under a full moon with open views to the northwest. About two o'clock one of my city friends, who was sleeping out for the first time, woke me up and whispered that wild animals were nearby. Sure enough, two skunks were prancing about in the moonlight near our feet.

We broke camp at sunrise. Vernooy Falls loomed large on the map, so we set our course that way. We found an inhabited farmhouse; all they had to sell us was thick, juicy lamb chops, milk, honey, and homemade bread. Total cost: fifty-five cents. We went through Samsonville without being aware of it, took the wrong fork and followed a narrow dirt road that went through a virgin stand of maple and beech, trees of such size as none of us had ever seen. We wandered through this twilight zone all afternoon, and just at dusk under a cold, threatening sky we came off the ridge at a farmhouse. Next door was a sign: "Sundown Post Office."

We stopped to ask permission to camp in the back field. A nice old lady greeted us, looked us over and then invited us in. We told her our business and she said, "You boys came just in time. You can do me a favor. My folks are away to the fair and I just got word they won't be home till late. I have a hot supper all ready for them. They won't be here, so you boys will have to eat it or else the pigs will get it." Thus urged, we did the pigs out of a meal.

After supper I soon suggested that we had better get our tents up as it might rain. That motherly old lady looked us over again and said, "Before you go, I want to show you something." She lit a lamp and we followed her up a flight of narrow stairs into a large chamber with two beds. She led me to one and bade me just feel of it. My arm sank to the elbow in a feather bed. "Now," she said, "there is no need for you boys to sleep on the ground. No one is going to use these beds tonight, so you might as well." To make a long story short, we used those beds, enjoyed a breakfast of specially fried eggs and a big platter of buckwheat cakes and maple syrup, and in payment all that lady would take was twenty-five cents from each of us. "Just to make you boys feel better," she said.

From Sundown, our route was west and north on an old road with the Red Hill Fire Tower as a landmark. Early in the afternoon we came down into the valley of the East Branch of the Neversink River at Ladletown and Claryville, an old tannery center. At the one occupied dwelling, we got lunch and extra food for supper for twenty-five cents. We crossed the river and took the road up the West Branch beyond the Round Pond road where our map showed an old trail heading north to the Beaver Kill.

We found a trail and headed into the unknown. By mid-afternoon we came to a stout fence and soon entered a clearing, located a good spring and made camp in the corner of a cellar hole. We had filled our baskets and were getting supper when trouble arrived in the form of a black bull. He pranced around while we hastily erected a barricade and collected a pile of stones for ammunition. The bull kept his distance; we tried to be nonchalant, but in truth we were scared. Here we were, besieged, with food for only half a meal. During the night the bull got curious, edged up close and his red eyes gleamed at us in the firelight.

Next morning a miracle happened. We were getting breakfast with the last of our supplies—with the bull a close observer—when a horse came up on the gallop, looked us over, then whirled and let fly with his hind legs. The bull dodged, the horse pranced and kicked, we helped out with a few well-thrown stones, and the bull finally ran away. The horse, evidently a pet, then came right into our camp, nuzzled us, sampled our food, cleaned up our dirty dishes, got into our salt and chewed up a sweater. We packed up hastily and got out of there. Not long after that we hit the swamp at the head of the Beaver Kill and started down the fisherman's trail on the north side.

The path was lined with big, ripe blackberries. Those black dots on the map where we'd expected to buy food were nothing but cellar holes. We found out later that we had been crossing the Gould property, where all the houses had been burned. We came to our first standing house at three o'clock, half-starved. A man answered and reckoned he could rustle us some grub, though all the women folks were away. What grub! Half a cheese, a gallon of cold milk, a bowl of soft maple sugar, two loaves of homemade bread, and a pan of doughnuts! He watched with mounting interest and admiration at the way we put away the food while we told of our experience with the bull. Then came the reckoning. What do we owe? After the usual argument, he drawled, "Well, if it suits you better, a quarter."

We continued down the Beaver Kill to Hardenburgh. At Turnwood we headed north and soon came to a farmhouse where we got permission to camp in the hayfield. As we were about to start cooking a rather meager supper, we noticed a lady and a small boy, heavily laden, coming our way. They had a pail of hot ox-tail soup for us, more milk and honey and a pan of hot cornbread. She would not take a quarter or even a penny! Said she came up to swap food for news, as she had not

Catskill woods. Photograph by Mark Schaefer.

seen a newspaper in a month. We had a pleasant evening around the campfire, and the small boy camped out with us.

The old dirt road from Turnwood to Mill Brook Road is one of beauty. Turning east on the latter, we descended via the Catladder to Dry Brook valley. We turned off at the White Church, and near Hanley Corner stopped at a farm to buy some food and had another chance to do a good turn and do the pigs out of a meal. There had been a family party. The guests had departed. "The table is loaded with food," said the lady of the house. "Go right in and help yourself. And if you are looking for a good place to sleep," she added, "halfway up the hill is Ralph Jones' farm. He hates women and likes company." He did, we discovered.

The next stopping place was well up on Belleayre Mountain, at a nice little home with views for miles in all directions. While we ate, the owner, one of the editors of the old *Brooklyn Eagle*, listened to our adventure tale.

We came off the mountain into the abode of summer people at Highmount. An auto truck gave us a lift to the Ashokan Reservoir Dam. The engineer in charge of the pumping station showed us around, took us swimming and supplied food and a good place to camp. Since that time, Catskill hospitality, Catskill people, Catskill food, and everything Catskill has had a deep meaning for me. ⚉

77

REMEMBRANCE OF THINGS PAST

RESERVOIR OF GOOD MEMORIES

Walter Gregory, #18, #8W
from Winter 1979 *Catskill Canister*

I read of the wildlife that abounds in the Catskills and, although I've never seen a bear, I have found their tracks and droppings on numerous mountains. I've seen deer, rabbits, squirrels, chipmunks, and mice. Winter is the best time to learn what animals are about, for the soft snow reveals much. Tracks go from tree to tree and then down a hole. They crisscross the trail frequently, and it seems that all the wildlife in the woodlands is out to enjoy the snow. One time, while resting on Panther Mountain looking quietly about— "There, what was that? Looked almost like a ghost, so sudden and then lost. There it goes again. Why, it's a snowshoe rabbit. He really scoots! Hard to see, as his snow-white winter coloring is a perfect camouflage." Winter climbs can be such great fun. I recall the many times we would slide and fall down and laugh at the plight of the other fellow as he banged around a tree or across a fallen log.

Once, we parked at a barn with permission from the owner and made off to climb North Dome in the deep snow. It was windy and cold. When we arrived back at the cars, I went to thank the owner and she remarked that she had watched us getting ready to go. "When I saw you fellers with all your gear, I wasn't worried no more. I just knew you'd be all right. You sure looked like you knew what you were doing."

Another time some of us needed a place to park while climbing Bearpen Mountain up the old ski slope. We stopped at the farmer's house whose land we must cross and asked his permission to park and climb. He looked out at us in the wind and snow and cold, and more snow coming down, and said, "Why, of course—but do you *have* to?"

It is great to remember the friends and companions sharing the fun and struggles of the trails and mountains. The beautiful views upon reaching the top, along with the wonderful feeling of having accomplished something, make it all so worthwhile. While writing this, I just felt like rambling along like on a bushwhack, bringing out a few of the things we experience and then remember with an inner glow of good feeling. 👣

78

CATSKILL MEMORIES

A LOVE AFFAIR WITH THE CATSKILLS

Fred H. Schroeder, #181, #74W
from April–June 1997 *Catskill Canister*

It's no secret that I have a love affair with the Catskills. They hold a place dear to my heart, not only because I'm so familiar with them and they are nearby, but because they have their own unique charm that I will defend at the drop of a hat. I bristle when they are compared, derisively, to the Adirondacks or the White Mountains; I protest remarks that the Catskills are too easy and that there are no views. Who could ask for a better view than the one from the Escarpment Trail near Acra Point in May, where one looks out over the valley of the Batavia Kill at the soft green of emerging buds with the nearby Blackhead Range as background?

The area is replete with history, with trails and mountain tops not half as crowded as the Adirondacks or the Whites, where one can stand in the col between Lone and Rocky and not wish for more wilderness, and where it's possible to experience the most delightful bushwhacking to be found anywhere, with open woods leading to interesting rock ledges, flowing streams, and a huge variety of flora. The woods—once cut over for their tannin and for homesteading—are once again pristine and nearly fully regrown, a joy to walk through. A bonus is to come suddenly upon a stand of virgin hemlock, a grand glimpse of the past. Nowhere else have I experienced so many long ridges without encountering another person, but caught sight of deer darting over the ridge, a porcupine lumbering along the path, or the footprints of a coyote.

Never will I forget my first snowshoe hike to Windham High Peak in deep powdery snow on a clear sparkling day. We emerged from the coniferous forest onto an open ridge into snowdrifts so deep they required enormous energy to plow through. On a snowshoe trip that started from Peekamoose Road and encompassed Peekamoose, Table, Lone, Rocky, and Balsam Cap, one of our party became trapped on a ledge while descending Balsam Cap. We had to fashion straps and ropes to haul him up and find a safer route to Moon Haw Road. On a Lincoln's birthday hike, a blinding snowstorm hit as we were descending to Stony Clove; the wind-swept snow had infiltrated the hood of the car, packing the engine so it wouldn't start. Eventually a plow crew came by and arranged to tow us to a garage where the engine thawed out. It was after 3:00 AM when we arrived home.

There are a few painful memories. Leading a hike on Southwest Hunter, I stepped on leaves and completely disappeared from view. The leaves had covered a crevasse, and I plunged about eight feet, landing on my pack with luckily only a scratch on my brow and a sore ankle. Another misadventure occurred on Plateau as we dipped into Mink Hollow on sheets of ice. Trying to help one of our group around a tricky bend, I neglected my own position and, despite crampons, slid off a rock onto a stump twenty feet below. That fall resulted in a chipped ankle and a massive hematoma that put me out of circulation for a while and effectively ended my jogging routine.

The rest has been pure joy: the bears on Panther, the bobcat on Balsam Lake Mountain; the fun of trying to hit, dead on, the connecting ridge between Fir and Big Indian when the visibility was nil and our compasses were doing amazing jigs because of iron deposits; finding a touching tribute to a deceased hunter near the canister on Halcott; discovering an unmarked trail on Hunter that turned a traditional trail hike into a bushwhacking adventure.

To me the Catskills are a potpourri of memories, beginning with an autumn hike around North and South lakes and seeing the vistas from the old Catskill Mountain House and Artist's Rock. Thereon, it was an easy progression from showing off the Catskills to my new wife, to introducing groups of Boys' Club members to an area far removed from their inner-city habitat, to sharing these mountains and my experiences of them with many others. My greatest reward has been, and remains, the number of hikers I've introduced to the Catskills—an area that, for me, symbolizes beauty and grandeur, a reminder that in the days of urban development such a treasure still exists. 🥾

79

THE FIRST OF MANY CATSKILL HIKES

A PIECE OF CAKE?

Lenny Stark
from Winter 1981 *Catskill Canister*

Having spent many years in active Boy Scouting, with mountain experience like escorting Explorer Scouts up Mount Whitney, a short hike to the 3,573-foot summit of Indian Head and possibly Twin would be the proverbial "piece of cake." No thought, however, was given to the fact that the Whitney climb was my most recent hike. My desire to get out is curtailed by those business commitments many of us seem to bump into; mine restrict weekend hiking, since the resort hotel I manage caters to weekend vacationers.

Formally becoming an aspirant to the Catskill 3500 Club, I attended its annual dinner and made a pitch to my table companions to find weekday hikers to show me the way. Richard Davis and I made plans to meet in Kingston at 7:30 to climb Indian Head. I had on my kangaroo leather boots, an old Boy Scout daypack, and layers of clothing to beat the cold. Davis met me with Sam Steen, and those two experienced Catskill climbers readied their gear for my car trunk. They had packs on pack frames, snowshoes, and crampons. Noting all of this, I wondered if I was under-equipped or if they were over-equipped. With due respect for my elders (by at least fifteen years each) and their experience, I opted neither to laugh at nor question them nor their knowledge and skills.

They decided snowshoes were probably not necessary as we hitched up our packs. I took a gulp of fresh air and off we went. After about twenty minutes of walking, I felt in the pink and told my companions that two peaks would indeed be my goal that morning. Richard, nodding his head with an encouraging smile, said he would certainly accommodate me, but advised me to wait till later before deciding. The walk began to ascend a bit and then get steeper. My legs understood this sooner than I. Soon, we were walking on snow and ice-covered parts of the trail. Footing became a little trickier. Time for a breather! Upon the urging of my companions, I took off the first layer of clothing. It was really not too cold out after all—or was it that I was warm? Outer jacket now strapped to my pack, shirt and sweater unbuttoned, we climbed higher (the ascent being measured inch-by-additional-inch through my legs), and the distance between us widened. The breathers came more often and lasted longer. What had happened to my once strong legs? Where had my stamina gone? Was the easy life evidenced around my waist telling me something? Had eleven years of inactivity ruined my hopes of earning a 3500 Club patch?

With great patience and encouragement, they helped me make it to the summit of Indian Head. Sitting on an overlook peering down at Ashokan Reservoir made it worth all the effort. The sound of quiet and the brush of the slightest of breezes melted together in the brightness of the unclouded sun. Isn't this what it's all about? Still, I decided not to subject my companions to the possibility of having to carry me down from the top of Twin. I'd defer that climb until some time after a substantial weight loss and a substantial gain in leg strength and stamina. Perhaps increased jogging and racquetball might help. Now, if I could only get rid of those business commitments …

Our trip down, with Richard's crampons on my boots, was much easier, even though some newly awakened muscles decided to renew their acquaintance with me. We met hikers on their way up and stopped to chat. I noted how smug I seemed even to myself when I smiled and wished them well on their trip. After all, I was finishing my ordeal and they were just starting. Then I realized that my trip was not really over, even though we were heading down. My trip, in fact, had just begun— thirty-three peaks left to go.[1] I couldn't wait to get down to start working on my physical conditioning. Watch out, Slide! 🏃🏃

[1] Southwest Hunter was added as a required peak in 1990.

Lookout Ledge near summit of Indian Head Mountain. Photograph by Carol White.

80

RETURN TO SLIDE MOUNTAIN

PASSING ON THE MEMORIES

John L. Slechta, #1054, #634W
from July–September 1997 *Catskill Canister*

As I hiked up Slide Mountain on a crisp, sunny day one recent February—my final required hike for entry into the 3500 Club—I remembered my father's words from 1958: "You've had more fun on this trip than you've ever had in your life." *I don't think so,* I had thought. But I didn't want to hurt his feelings, so I just nodded my head. I was ten years old at the time. For the first time in my life I had climbed a mountain—and the tallest mountain in the Catskills!

In retrospect, my father's statement was probably correct. I had loved every minute of that trip. We did it together, just the two of us. That in itself was a rare event for a boy with two younger brothers and a father who worked two jobs. And, I'd hiked to the top of a *real* mountain. As a native Long Islander, I was accustomed to seeing mountains only in pictures.

My father and I never hiked up another mountain together. He was too busy working in order to feed and clothe us boys. Thankfully, though, he did manage to schedule two more hikes up Slide—one with each of my brothers.

My next Catskill hike was almost twenty-four years later, in August 1982, with my eleven-year-old daughter Stephanie. At the time I was an inexperienced and woefully ill-equipped hiker, and my route choice almost did me in. We camped at Woodland Valley and hiked up over Wittenberg and Cornell to the summit of Slide; then we backtracked—for a total of fourteen miles on the trail and almost a mile of total ascent. My daughter, with her unlimited supply of youthful energy, had a ball. I was absolutely exhausted and extremely sore, but not discouraged.

Since then, there have been many more hikes in the Catskills and elsewhere. As my other two children, Julie and Matthew, got older, they joined us. While our journeys to the Catskills did not entail the long drive my father and I had endured, the seven-hour round trip from our home in the Finger Lakes region of New York meant that we could only manage an occasional Catskill trek.

February's hike up Slide was a dual milestone. My goal of qualifying for the 3500 Club, a thirty-nine-year odyssey, was about to be achieved—a noteworthy event, and one that was all the more satisfying because Julie and Matthew, now adults, were able to accompany me. But the most significant aspect of the hike to me was that after all these years I was returning to Slide with my father.

Dad had died almost a year earlier, after an extended illness. A humanitarian to the end, he had arranged for his body to be donated to medical science and then to be cremated. Years ago I had asked him what he wanted me to do with his ashes when they were returned to us. "I'd like you to scatter them on top of Slide Mountain," was his reply.

You got your wish, Dad. Thanks for all the wonderful memories. ⚐

Memorial to William Curtis and Allen Ormsbee, builders of the Curtis-Ormsbee Trail to Slide Mountain, who died in a snowstorm on Mount Washington on June 30, 1900. This trail leaves the Phoenicia-East Branch Trail, 0.85 miles south of the Slide-Cornell-Wittenberg Trail. Photograph by Larry Gambon.

81

HELIOGRAPHY ON THOMAS COLE

An Ingenious Experiment

Edward G. West, #45, #40W
from Winter 1973 *Catskill Canister*

Editor's Note: Richard DeLisser wrote in Picturesque Ulster that 3,940-foot Thomas Cole Mountain is visible from 4,180-foot Slide Mountain, but Edward West of Shandaken, former Superintendent of Land Acquisition for the New York State Conservation Department, contended that all the high peaks are visible from Slide except Thomas Cole, for between Slide and Cole arises 4,040-foot Hunter Mountain, 10.6 feet above the line of sight. The direct line of sight, however, is twenty yards lower, 494.6 yards southeast of Hunter's summit fire tower. Factor in a forty-foot fall-away because of the curvature of the earth, and it is nip and tuck!

We proposed an exercise to find out once and for all whether Thomas Cole Mountain can be seen from Slide Mountain. One party would give signals by mirror and light from Thomas Cole, and the other would observe with a Wild T 1 theodolite telescope on Slide. Franklin and Winifred Clark climbed Black Dome with Bill and Elinore Leavitt, David and Ann Clapper, and Bill, Anneliese, and Erika Lawson (#90, the youngest 3500er in 1971, at age 6). The Slide team was made up of myself, Professor Samuel Owen of the College of Engineering at Rutgers University, Richard King, John Mayer, Wayne Hartman, and Rickey, Tommy, and Jim Brooks.

The Cole party would test with the mirror at 2:00 and 2:30 PM from the summit of 3,980-foot Black Dome Mountain, then move quickly to Cole and flash the signal every half hour 3:00 to 4:30. Beginning at 7:30 and continuing until 9:00, signals were to be given with a small searchlight borrowed from the Shandaken Fire Company, concluding with another "dry run" from Black Dome at 9:30 to check the method.

The mirror is an ingenious device for long-distance signaling. A small cross-shaped slit at the center enables the user to look at his target. The sunlight coming through the slit makes a bright cross on the clothing or face of the user, and a small mirror on the reverse side makes it possible to tilt the mirror so that the reflection of the bright cross is superimposed on the slit. Since the angle of incidence equals the angle of reflection, the sun's rays are now directed toward the target. The mirror signal from Black Dome came across the intervening twenty-one miles and, without a glass, looked like a diamond in the sky; through the Wild T 1 theodolite, it was dazzling! Thirty people witnessed the exhibition in amazement.

On Thomas Cole it was necessary to climb a thirty-foot fir tree, and Franklin, Anneliese, and Bill Leavitt took turns climbing it and giving the signal. Franklin hurt a knee in the climb and has had arthritis in that knee ever since. After the 4:30 signal, they made camp and prepared dinner. Then, after dark at 7:30, Bill did all the tree climbing. The light could be seen without the telescope! At 8:30 the signal was exceptionally bright and was seen by eight observers. A spontaneous cheer went up from all. The party on Cole had to wait until the next day to learn whether their efforts had been successful. 𓀀

View north from lookout ledge below Slide Mountain summit. Photograph by David White.

82

FOLLOWING IN MY FATHER'S FOOTSTEPS

HIKE INTO THE PAST

Richard Levine, #852
from July–September 1996 *Catskill Canister*

I was telling my father about some of my hiking experiences, when he interrupted me. "I hiked a peak once," he said. My father was a walker—not one of those vigorous, power walkers of today, but at his prime he kept a fairly steady pace. He told me he climbed Mount Tremper when he was forty. (I started hiking and climbing at age forty-six.) "It was difficult going up, but much easier going down," he went on. After he described his hike, I resolved some day to duplicate it.

At 2,740 feet, Mount Tremper is not one of those peaks sought after by hardcore hikers and climbers, although the total elevation gain is 2,000 feet in three miles. The mountain poses no challenge; it is a straightforward, simple walk up a wide path, much of it smooth.

The day arrived to climb Mount Tremper when two of my hiking companions weren't able to go for a planned weekend outing. So I decided to make the hike an overnight trip, backpacking to the first lean-to on the western slope at 2,100 feet, about two miles from the trailhead. There I set up my tent, left my heavy gear and started toward the summit.

It was a cool day for November, with sudden bursts of wind. The patchy cloud cover constantly changed as I approached the summit. There was no one else about. The closer I came to the summit, the more aware I was of my father's presence. It was sixty years since he had climbed Tremper. I was sixty-five years old now. My father had been dead for twelve years, but his presence, here on Tremper, was overwhelming.

I slowly approached the base of the fire tower at the top of the peak. Looking across the valley, I saw other mountains silhouetted against the sky. My eyes filled with tears as I realized that my father had stood on this same ground. I stooped and picked up some stones, put them in my pocket, and then continued on the trail. 🏃

83

NUMBER TWENTY-SIX

WHERE SLIDE MOUNTAIN GOT ITS NAME

Benjamin Sadock
from Spring 1982 *Catskill Canister*

It was late October, early for the two inches of snow that had fallen the night before. On the way to the summit of Slide Mountain, at times I thought myself to be in another world. There were the ruby and gold leaves, the new snow, branches with melting ice, a strong sun—all the seasons at once. I was with my sixteen-year-old son on my third climb ever.

He popped up out of the woods. The woodsman had two small boys with him. He asked if we would like to see the slide. "That's how the mountain got its name," he said. We dropped off the trail and seemed to fly down and across, down again, snow and wet leaves covering my boots, hands soon numbed by holding myself back by hanging onto the trees. In a few moments they all outdistanced me. I followed their tracks, listening for the cracks of branches breaking, and fighting to keep up. I felt my age. Then, silence. Not even their voices!

I was deep in the woods, out of breath, the slope falling away; then more tracks and I found them, standing at the top of a slide—a white gash in the mountain that seemed to fall away forever as I craned my neck to look downhill. "Would you like to go farther?" he asked, unaware of my just having caught up with them. "Not me," I said. "You all go and I'll wait here." He told me not to stray, that they would be gone just a few minutes." Off they went to see more of the awesome slide.

I was alone, no sound except for the wind whistling through the trees and bringing down ice-heavy branches, the sun still strong, in and out of clouds. I relaxed and took in the uniqueness of the setting, wondering about the forces of nature that caused the falling away of so much of the mountain. It had happened in 1820. In the 1960s the other slide happened—the one they were off to see. The woodsman had seen the new gash from another mountain and come over "and hustled up," as he put it. The fellow was beginning to take on an unreal aspect to me, like some Norse mythological figure who lived in the mountains in winter. Clear-eyed, his body moved effortlessly and gracefully through the woods, not a step wasted. I guessed his age at sixty, but it was difficult to tell—he could have been seventy. He loved the woods, especially the snow. And the boys with him felt safe, learning things just by being with him.

Suddenly there was a twack and he popped up from behind a large pine, pleased, I could tell, at having arrived back at the place where he had left me. I followed them up, taking long, high steps on that steeply angled part of the mountain. My heart was pounding trying to keep up, afraid I might lose them, listening for sounds, looking for tracks in the snow. With a last hard push I was up on the trail. He was there, not breathing hard at all. He smiled and asked if I'd enjoyed the side trip. "That was my first bushwhack," I said, "and now I know what it's like."

Following them down, my son was full of the view of the slide, how steep it was, and that the old man had told him how he had climbed up hand over hand. I had told the man how my son and I hoped to become 3500 Club members, and I asked him his number. "Twenty-six," he said.[1] He volunteered that he had climbed all thirty-four of the mountains in winter, too. "What's left?" I asked. "Well," he said, "we're thinking of getting a patch that is entirely black for those members who climb them all in the dark." I didn't know if he was pulling my leg, but he said that he'd already climbed two that way. ‍🏃🏃

---

[1] George Gyukanov, a charter member of the Catskill 3500 Club.

View of slides on Slide Mountain's north face from a bushwhack to Wittenberg Mountain. Photograph by David White.

84

THE SECRET TO STAYING YOUNG

EIGHTY-THREE AND NOT SHOWING AGE

Ann L. Clapper, #13, #21W

When I was a teenager, my dad, Bill Leavitt, #1 of the Catskill 3500 Club members, and I used to sit on the floor on a Friday night and study topo maps. We would look for places where the contour lines were very close together, and then we would plan a trip to those places. We saw some amazingly beautiful country in the Catskills that way. We would search our way up through the cliffs and delight in the adventure.

Bill (I called him "Will") was eighty-three and not showing his age at all when we did the following hikes in 1995:

On May 6 we hiked to Overlook Mountain from Platte Clove Road via the Catskill Center Trail and the old Overlook Turnpike (built in 1880, now the Overlook Trail.) Beyond the Devil's Kitchen lean-to, the trail crosses the Cold Kill brook and climbs to Codfish Point—the remains of an old bluestone quarry on a short spur trail. We explored the large quarry and talked about life here a century ago. Once, workers were stranded at the quarry for a week during an early spring snow and all they had to eat was codfish. They consumed many boxes and nailed the box lids on trees.

We continued at the 2,600-foot level to the spring, due east of the summit of Plattekill Mountain, and another 0.8 miles to the junction of the trail to Echo Lake. This body of water, formerly called Shues Lake, was a stronghold of Native Americans in the Revolutionary War. It is the only natural lake in a designated wilderness area in the Catskills, and it is the headwaters of the Saw Kill brook. From the Echo Lake junction we climbed 1.4 miles to the junction with the trail from Woodstock, a half mile from the summit.

We took the short side trip to the old Overlook Mountain House ruins, a hotel first built in 1871. The first hotel was destroyed by fire in 1875; rebuilding ceased with the stock market crash in 1929. We explored the old cellar where the bar had been, and remembered great family lunches there. We explored upper floors where the view was great—but the floors and stairs were not in good condition. I fell on rotten stairs and crawled across a floor where floorboards were missing. We saw music staffs and notes painted on the side of the building, and musical notations were painted on rocks all along the old road.

My brother had fallen in the Cold Kill brook on a winter hike in the early 1950s, and we then continued to hike four miles with him in wet clothing. We built a fire in the big hotel fireplace to dry him out. My dad and I marveled that we'd continued the hike with my brother in wet clothes; we didn't know as much about hypothermia back then! The boy was always falling in the water, and we usually tried not to let it ruin our day.

After exploring the hotel, we climbed toward the summit and found a sunny ledge for lunch with good views of Woodstock, the Ashokan Reservoir, and Slide Mountain. We bushwhacked off the summit and came to Eagle Cliff, a famous old summit landmark. The route down to the trail was beautiful with purple trillium, spring beauty, trout lily, and bluets.

On May 19 we explored the col between Indian Head and Plattekill Mountain. At Devil's Kitchen lean-to we left the trail to follow the Cold Kill up to its source. We found campsites in a beautiful hemlock stand, continued until the stream petered out, followed plastic flags and found ourselves on the DEC trail to Indian Head—this would never do! We'd been on a Cold Kill tributary. We headed southwest and found the elusive Cold Kill, stopping at a hunters' camp. The col was

Echo Lake. Photograph by Larry Gambon.

beautiful, long and flat with a dry streambed winding across it. We hiked across to an old trail that headed down into the Sawkill Valley and east up Plattekill, passing the remains of a house, an old bluestone quarry, and an old road ascending toward Indian Head. We had to know all about that—so we'd be back!

The climb up Plattekill through rock outcrops was very beautiful. We found a good view east for a summit lunch. Descending the south ridge was a great choice, with fine views of Overlook and Echo Lake. Someone was rowing a boat across the lake, leaving a large wake. We cut east in an area with mountain laurel, and descended quickly to the Overlook Turnpike.

On May 27 we explored more. I had to know how we'd lost our way! Our friend Bonnie Maroney came along for another great adventure, and this time when we left the lean-to we were prepared with a compass bearing. The brook disappeared, so no wonder we lost it! We hiked at 245° and found it again. The top of the col is an hour away from the lean-to. We found the old road heading up Indian Head and followed it to another interesting bluestone quarry where a large pile of quarried stone was ready to be transported out. We bushwhacked through very steep cliffs up the east side of Indian Head, with Will scouting the best routes. Once he even found a way through a cave! He said he found that just to keep things interesting. We came to the Indian Head trail at 3400 feet and went up to Pulpit Rock for lunch. 🏃

85

TAKE TIME TO SMELL THE FLOWERS

EXPLORING KAATERSKILL HIGH PEAK

Ann L. Clapper, #13, #21W

It looked as though it would rain on this mid-June day. The weatherman said we should take advantage of the day, however, so we did. My father, Will, and I left the car at Devil's Kitchen on Platte Clove Road and hiked the DEC trail north toward High Peak. We met a couple who said it was socked-in at the top. Another couple was looking for Huckleberry Point, so I gave them a map. At 3,000 feet we decided to bushwhack up the east ridge of High Peak. After a quarter mile we came to the snowmobile trail that encircles the mountain. We continued our course and soon were following an old trail that stayed to the south side of the ridge, which explained why we'd never found it before. It provided a gentle ascent and was quite easy to follow. In an overgrown section, three fluffy baby partridges flew out; their mother was right behind them, scolding us severely. She tried to lure us away, and I apologized to her for the inconvenience.

We lost the trail at very steep cliffs and scrambled up looking for the best route. It was beautiful here, with pinkster and bluets in bloom all over. I took time to smell the flowers and pointed out that it was important to do this ... life is too short. The ascent was very interesting now. We were crawling up and clinging to trees and rocks. On top, we heard an engine running—a very steady sound. We came to an old airplane crash site, and the sound seemed to be coming from the plane itself. This was eerie! I couldn't see any engine. Will noticed the end of a porcupine sticking out of one of the wing sections. He was chewing on the aluminum—the source of the "engine" sound. I couldn't believe his chewing could be that regular for such a long time! We didn't disturb him, and he kept chewing.

Just above the crash site we discovered a trail toward the summit that connected with the trail we'd been following, and we were on top in five minutes. We headed toward the southern lookout for lunch and watched ominous clouds over on Indian Head; it looked like we were going to get wet. I had a ham radio and called my husband David on two meters. I tried the .21 repeater and accessed at least three machines. I'm sure folks on Long Island could hear me well! David came on, and we decided on a direct frequency that was much quieter. Will also called David on his cell phone. We heard the phone ringing over the radio, and soon David was talking to us through two speakers. It was probably a good thing we were alone on the mountain!

We took our time descending the very steep south face of High Peak and walked through fields of nettles on the snowmobile trail. I used my rain jacket to protect my legs from the stings. We headed east toward the trail where we'd come in, and after fifteen minutes still hadn't found it. I announced that we were lost. We both laughed and Will said, "When all else fails, use the map and compass." We'd been traveling almost south, instead of east, walking parallel to the trail we were trying to find. We came to the trail in five minutes. It's easy to get turned around on a cloudy day if you are not watching your compass. Could that be a lesson? 🏃

Vista to Kaaterskill High Peak and Roundtop Mountain above North-South Lake.
Photograph by Larry Gambon.

Part IX:
CATSKILL
MOUNTAIN HIGHS

Any trail you hike will offer new wonders in each season. The woods will grow and change, the wildlife will move with the food and water supply. Go and enjoy your discoveries. As John Muir said, "Climb the mountains and get their good tidings. Nature's peace will flow into you as sunshine into flowers, the winds will blow their freshness into you and the storm their energy, and cares will drop off like autumn leaves."

Joan Dean

Photograph by Larry Gambon.

86

FRANK'S STORY

HOOKED ON HIKING AT AGE SEVENTY-THREE

Dr. Susan L. Puretz, #1208, #455W
from the *Saugerties Times,* September 2005

What do you do to celebrate your eighty-second birthday? If you are Frank Serravallo, you invite twenty-four people to join you on a hike up Balsam Lake Mountain—a 3,720-foot Catskill peak—not to commemorate your birthday, but to share the completion of your latest goal to climb all thirty-five Catskill peaks over 3,500 feet high, over the age of eighty.

Frank has both the summer and winter Catskill 3500 Club patches, but what was significant about the Balsam Lake hike on August 13, 2005, was that he had re-climbed all thirty-five peaks for the third time, but this go-round he was over eighty!

While Frank has lived in the Catskills all his life, he is relatively new to hiking the mountains. He took his first Catskill 3500 hike at the age of seventy-three. Although he didn't hike until recently, Frank has always been physically active. As a young boy growing up in Glasco, Frank organized, managed and played sand-lot baseball—later turning that passion into managing Little League and Babe Ruth teams for fourteen years. Frank also wanted to be a professional fighter and trained daily for two and a half years by running six miles and then working out with a punching bag before going to work. An interest in roller-skating followed, and for almost four years he could be found every night of the week at the Route 9W roller rink.

Then along came Vivian, whom he married in 1946, and he rechanneled his energy into raising a family and community service. He is the proud father of two, grandfather of four, and great-grandfather of four. He is also a member of St. Mary's of the Snow, where he has been an usher since 1960 and a head usher for the last seventeen years. He began his work life in the Ice Houses of Glasco. That was followed by work in the brickyards, where he loaded boats, then came work in dress factories, and finally he became a construction worker.

During that time, his enthusiasm for activity never waned. He became interested in water skiing in the early 1970s. For five years it would not be uncommon to see Frank and his two sons starting out on the Hudson River in Saugerties, water skiing to Kingston, turning around and heading up to Catskill, then back to Kingston, and finally finishing in Saugerties. Frank and Vivian walk regularly, and Frank also rode his bike around town. It was because he had ridden his bike to a defensive driving course at the Saugerties American Legion that he became involved with the Rip Van Winkle Hikers—a local Saugerties hiking group. Frank had newly met a fellow participant, Gil Hales, during the driving course. At day's end Gil saw Frank get on his bike and asked what Frank did for other exercise. Satisfied with Frank's answer, Gil invited him to join the hiking club, and the rest is history.

Once he took that first hike, he knew hiking was for him; he was hooked. Frank found the mountain a challenge and, as he says, "I have always liked challenges." One particular challenge occurred on March 11, 2002, climbing up the back end of Slide Mountain, at 4,180 feet the highest peak in the Catskills.[1] The mountain was covered with a layer of ice because of a late-winter storm, and the footing was treacherous. Frank fell, slid upside down over the boulders and came close to plunging down the mountain, but grabbed a fir branch that stopped his slide. It was a close call. Because of the hand injury he sustained during the episode and the icy conditions, the hikers did not get off the mountain until 9:00 PM. They hiked the last three or so hours in the dark with the aid of a few headlamps. When they got back to the parking lot, they had a champagne celebration to honor a fellow hiker's accomplishment of climbing all thirty-five peaks in the winter. Frank was very proud that the champagne he was carrying for the celebration didn't break during his fall.

Frank is known to be afraid of bears, especially one with cubs, and after two years of yodeling to scare bears, the inevitable finally happened. On a descent from Friday Mountain in the Slide Wilderness, Frank was out in the lead by himself and encountered a bear. Lucky for all concerned, neither party wanted to get acquainted.

Frank has lots of hiking memories. Two years ago on a Rip Van Winkle moonlight hike up Overlook Mountain, Frank and two other men ran down the mountain so that they could get home in time to see a Monday night football game. Frank was a young eighty years old. He has also participated in the Rip Van Winkle Hikers annual Halloween Hike. It is a dress–up affair, and what better costume for Frank for the first inaugural event than to go as Rip Van Winkle? His picture taken on that hike is now the logo and adorns the club patch and business cards. Frank's second costume hasn't been topped; he went as a pregnant woman who ended up breaking water and delivering her baby on a bench below the Overlook Fire Tower—with the able assistance of several club members. So good was Frank's costume, that even many of his close friends had trouble identifying him.

It's not surprising that when Frank took up hiking, he would do it enthusiastically and with commitment. He has lived his life that way. Often on hikes he'll recount how he met Vivian, his wife of fifty-nine years, their dancing to the local bands, their favorite hangouts and music, and raising their sons. When a hike is done he looks forward to a warm meal and spending the evening with her. Vivian, according to Frank, is the best cook the world has ever seen. She is also, fortunately for him, completely supportive of his hiking.

When asked if he had a favorite hike, he answered that all his hikes were good ones and that the last mountain he had climbed always seemed the best … that is, until the next hike. He continued, "It is also good to know that with every hike, I've accomplished something." A notable goal for someone who first started hiking when he was seventy-three!

With his presence on the Monday hikes of the Rip Van Winkle Hikers, he has become a role model for many club members who are approaching or are in their seventies. Don Dobbs, a club member, summed it up: "Frank proves to them that older people can continue to challenge themselves and accomplish many physical feats once thought to be the sole province of younger people." 🏃

---

[1] See "Night Falls Early."

Frank Serravallo. Photograph by Susan Puretz.

87

THE CATSKILLS:
A NEW ENGLANDER'S PERSPECTIVE

A CATSKILLS CONVERT

Bob Parlee, #1661
from July–September 1999 *Catskill Canister*

A New Englander from the Boston area, I have hiked extensively throughout the Northeast for many years, from the summits of Baxter Park in Maine to the Taconic Hills near the Massachusetts-Connecticut border. As a card-carrying member of the Appalachian Mountain Club (AMC), it seems I'm supposed to have regional myopia in terms of hiking destinations. We're allowed the occasional fray into the Adirondack High Peaks. Other mountain ranges west of the Hudson are either unknown or have been deemed unworthy by the New England hiking establishment.[1]

On countless occasions while hiking in northern New England, I've mentioned the Catskills as a worthwhile destination. The response is usually one of lukewarm interest: "Are there mountains there?" or, "Isn't that a hilly place with a lot of big hotels?" I've been making two or three trips a year to the Catskills for the last ten years. I'm truly shocked that more New Englanders haven't discovered these fine mountains.

When I was a youngster, my family made an extended camping trip one summer down the Eastern Seaboard. On our way back we stopped for a few nights at North Lake Campground. The beautiful escarpment cliffside and the deer roaming through the campground cemented my love for this area. Ten years later, while visiting a friend, we made a trip to Wittenberg Mountain on a sunny fall day. From then on, I've been a true Catskill devotee. I've managed to persuade my girlfriend to give the Catskills a chance, and she's hooked, too. Our trips to the Catskills have provided me with enduring memories as cherished as those from anywhere else: seeing a deer drinking midstream from the East Branch of the Neversink River near Denning; spying a speckled native brook trout finning in a clear pool in Donovan Brook on the slopes of Lone Mountain. I've witnessed beautiful mountain vistas such as the endless waves of hills that can be seen from Doubletop's summit ledges. While descending the north slope of Panther, I passed through a cathedral grove of hardwoods. My girlfriend and I have found our way through the thick evergreen growth between Friday and Cornell to emerge at Cornell's fine summit outlook. We've marveled at the diverse old-growth forest of maple, hemlock, spruce and yellow birch on the middle slopes of West Kill. On the same trip, we enjoyed a sun-warmed, late-spring day atop West Kill looking south at the pastel-green valley that leads to Phoenicia and the Esopus Valley.

I feel lucky and privileged to be a New Englander who loves the Catskills. The drive time from the Boston area to the Catskills is about the same as to the mountains of western Maine. If more New Englanders took the time to venture into the Catskills, I'm sure they would become Catskill converts. To me, the Catskills truly represent our eastern mountains and need not be defended against any other "competing" mountain region. 🏃

[1] Since then, AMC has published a guide to Catskill trails.

Kaaterskill Falls. Photograph by Larry Gambon.

88

THE KATSKILL KID

A MOUNTAIN JUNKIE IS HOOKED ON THE CATSKILLS

Robert A. Forrest, #278
from Summer 1978 *Catskill Canister*

Sometimes at parties I am introduced as a mountain junkie, and people expect me to regale them with stories of clinging to precipices with my eyelashes while dodging falling rocks. I do have some of these tales to tell, but a number of my best stories—and some of my favorite memories—concern the Catskills, which makes some people downright uncomfortable.

When I first approached the Catskills, I did so with ambivalence. Yes, I wanted to climb mountains, but no, I did not want to climb the Catskills. I suffered under the delusion, borne by most people, that the Catskills are a region of decaying hotels, racetracks, and neon signs that could blind anyone not wearing sunglasses. The Catskills are composed of sedimentary rock, slippery moss, a bit of blowdown, and a lot of bugs—or snow—depending on the season. The word "peak" brings to mind a pinnacle cleaving the sky, so climbing in the Catskills is not strictly speaking "peak bagging"; think of it, rather, as "plateau collecting." Initially I cared only to climb the two 4,000-footers toward my 111, and I did so. I found not wilderness, but wildness, which was quite satisfying. So I returned.

My impecunious status as a graduate student and later as a researcher made me firmly tied to New Jersey and vicinity. The White Mountains were assuredly beyond a weekend's striking distance. My first trip to the Catskills was late in the winter, and I spent the first night sleeping on a miniature glacier in the cave on Wittenberg Mountain. The wind was blowing a mixture of rain and pine needles onto my upturned face, and I could not quite make up my mind whether to swallow or to spit. Later on, fog moved in and I could not see the foot of my sleeping bag. Still later, I felt something at my back and turned to find the world's biggest raccoon grinning at me.

Then, one evening in June, I stood at the edge of the escarpment on the site of the Catskill Mountain House. The sun was low in the sky and my shadow cast itself halfway to the Hudson River. At that moment I realized I was hooked on the Catskill region. I have returned often since then, mostly to climb the 3,500-foot peaks. I started haphazardly, and had racked up over a dozen Catskill peaks before I ever saw a topographical map of the area.

I determined that I wanted to complete the project alone. Some people have asked me, "Is climbing trailless peaks, alone, the safest thing in the world?" I can only answer, "It's safer than driving." Being alone in the mountains has never bothered me, but it does bother me to be alone while I drive home. I sometimes wish for a companion capable of doing some of the driving or of keeping me awake with conversation. Instead, I rely on the car's irritating radio to stave off sleep. Once, I considered wearing my Joe Brown rock-climbing hat so that if I fell asleep at the wheel I would stand a chance of surviving a crash; but I decided to camp instead, and thereby keep everyone safer. Sometimes I found myself talking to the trees and shrubs by Sunday morning. All the same, I was reluctant to share my Catskill trips. Several times, when the girl I was seeing suggested that we hike together in the Catskills, I changed the topic of conversation.

Unlike other Eastern ranges, I see more deer than people in the Catskills. I've seen many porcupines, one of them trying to eat my car and another menacing me with thousands of quills when I criticized its choice of breakfast. It ambled off only when I yelled too loud for it to enjoy the feast.

Twin Mountain from Sugarloaf Mountain. Photograph by Larry Gambon.

As spring moved the green leaves higher up the mountains, finding the summit registers on the trailless peaks became challenging and, on Friday and Fir, time-consuming. I praised orange canisters for their high visibility.

The worst blowdown I encountered was on a bushwhack up Friday Mountain when I came up from the Neversink too close to Cornell. There I learned the origin of the expression, "That's as easy as falling off a log." Persevering—at a snail's pace—I won through and chalked up the conquest of Friday to clean living, a liberal education, and being thin enough to pass through the scrubby trees. Blowdown resulted in bloodshed on Rocky; I lost a fight with a branch that took a chunk out of my right hand. I bled like a stuck pig until I bandaged myself; later I enjoyed the sympathy of my co-workers, who thought I had been seriously injured.

Every time I am on the Devil's Path, I look everywhere for covens of witches performing their odd rituals, but so far I have had no luck. In gloomy weather the Devil's Path is aptly named, for the dark rock ledges, the sound of running water, and the absence of light beneath the tree canopies, all contribute to a nether-world effect. It is a special place.

There have been disagreeable times, too. On Doubletop one August, a thunderstorm overtook me just after I left the summit, and the streambed I was following down became an inclined skating rink. I slipped and stumbled endlessly. On Bearpen one October, a careless hunter zinged a shot over my head. Appropriately outraged, I cursed him roundly and then shouted, "Do I look like a grouse?" I was nervous for days afterwards and had to give up watching violent shows like Kojak. For the rest of the fall I cowered in the deepest recesses of the library.

Mountains, in general, and the Catskills in particular, mean a great deal to me. I was very proud when, having written of some of my Catskill adventures to a friend in Seattle, I received by return mail a postcard addressed to "The Katskill Kid." 𝄆

89

AUTUMN IN THE CATSKILLS

No Place I'd Rather Be

Peter C. Ricci, #475, #171W
from October–December 2001 *Catskill Canister*

The crumple of leaves beneath my feet and cool, evergreen-scented air filling my nostrils with each breath I take remind me why autumn is my favorite time in the woods. The trail is covered with a carpet of brightly colored leaves with fingers of gnarled roots stretched out across the trail as if to grasp the remaining days of summer. As I scramble up ledges, the gentle breeze soon accelerates to a roar and trees sway in a hypnotic dance to a haunting tune. My breath is swept away by cold currents. Out upon the open ledges of Wittenberg Mountain, I look through crisp, clear air towards the Ashokan Reservoir laid out below like a pane of glass with jagged edges offering no reflection on this windy day. Dramatic clouds with hues of gray, shaped like figurines, parade in the sky.

Onward through the causeway to Cornell Mountain, where a couple of good handholds and moves short of gymnastic maneuvers help me get up the V-shaped cliff and onto the summit. Looking back at Wittenberg, I see the definite profile of the southeast face plunge down into the hollow. The long stroll through the Cornell-Slide col is accompanied by the sound of branches interacting, a sound that crescendos as wind funnels through the col. A day like today instills a sense of peace, but it is not a quiet serenity.

Finally, the base of Slide Mountain, where I look up and see ledge upon ledge that form the battlements of the mountains, wondering where I go from here. As I ascend, the trail bobs and weaves through weaknesses and cracks in the rock walls. Months ago I would be struggling with heat and humidity that saps even robust hikers of strength, but with cool air that seems to caress and invigorate, the pipe spring high up on Slide's east shoulder is easily reached—a spring that retains its magical aura and provides water for the parched no matter what time of the year.[1]

On the summit, expansive views provide feasts for the eyes. I scan down to the undulating field of colors dropping into dark abysses of the valley, and then seek out far horizons and clouds giving way to hues of blue. The wind is dying down

Autumn woods in the Catskill Forest Preserve. Photograph by Larry Gambon.

and the air seems to be at peace with itself. There is no other place in this world I would rather be but here. On the back of Slide, the trail takes me down gently. I look over the east side to the ridge that forms the backbone of the Giant Ledge-Panther massif; Giant Ledge will be this evening's campsite.

Leaving the spruce, pines, and ferns, I enter hardwood forest and carefully make my way down on leaves that cover rocks waiting for the unsuspecting hiker to make a false move. With camp set up on Giant Ledge, I relax after dinner taking in the sunset. A woodpecker jackhammers a distance away; chipmunks gather their winter supply. Woods can be so quiet, yet so alive. Sunset signals the end of another day; once-bright rays tempered to a soft yellow glow reflect a fiery inferno through thin layers of wispy clouds.

The next day is overcast, and I pack up and start the long and gentle descent to Woodland Valley. In spite of being overcast, however, the vivid colors shout brilliance. Reds, yellows and oranges compete for attention. Even the bark from trees stands out. Every now and then I look to my right, up to the top of Slide, to see its crown of firs peek through as though the mountain is saying "until next time."

---

[1] I have seen this spring dry only once. *Ed.*

90

FINDING PEACE IN THE CATSKILLS

AFTER 9/11

Snapper Petta

It was September 25, 2001. As the director of outdoor programs for the State University College in Oneonta, New York, I should have been getting ready to leave on an extended trip that was planned for our September break. Unfortunately, the events of two weeks prior had put a halt to that. Every student I knew wanted nothing more than the opportunity to go home and spend time with family. Even our "die hard" outdoor kids were craving the security and warmth of being home. The tragedy of September 11 had affected all of them in ways with which they were only beginning to come to grips.

For me it was the opposite. I needed to get away. The woods have always been my sanctuary. As I've told many a clergy member, I feel closer to my Creator when I'm in the woods than anywhere else. Thankfully I also have a loving and understanding wife who is willing to put up with this small quirk of mine. So for me it was set: I would still be going to the woods, albeit alone and for a much shorter period of time—just overnight.

Although my wife loves and understands me, she's still not thrilled when I go off alone. I didn't want to worry her any more than necessary, so the idea of one night away seemed to fit what both of us needed—time away for me, but not too much time for her. As it turned out, she was hosting a household of friends the evening I planned to be gone, so my presence wouldn't be missed.

Now—where to go? Living in central New York, the Catskills were the perfect location. It's a region that has shaped my very being; I've been a frequent visitor since childhood. As a kid my dad regularly took me trout fishing on the fabled Esopus. We would fish near Phoenicia and occasionally climb Mount Tremper to visit with the ranger who manned the fire tower. I can still remember our post-trip outings to Folkert's store, where we'd look over the colorful trout flies, housed in their glass display cases, while eating the best ice cream imaginable.

My years at scout camp were spent in the region as well. One of my favorite trips was to hike from the main camp over to Alder Lake (then owned by the Nassau County, New York, Boy Scouts of America Council) which served as an outpost site. Sometimes we would hike over and back in one day; this was the goal for achieving my hiking merit badge. On other occasions we'd pack our canvas "Yucca" packs and spend the night, hiking back the next day after an evening of sleeping under the stars. While there, we heard stories about the former caretaker who trained animals for Walt Disney movies. Our imaginations also worked overtime whenever we walked past the old Coykendall mansion; especially at night when visions of ghosts and other specters filled our young heads.

I've spent the last twenty-six years leading college students on trips in the region. About twenty weekends a year I'm out sharing the history, lore and mystique of the Catskills with my students while we hike, snowshoe, cross-country ski, or work at our two "adopted" lean-tos. Each trip is its own unique adventure of discovery and reassurance. Regardless of the season, the Catskills continue to enrich my life.

So, there it was … my decision was made … I was going to the Catskills! But where? Although small in comparison to other wilderness regions, the Catskills still cover a considerable amount of terrain. After consulting my maps and guidebooks, I settled on hiking to a lean-to that sits on the western flank of Balsam Lake Mountain. The hike in would take me back to Alder Lake and along the new hiking trail that traverses from the lake to the mountain's summit. I hadn't been back there since my old scout days, so it would be a chance to become reacquainted with an old friend. The morning of the 27th dawned brightly, and with it my escape began. Autumn colors had crept quietly into the surrounding hillsides. Peak color hadn't arrived yet and there was a nice mixture of green in amongst the red, yellow and golden leaves. It was the perfect appetizer to the main course that still lay ahead.

Just yards from the Alder Lake registration box I came upon the old manor house. Set off by elaborate stone walls that line the drive, Mr. Coykendall's former lodge still allows a glimpse into its magnificent past. Every window is broken, yet it's easy to imagine the sublime views they once offered of the lake and surrounding mountains. The substantial porch, where guests were once greeted before being swallowed by the huge entryway, still stands as a testament to the wealth of its former owner.

A short walk down the lawn led me to the lake. The dam that created Alder Lake continues to be rock solid, while the spillway under the bridge remains a focal point of interest. As Catskill lakes go, Alder Lake is a rather large sheet of water. Surrounded by Balsam Lake Mountain to the east and rolling hills to the west, the peacefulness of the setting quickly settled my mind. The solitude and quiet were exactly what I was seeking. Heading counterclockwise on the trail, it didn't take long to discover why the old-timers say the Catskills are made up of "one part dirt to three parts rock." Loose rock and small stones are constant companions on many Catskill trails, and this one is no exception. Since sound footing requires constant vigilance, I was fortunate to get an occasional glimpse of the lake through the forest. Within a half mile of leaving the lake, I came upon the intersection where a new trail headed east to the lean-to.

From this point on I was in new territory. This trail didn't exist when I was a scout; it wasn't built until 1997. I instantly felt comfortable on this new route. A small stream paralleled my travel, accompanying me most of the way up to the campsite. My fluid companion made itself known through its tumbling waters, still pools and cool air as I hiked the trail corridor. It was the quintessential Catskill scene, exactly as I had hoped it would be.

Even taking time to "stop and smell the roses," it didn't take long to cover the one and a half miles up to the shelter. As I'd anticipated (and hoped), there wasn't another person in the woods that day. Although the flight ban had been lifted, no planes flew over the local airspace that afternoon. It seemed to me that this could be the closest anyone would ever get in the twenty-first century to experiencing the quiet sounds of the woods all people knew prior to the Wright brothers' creation.

Arriving at the lean-to, I dropped my pack and took a breather. Sitting on the deacon's bench, sipping from my water bottle, I looked over the old beaver meadow that fronts the site. Russet-tinged grasses seemed alive as they swayed to and fro in the gentle breeze. Across the meadow dappled leaves fell lazily to the ground, adding to the movement of the scene. It was impossible to sit there and not be embraced by a feeling of serenity.

I set about getting ready for the night. The guidebook informed me that there was a spring behind the lean-to on the other side of the trail, so I set off to find it. I heard the rushing water before I actually saw it, and filled my water bag. I rummaged in my pack for the forty feet of rope I was carrying to throw my "bear bag" line, while it was still light; I've watched too many people wait until dark to do this simple chore. If they're lucky, it only leads to some frustrating moments in the darkness, but I've witnessed more than one person narrowly escape being hit by the weight, usually a rock, attached to the end of their line as it bounces off the tree limb at which they've aimed. Being alone, it was important to eliminate any chance of potential injury, major or minor.

Next on my agenda was setting up housekeeping for the evening. I laid out my down sleeping bag, fluffing up the loft to ensure maximum insulation, and opened the valve on my sleeping pad. Numerous knee operations have sold me on the value of an air- and foam-filled mattress for sleeping. I set off to gather a small supply of firewood. I'm a firm believer in cooking with a stove, but I still enjoy a small evening campfire. Since a well-maintained fireplace was part of this campsite, I wasn't going to miss out on spending quality time gazing into the glowing coals of the wilderness version of television.

Coykendall Lodge, Alder Lake.
Photograph by Larry Gambon.

Then I noticed the slight change in the clouds. The forecast had suggested a quick-moving front would travel through the area sometime that night. It was apparent from the clouds' changing shapes and graying coloration that the rain would arrive soon. With the weather on a downward trend, I got out my stove, fired it up and quickly prepared dinner. Being alone, I hadn't planned on anything elaborate; the standard one-pot rice meal embellished with cashews and curry was more than enough for me. It was only a matter of minutes until I was dining "al fresco" along the banks of the stream. With dinner cooked and eaten and the pot washed, I brushed my teeth, hung my food bag and settled in for a soggy evening.

Since the rain was still in the offing, I made a small campfire in the fireplace by the lean-to. Enthroned once again on the deacon's bench, reveling in the luxury of my sleeping pad/chair, it wasn't long before I was entranced by the fire. Delicate yellow-orange flames danced amongst the fuel, creating life from the dead wood as freshly exposed pockets of gas popped, exploded and hissed, sending sparks skyward. As the evening progressed, the flames died down to a bed of glowing red, casting an eerie shadow of light inside the shelter. Staring into the dying embers, a feeling of everything "being right with the world" came over me. The comfort, solitude and serenity I had earnestly searched for now wrapped me in their collective warmth. I was at peace in the Catskills.

It wasn't long before that reflective mood was broken. A *hissss* came from the fireplace; a soft but steady drizzle had begun. Knowing the rain would keep the remaining coals in check, I dashed to the outhouse for a last visit. Back in the shelter, my chair was rapidly transformed into a sleeping pad and, snuggled inside my personal cocoon, I listened to one of my favorite sounds—rain falling on the shelter roof. With nature's lullaby playing softly overhead, sleep came quickly.

An hour or so later I awoke to moonlight flooding the interior of the lean-to. The rain had stopped and there was enough light to see a breakup in the clouds. I picked out the Big Dipper and heard a familiar seasonal sound. The honking of Canada geese grew louder as their V came into sight. Silhouetted against the sky, the intensity of their calls added to the moment. I listened as the gradually retreating sound winged its way out of earshot.

The next morning dawned bright, beautiful and damp. Rain had drenched the area; my surroundings were dressed in droplets of water. The world had been washed clean overnight. Soon breakfast was ready to go. Oatmeal energized with granola, a heavily laden bagel (oh how I love crunchy peanut butter), a steaming mug of cocoa and a handful of raisins were a fitting beginning to the new day. Within an hour I was on my way. All the vegetation lining the trail was wet.

Not long into the morning I stopped dead in my tracks. I wasn't sure if my eyes were playing tricks with my mind. A small bear, about twenty yards off the trail, was clinging to a tree's main trunk. The bruin's coloration blended in well with the forest shadows, but movement gave his location away. What an incredible gift! To be able to observe this animal in its natural setting was truly awesome. I watched as the bear held tightly to its anchor. He neither went up nor down. He was as frozen in his tracks as I was. In order not to disturb the critter any further, I slowly slipped away. Watching carefully out of the corner of my eye, I lost sight of the bear as my travels took me through a hedgerow of elderberry bushes that lined the trail. It was here that the next surprise ambushed me.

Glancing downward my eyes came to rest on a large, purple, seed-filled pile of scat! Bear scat!! BIG BEAR SCAT!!! The hairs on my neck instantly stood at attention; Momma was somewhere nearby. Suddenly the morning's silence was interrupted by a startled voice—mine. "Hey, Momma, it's okay, Momma, I'm on my way out of here, Momma …" Loud, non-rhythmic whistling followed. My pace and pulse quickened. Whatever calm demeanor I might have displayed moments before was now replaced with a dedicated urge to get out of there. I was a guest in the bear's home, and I wasn't about to overstay my welcome. Although the small bear I had seen was no longer a cub, I knew his maternal protector couldn't be far off. Not wanting to rile her, I hotfooted it out of there.

The furiousness of my pace brought the lake into view much sooner than expected. With the trip's end being less than a half hour away, it was an appropriate moment to take a break and put my journey into perspective. Why had I come? That was the question that repeated itself. The initial reason was to get away from everything that had occurred as a result of the September 11 tragedy. I wanted to get away, find solace, and reconnect with nature to find life's beauty again. Had that been accomplished? The answer was a resounding yes! Once again the Catskill Mountains had lifted my soul. Their magic and hidden treasures, available to all who seek them, rewarded me with an inner calm. It was this sense of peace and tranquility that would carry me through the trying times that lay ahead of us all. 🥾

91

THE LAST TRIP IS ALWAYS THE BEST ONE[1]

FOLLOWING IN MY SON'S FOOTSTEPS

Dick Sederquist, #905, #349W

The last hiking trip I took with my son is always the best one we've ever had. Each trip builds on the past. We remember all the good times and look forward to many more. Our conversations touch on many topics, a lot of them just plain funny and inane, like weird and disgusting food groups and "What would you rather do?" questions Jeff asks, with totally irrational choices to pick from. We talk about what we are doing, what we did last time, and what we will do next time. Sometimes we talk seriously about life and death, how the forest and mountains transcend us all, how we owe our very existence to the wilderness.

Some of our trips are single-day excursions; often we backpack. Sometimes we stay in a motel for a few nights and hike each day. That's best during really cold weather; I've never been keen on winter camping. Even in cold weather, carrying a heavy pack makes me sweat, despite layering down next to nothing. The extra weight in dry clothes just compounds the discomfort. I'd rather slog from dawn to dusk and stay in a warm motel. A hot shower, a few beers, a satisfying meal and a warm, dry bed are my rewards for a good day. Hiking, I rationalize, is all about rewards.

Jeff and I have been doing this for thirty-four years, since he was four years old. The only change is, now I'm the one keeping up with him! I don't mind following in his footsteps, particularly when he is breaking trail on snowshoes. Nowadays, we're able to make most of our winter objectives because he takes the lead and tirelessly tramples down the deep snow.

The last time I led in winter was when he came home from college for a quick two-day, end-of-winter hiking trip to the Catskills. That late in the season, I hoped that previous ice storms would have consolidated the snow, but there were two feet of soft powder at the trailhead. After a mile, we left the trail for the bushwhack to Doubletop Mountain. The higher we climbed, the deeper the snow became. I started out in the lead, hoping Jeff would spell me as the terrain steepened; I'd stop and let him pass. Within minutes, I'd find myself back in the lead, waist-deep in snow on an ever-increasing pitch. Jeff silently pursued me, without his usual enthusiasm. Too many beers with a high-school buddy the night before had resulted in a queasy stomach and throbbing head. Was this not going to be one of those memorable trips?

When we finally summited Doubletop, Jeff plopped down in a clearing among the spruce. I tossed him a bag of sliced pepperoni. "See if this helps!" As I peered at Graham Mountain, our next objective, a hand touched my shoulder. My son was grinning. Either pepperoni contains an instant wonder drug, or it was the miracle of youth, but something had kicked in. He led the rest of the hike. Conversation poured out of him. "What would you rather do," he asked, "jump off this cliff or be eaten by a mountain lion?" Jeff, with his "what would you rather do?" questions, was back. The rest of the day passed without any hint of his earlier malaise. That night after dinner, he fell asleep at 7:30, and I was asleep a half hour later. Another great trip to remember! 🏃

---

[1] This is an earlier, edited version of "The Last Trip," published in *Hiking Out: Surviving Depression with Humor and Insight along the Way*, by Dick Sederquist, 2007, Publishing-Works, Inc., Exeter, New Hampshire.

Catskill stream. Photograph by Larry Gambon.

92

ASHOKAN HIGH POINT HIGH

HIGH POINT HIGHS

Jeff Green

Kanape Brook is beautiful. Stunning. Incredible. Fantabulous. I'm a flatlander (do the Hudson Highlands count?), 220 pounds (forty excess), my knees are bad and I've got asthma, so hikes like this are special for me. If I don't "bag the peak," I don't get upset; I just find other aspects of the hike that satisfy. If one only walks to the col between Ashokan High Peak and Mombaccus Mountain on this hike, one should be filled with satisfaction.

I start walking and it's really nice; there's oxygen in the air, and the trail isn't too steep or rocky. When I start to huff and puff, I just look into the chasm and admire the rushing brook. You pass an old stone well whose water looks potable. At just over two and a half miles and after about one hour of walking/climbing, I reach the grassy col between the mountains. People ask me if I thought the loop would be a better ascent than directly up the mountain. There's a loop? No one's ever mentioned a loop before. Not in my books, and my 1996 fifth edition maps have only a broken black line going up the mountain.

I tell them that slow and steady is my motto, so I'll be going straight up— and off I go. Slow and steady. Up and up and up. It's not bad; the six ledges are well-marked and easily within the skills of almost any hiker. To prove it, I pass a couple from Poughkeepsie with two five-year-old kids hopping up the trail. I am sweating, breathing really hard. So, slow and steady. I stop, breathe, take a bunch of steps, repeat. It's a one-mile climb with an elevation gain of 1,000 feet from the col to the summit. I reach the top ledge at 12:45. It's amazing how you can crawl on your hands and knees to a mountaintop, and the very second you get there all this energy flows from somewhere and you're on your feet, looking around and feeling no weariness—at least for a few minutes.

Now, this herd path to a better view I've heard so much about? I scramble down the mountain in the opposite direction from my ascent, thinking I'm on a path, but there's so much debris and downed trees that I can't tell, but … what? There! Yes, I'm on it and … where'd it go? And it goes down, down, down and reaches a ledge. You think, *How can I get down there*? You see a tree on its side that you follow and then pass under, and you're at the bottom in a col between Ashokan

High Peak and Ashokan High mini-Peak at a large stone monument. Bushwhack up the other side and the trees break and the world opens up beneath your feet. Schunemunk, Nimham, Alandar, right into the Gap, and more—a great view. If the leaves were down, all the Catskills would show to the north, but the oaks block the view this time of year. Getting back to the main mountain seems to take a lot less time than I thought it would, though it does tower over you and you think the climb will be considerable.

Now, this loop I've heard so much about. I continue on the red trail over the summit and pass a small view to the south, then pass a hand-dug cistern, blueberry patches and another hand-dug cistern, followed by a wide field with the higher mountains nicely lined up for our viewing pleasure: Peekamoose, Table, Friday, Lone, Wittenberg, and Slide standing above them all. Quite grand. A couple is setting up a tent in the field and, looking at all the gear they've got with them, I ask how long they're going to be there. "Oh, just for the night," the guy says. Just for the night? These folks even brought a stereo.

It's hard to stay on the red trail here as it wanders among the blueberries. It stays to the ridge top, drops into a minor col, tops the ridge again, and then turns south, where the forest changes and the road levels and becomes easier

Don't miss the mountain laurel on Ashokan High Point. Photograph by Larry Gambon.

underfoot. This trail follows along the side of the mountain when, all of a sudden, it drops steeply into a maple forest and becomes a rocky watercourse with dangerous footing. After carefully navigating this for too long, you hear the sound of rushing water off to your right. As it gets louder you look to the right, but don't see any water flowing anywhere and then—there it is!—I must investigate. There's a stream shooting out from some rocks. I walk upward a bit, away from where the water is coming out and listen to the ground. I don't hear any gurgling or running, yet there it is, 100 feet farther down! This is where the Kanape begins, so no wonder the place is magical.

The creek quickly forms a deep ravine, and the trail, still dangerous and rocky (and now muddy), follows a contour around the slope of the mountain, enters a forest of hemlock, white pine and mountain laurel (an interesting mix), and the footing becomes much better. This is a pretty forest and has a nice spicy odor to it. The loop trail finally meets the main trail just this side of the col at about two miles from the top of the mountain. This is not a shortcut, nor do I think it easier taking this to the top than the direct route.

As I head back down the valley, I am again stunned at the incredible beauty of this place. When the sun sets behind Mombaccus Mountain, the trees over my head are still in the sun. I see a stream falling over dozens of cascades and waterfalls into the main Kanape Brook, and then I notice that there are more little streams like this everywhere. As I walk farther down the mountain, the sun peaks out from behind the mountain throwing this red maple forest (huge trees!) into an orange and golden light that makes the world seem endless. I look over into the ravine again and see yet another rill falling and leaping and splashing down a ravine to meet the Kanape. I can do nothing but applaud and say "bravo."

Still, I'm tired. At about six o'clock I reach the car after hiking nine miles and climbing about 2,500 feet. For me, this is a really good day. (I miss the days when a hike like this was a "walk in the park"). I decide to drive back through Kingston because I can drive across the Ashokan Reservoir dam, which has one of the grandest views on the planet: looking back at the high peaks and there, just as I come to the top of the ramp, is Ashokan High Point and it's *HUGE*! Imposing! Giant!

And I climbed it. 🏃

93

WINDHAM HIGH PEAK

THIS MOUNTAIN HAS EVERYTHING

Lawrence D. (Larry) David, #703
from April–June 1994 *Catskill Canister*

From 1990 to 1992, Salley Decker and I were the trail maintainers for the section of the Long Path from NY 23 to the summit of Windham High Peak. We climbed the mountain eleven times, seeing it in spring, summer, fall, and winter. It became my favorite peak. The trail to Windham is unique to the Catskills. It passes through a meadow, a hardwood forest, evergreens, second-growth deciduous trees, more evergreens, black cherry, and swamps before reaching the top.

A century ago the entire mountain was cultivated as a giant hayfield. You can still see a remnant of the field about halfway up, just beyond the last stone wall. The "enchanted forest" of Norway spruce, which is not native to the Catskills, was planted by farmers. The stone walls, the spruce groves, the lush vegetation near the top (a result of rich farm soil generated by hay growth), and the nineteenth century carvings uncovered by Jack Sencabaugh of the DEC when he cut one of the summit vistas, are the farmers' legacies. To walk this trail is to step back in time.

Maintaining this trail with its water bars, blowdowns, and a lean-to that always needed a cleanup, was a challenge. Most of the tree work and digging was required below the old hayfield. Above the steep pitch, rich soil yielded bumper crops of grass, ferns, and stinging nettles. Despite the weed whacking, every July the nettles grew back thick as ever. Mowing the nettles, dismantling a blowdown with a crosscut saw and axe, digging out water bars—these were the tasks of our ancestors. I felt I had journeyed back a century each time I worked that trail.

We had our share of characters on Windham High Peak. Jim Daley was a genius at scheduling work trips during downpours or snowstorms. One day we met Cal Johnson and his son Eric clearing the Route 23 trailhead for the Escarpment Trail race held in July; every year, over a hundred people race eighteen and a half miles over Windham, Blackhead, and Stoppel Point to North Lake. Windham attracts amateur hikers as well, such as one couple—he in sneakers and she in penny loafers—who found the mud half a mile below the summit impassable.

Windham also has its share of animal life. Porkies besieged the Elm Ridge lean-to, chomping up the seat of the new outhouse. Ranger Dennis Martin said bears wallowed at the base of the small cliff above the lean-to, where the Elm Ridge Trail loops over to an old, grown-in vista. We also once spotted a male scarlet tanager on the old road just below the lean-to. The little fellow was bright orange, a rarity among the species.

The views from the top of Windham High Peak, which is said to have a five-state view, were another reason it was my favorite mountain. From the eastern-most lookout point you can pick out the dome of Mount Everett on the Appalachian Trail in Massachusetts. As you scan the horizon to the northeast you can spot Mount Greylock in Massachusetts, Mount Equinox in Vermont, and the four Empire Plaza towers in Albany on a clear day. North-facing vistas feature the Mohawk Valley and the southern Adirondacks. That first vista to the south of the nearby Blackhead Range is always pleasant.

Caring for Windham, I got back much more than I ever gave. I was nourished by the peaceful wilderness, the beauty of the vistas, the working of muscles and tools, and a feeling of coming home to the mountain again and again. So, if you are ever up on Windham, take your time and stroll through the spruce. And, oh yes, keep an eye out for that orange tanager. 🏃

Black Dome Valley. Photograph by Larry Gambon.

94

A MOUNTAIN THAT DOES NOT QUITE MAKE IT

BEAUTY AND SOLITUDE OFF THE BEATEN TRACK

Friedel Schunk, #248, #87W
from Winter 1980 *Catskill Canister*

There is an advantage to completing a hiking list. It gives you a better perspective on what you do not want to do again. It also raises your awareness of other areas that find less usage.

On the first autumn Sunday of the last year of the 1970s, Catskills hikers were blessed with a gorgeous late-summer day—a little brisk if you were in the shade, but beautifully warm in the sun. A cold front from Canada had muscled its way into the area. It was one of those hiking days when one feels sorry for those who have other things to do.

My destination was Dry Brook Ridge. Starting at the German Hollow trailhead, my altimeter read 1,460 feet. The trail starts climbing immediately and continues to do so, steadily ascending 1,280 feet in 1.7 miles, where it meets the ridge trail that comes from Margaretville over Pakatakan Mountain. Hiking conditions are marvelous. The dry trail is an old logging road, but not the washed-out variety. The initial hemlock forest is soon replaced by hardwood; it really smells like woods. A pipe spring is on the right before reaching German Hollow lean-to. You don't have to be afraid of overcrowding; the trail tells you nobody else is there. You meet squirrels that hurry away, chipmunks that act disturbed, and you scare up some grouse.

The trail becomes level on the ridge, then dips 150 feet, followed by a seemingly endless quest upward for the high point, 3,460 feet. On several occasions you feel you are there, but you are not. And you soon learn that it does not matter: the trail does not go over the very top (and blessed be the one who made that decision!) Instead, the trail leads the hiker along the edge of the escarpment, offering several magnificent views to the west and southwest, particularly of the Huckleberry Brook Valley and Mill Brook Ridge. In the distance can be seen the arms of the Pepacton Reservoir.

This sure beats some of the 3,500-foot-plus "high peaks." I find solitude here in this beautiful setting, enjoying each lookout for long periods of time. 🚶

95

DELAWARE TRAILS OF THE CATSKILL MOUNTAINS

DELIGHTS OF THE WESTERN CATSKILLS

Joan Dean, #360, #135W
originally published in the April 1983 *Adirondac,* the magazine
of the Adirondack Mountain Club, Inc. (ADK, www.adk.org)

The red fox trotted up the side trail by the beaver pond. His coat was shining and red-gold in the rays of the late afternoon sun. I noticed the pointed red and white face, the cowering stance. Not more than three feet away from my "blind"—I was seated on a rock between some bushes—a large raccoon washed its supper at the water's edge. Out on the pond two beavers sped back and forth, to and from a bank around a hidden corner of the pond. A small face would pop up from time to time, only to quickly disappear, showing me that there were beaver pups there. Frogs jumped at the edge of the pond and their croaking was constant. On the other side of the pond, four deer fed, two of them fawns. I almost didn't notice a large bird take to the air from the corner of the pond; I recognized it from its size, color and flight—a great blue heron. Fish leaped out of the water for insects. I sat enchanted as I drank in the wonder of this scene.

Whack! Splash! Gone were the beavers! The raccoon hunched up, turned and moved away quickly. The deer snorted, stomped their feet and fled, tails up. Only the fox seemed unperturbed. He stopped, turned back down the trail and quietly disappeared into the woods. I was surprised by the sudden disappearance of my companions. I looked all around this small gem of water that lies midway between Little Pond and Trout Pond, connected by the Delaware Trails—an area just south of the Pepacton Reservoir.

Two or three minutes passed before I heard the voices that the animals had heard minutes before. Two youngsters came up the trail that led to the pond from Little Spring Brook. As these young girls approached me I greeted them. Their look was one I've often seen when I am backpacking alone. Wasn't I afraid to be in the woods alone? I replied that it was not a good idea to hike alone if one could find a companion to hike with, but I usually had nothing to fear as long as I was careful. The girls had come from the last house off the dirt road near the trailhead, about ten minutes away. After we talked about beavers and foxes and the trails, the girls ran back down the trail. Fifteen minutes after they had left, the beavers went back to work.

I was here in the early summer of 1972 because a friend had told me how beautiful and pristine the Delaware Trails[1] were, so little used that the ferns and grasses would brush your legs as you hiked and the wildflowers were spectacular. Since I usually hiked the overused trails to the high peaks of the Catskill Mountains, his invitation to experience this area was very welcome. My backpack then started from Little Pond Public Campground. After a short, steep climb to Touch-me-not Mountain (now viewless), there was a profusion of columbine; the path was verdant with spreads of daisies, Indian paintbrush, and buttercups. The viburnum flowers dusted the woods like snow, and the wood sorrel flowers carpeted the ground. I made no attempt to move at a fast clip for there was too much to see and hear.

Because I moved quietly, I came across many deer that often did not flee. I heard a mewing and squealing sound where trees had fallen and there were many branches on the ground. I had surprised a mama raccoon and she was angry with me; she was laden down with suckling young and had to slowly wend her way under the fallen tree, scolding me the whole time. My progress through the ferns flushed out two sets of game birds—the first had young that were very small, seven or eight of them. I stood still for a long time, first hearing her cries as she scattered them and then her clucking as she gathered them to her again. The mother of the second set, five larger chicks, scattered her brood with a cry. After a while she called to them with the same cry and they responded likewise, but did not regather as the younger brood had. I felt I'd experienced two stages in the growth of these birds.

In 1982 I rehiked the Delaware trails, this time on the new yellow-blazed trail from the end of Little Pond. An hour's gradual climb, connecting with the red-blazed trail I'd taken before, this trail is uniquely beautiful, going along a brook, through pine stands, past ruins and over a flower-strewn meadow with the most spectacular open views of rolling hills I have seen in the Catskills.[1] One could easily spend a day browsing along this trail with its old stone walls, stands of hawthorn and evergreen trees and, in July, its bountiful wild raspberries.

Any trail you hike will offer new wonders in each season. The woods will grow and change, the wildlife will move with the food and water supply. Go and enjoy your discoveries. As John Muir said, "Climb the mountains and get their good tidings. Nature's peace will flow into you as sunshine into flowers, the winds will blow their freshness into you and the storm their energy, and cares will drop off like autumn leaves." 👣

---

[1] These trails have been newly measured and described in *Catskill Trails*, 3rd Edition, published in 2005 by the Adirondack Mountain Club (ADK), Volume 8 of ADK's Forest Preserve Series of guidebooks.

[2] The entire loop is described in ADK's *Catskill Day Hikes for All Seasons*.

96

STORIES OF A FIRE OBSERVER

ON BALSAM LAKE MOUNTAIN

Larry and Betty Baker

Lost on the Mountain

A call was received at our residence at 9:00 PM from a caretaker on the Balsam Lake side of the mountain, reporting a missing hiker. The two hikers who had lost their friend were instructed to return to the fire tower where they would be met. Both the ranger and district ranger were not at home, so the fire observer alone proceeded to the tower from the Millbrook Road side. Muddy areas were checked en route, and they revealed that a person had run down the mountain after the observer had left the tower. The two hikers were met at the tower, and the consensus was that their companion must have exited the mountain on the Millbrook side. Everyone returned to our home, tired, hungry, and very concerned. The Sidney State Police headquarters was notified, and the hikers were given hot soup and coffee.

It was eventually learned that, indeed, a very distraught, confused, lost person had been picked up on Millbrook Road. The driver took him to the Margaretville police barracks, and the troopers placed him in a local motel. Because of the late hour, the State Police wanted everyone to make certain that his lodging was paid before he was reunited with his party. (This was most amusing to me.) In our personal vehicle, all three hikers were returned to their vehicle at the Balsam Lake trailhead. Eventually the fire observer got to bed at 6:00 AM.

The following letter was received at the Department of Conservation:

> The night of August 19th, when my brother and I could not locate the third man in our party—from whom we had separated when he had lagged behind in climbing with us to the Balsam Lake Mountain fire tower—Larry Baker calmed our anxieties with his coolness and level-headedness. He methodically proceeded with the search that we had started at 9:00 PM and carried it to its happy conclusion circa 3:30 AM. Mention must be made, too, of the warm hospitality extended by Mrs. Baker at 1:00 AM when we had still not located our friend. We have always met with courtesy

Balsam Lake Mountain fire tower.
Photograph by Laurie Rankin.

and helpfulness from your rangers; but we feel special gratitude towards, and think one of your best is, Larry Baker.

Things of Value

One October day in 1961, several members of a nearby elite fishing club journeyed to the summit of Balsam Lake Mountain to visit the observatory. Later the fire observer discovered a wallet belonging to a member of the party. The observer knew there was no telephone available at the club, the nearest one being at the caretaker's residence some distance away. Eventually, the wallet's owner was notified and directions were given for its return.

A note of thanks was received:

> It was a great relief to hear that you had found my wallet. With no money and no driver's license, I was completely depressed. I'd already made a careful search of all likely places I thought I'd lost it. Thank you for the ingenuity and effort it must have taken to contact me so promptly. My wallet is much more valuable to me now than when I lost it, for it is a constant reminder that there is still the kind of honesty, thoughtfulness and consideration of others that makes life worth living in this world of chaos. 👣

97

IN THE MOUNTAINS WE FORGET
TO COUNT THE HOURS

Sharing Good Times
Arlene Scholer, #441, #142W

How could the hiking bug bite me after simply taking a chair lift up a mountain in Austria? Walking down that mountain left my friend and me virtually crippled for several days. We decided that Europeans, with their boots and walking sticks, knew more than we did so, once home, we inquired about hiking clubs.

Exercise is as necessary as insulin for diabetics to maintain control of their blood sugar levels. As an insulin-dependent diabetic, I joined the Long Island Chapter of the Adirondack Mountain Club in 1977 to guarantee me year-round exercise options. After hiking in the Hudson Valley for almost two years, a small group of us decided to head to the Catskills once a month. Little did I realize how far that decision would take me.

I led two hikes per month, with more than 90 percent of them being in the Catskills. The Catskills outings were the most visually appealing and physically demanding within a reasonable distance from my home on Long Island. With physical exertion, I needed to match insulin to calories consumed and calories burned. My endocrinologist said that he could offer little advice, because most of his patients were couch potatoes. I experimented independently and made my own decisions as I earned my Catskill 3500 Club numbers by the mid-eighties. In the 1980s I also headed up an Empowerment Program. Starting in September, each hike involved more distance and elevation gain than the previous hike, with the promise of learning how to snowshoe come January. By 1990 I offered Catskill winter weekends, which continued for almost a dozen years.

Wanting to reach some summits that would be easier if done by backpacking over a weekend, I contacted a club member to teach a backpacking course for the chapter in the late 1970s. I was humorously dubbed his "first failure," because I packed anything I might need for the class's first weekend in the woods. This "when in doubt, pack it" mentality created a heavy load as we headed into the woods, but carrying sufficient carbs for daily demands and possible emergencies gave me peace of mind. I volunteered to work as that same instructor's "Girl Friday" for fifteen years. We'd head to Catskill summits, meadows and valleys every

Memorial weekend to give the recent graduates their first wilderness experiences. Winter classes faced colder conditions in February.

In the stillness of our May campsites, the songs of birds were heard when most of the world was still sleeping. As we were curious to see the birds singing their beautiful songs, binoculars were added to the list of essential gear. Catskill wildflowers and birding in the spring became traditions, as did snowshoeing that welcomed beginners every winter.

More than twenty-five years of Catskill hiking took its toll on my body, however. My hammered knees recently required replacement surgery. Fortunately, various experienced members generously started offering the Empowerment Series and winter weekends to ADK-LI members. I'm especially eager to regain the strength to revisit winter summits.

Sharing the good times introduced me to countless members, and together we logged great hours of fun in all seasons. Catskill hiking put me in shape to finish the forty-six Adirondack peaks in 1993, and now forty-two of New Hampshire's forty-eight summits. A major benefit of participating in a variety of outings is the weaving of a memory blanket that incorporates friendships as well as good times. 🏃

On the trail. Photograph by Larry Gambon.

98

FIRST-GROWTH FORESTS vs. SKI SLOPES

THE UNKINDEST CUT

Michael Kudish, #147

Belleayre Mountain

First-growth forest is defined as forest that has never been used commercially. There are over 100 square miles of first-growth forest still left in the Catskills, in nearly fifty separate parcels. Reasons for the removal of first-growth forest are logging, tanbark peeling, quarrying, agriculture, and forest fires (often caused by people). Many would not consider skiing as yet another cause of first-growth forest removal.

I spoke in 1996 at a lecture series organized by the New York State Department of Environmental Conservation, Purple Mountain Press, and the Catskill Center, held at Discovery Lodge on Belleayre Mountain. Richard Parisio, Catskills naturalist and series host, and I led a hike of lecture attendees up the mountain after my lecture to see first-growth remnants at the top of the ridge. All the ski slopes and access roads above 2,800 to 2,900 feet had been cut through first-growth forest, beginning in the 1940s, but the area surrounding the summit had been all in first growth the last time I had visited, several years before.

You can imagine the look on our faces when, on arriving at the 3,429-foot summit, we faced southeast and saw a brand new ski lift, the Handle Bar, where first-growth forest had been! This lift descended downslope gently for 125 feet in an open swath 100–125 feet wide to the top of an older lift, the Triple Chair. The embarrassment was acute for the DEC personnel with us, who had not been aware of this!

Hunter Mountain

In 1996, Hunter Mountain Ski Bowl proposed a land exchange with the State of New York: if forest preserve lands adjacent to the ski bowl could be added to the facility, nearby privately owned ski bowl lands of near-equal acreage would be donated to the state. This proposal was not agreeable to everyone. Some feared it would set a precedent for other land swaps, but the primary fear was that more ski slopes would require more water from the Schoharie Creek for snow making. This would damage one of the Catskill's best trout fishing streams. Others among us wondered if any of the land in question was in first-growth forest.

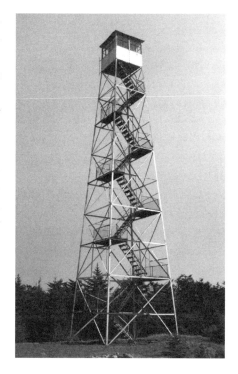

Fire tower on Hunter Mountain.
Photograph by Larry Gambon.

The Catskill Center and the Adirondack Mountain Club consulted me. I had not thoroughly mapped the Hunter Mountain forests, so from June 5 to June 11, botanist Jack Bierhorst, foresters Sean McCarthy and Chuck Schirner, and ADK's Jack Freeman joined me at different times on nine hikes, mostly bushwhacks, in search of first-growth: up one spur and down another, up one hollow and down another, crisscrossing the north, northeast, and east slopes of the mountain many times. We explored the watersheds of Becker Hollow, Mossy Brook, Shanty Hollow, and Taylor Hollow.

We did, indeed, find first-growth forest, in two separate parcels! About 360 acres were in the Becker Hollow watershed, and 100 acres were in the Shanty Hollow watershed. Both areas were included in the exchange proposal.[1] Neil Woodworth, writing in ADK's July–August 1996 *Adirondac* magazine, reported that Hunter Mountain Ski Bowl had changed their proposal to a lease of state lands, instead of an exchange. The Catskill Center's board of directors voted eight to seven in favor of conditional support for the proposed lease, because of the importance of skiing to the Catskills' economy. This narrow vote nearly tore the Catskill Center in two: the executive director and many staff resigned in protest over this vote.

Such a land exchange or lease of forest preserve land would require a New York State constitutional amendment and passage in two successive years by the state legislature, because New York is the only state that constitutionally protects its forest preserve lands. In 1997 the legislature voted against such exchange or lease, and the 460 acres of first-growth remains unbroken by ski slopes on Hunter Mountain. ⚇

---

[1] Refer to *The Catskill Forest: a History* by Michael Kudish, published by Purple Mountain Press, for complete information on first-growth forest.

Part X:
CATSKILL
MYSTERIES

*We had not yet found the wreckage of the plane at
that point, and we didn't know we were there on the
anniversary of the crash and the pilot's death. Could
the Catskills be haunted?*

Chris Maget

Photograph by Tom Farre.

99

A CATSKILLS QUEST:
HUNTING FOR THE ADK PLAQUE

THE CATSKILLS QUEST COMPETITION

Tom Farre, #1296, #482W

Achieving membership in the Catskill 3500 Club imparts a certain overconfidence. When you've bagged all thirty-five of the Catskills' highest peaks, you experience a kind of "been there, done that" attitude about all things pertaining to that noble plateau north and west of Kingston, New York. It was in this frame of mind, fresh from earning my summer and winter 3500 Club patches, that I began my quest for ADK Long Island's plaque, hidden somewhere in the Catskills and marked by clues devised by the previous finder. Over the next three years the quest would take me to four summits, where once I crawled on my belly in the snow, clawing at the dirt in snake-infested crevices (at least they could have been!) Facing failure, I gave up in disgust before experiencing a Eureka! moment worthy (in my mind) of Archimedes in the tub or Newton under the apple tree.

The plaque has a special place in the Long Island chapter's history. In 1984 Richard Furman created a "Catskills Quest" competition around a palm-sized brass plaque engraved with the letters "LI-ADK." It was first hidden on Peekamoose Mountain, and clues were published in the club's newsletter, the *Mountaineer*, from the perspective of the hiding place. For instance:

"Though I belong to a select, trailed Catskill 3500+ group, I am but one of a lofty eight. The sum of the elevation's individual digits is equal to the total letters of my title in full."

The quest was fun, but it also entailed map study, compass work and Catskills lore—nicely complementing ADK's mission to encourage responsible, competent, outdoor recreation. Since those early days, the plaque has repeatedly been found and hidden, with a new set of clues published for each new location. Whoever finds it wins free club dues for the next year and a footnote in chapter history.

When club members gather, especially after a drink or two, the conversation often turns to tales of the plaque. Like the time at a post-hike dinner that Arlene Scholer said, "I wonder if anyone found the plaque on Peekamoose?" All those at the table were sworn to secrecy, and the quest continued. Or when a plaque finder bragged that his clues were so clever that it would take years before anyone deciphered them. Rich Moore found the plaque the next weekend.

That's where my story begins: reading Rich's four clues in the spring 1999 *Mountaineer*:

"Clue 1. You do not have to wait for the solstice to rest your weary head on my summit.

"Clue 2. If you travel approximately 3.5 miles from my summit on the cerulean (hint: John Paul would know) colored trail, you will come to the Great Northern Viewpoint.

"Clue 3. If approaching from far to the south, enjoy the sunset view. However, watch your step and don't be caught napping, or you will arrive much later than you think. Also, be careful not to wander off to the left or you may find yourself in a shady little vale named in honor of Mrs. Scribner.

Clue 4. Upon reaching my summit, look for a herd path leading to an overlook looking to the south where you will find a large flat rock and a "No Camping" sign. From this rock, take a compass bearing of 286°. This should point you in the right direction. However, don't jump, but scramble down to your right to the base of the cliff. There you will find a ring of fire behind which is the object of your desire. I hope you don't forget your flashlight!"

I was baffled, but intrigued enough to begin the quest. The "cerulean-colored trail" in clue two must refer to the Devil's Path (which is red), I thought, confirmed by the reference to (Pope) John Paul, a great general in the church's war against the devil. Smug in my brilliance, I tried interpreting the other clues in light of the Devil's Path—a mistake that put me off the trail for a couple of years.

I eventually discussed the clues with two ADK friends and 3500 Club members, Joan McNulty and Diane Bamford. About the cerulean trail Diane remarked, "Isn't cerulean blue?" Of course it is, and thus began a new intensive study. "The Great Northern Viewpoint," though unknown to us, suggested the northern Catskills, and perhaps the Escarpment Trail. This beautiful, twenty-four-mile woods path, blazed blue, runs roughly north to southeast, from Route 23 near Windham over two peaks to North Lake and beyond, with side trails to Black Dome and Thomas Cole. Plenty of summits to hide a plaque!

Was the plaque hidden along the Escarpment? Diane reasoned that "John Paul would know" could refer to Christianity's long path to salvation, and the Long Path does join the Escarpment Trail for a while. Perhaps ... But confirmation would come from clue three, where Joan recognized a reference to the Sleepy Hollow Horse Trail (Irving's Rip Van Winkle napped there after several flagons of enchanted beer and awoke twenty years later). The Sleepy Hollow Trail meets the Escarpment Trail north of North Lake, but which way to the plaque?

Clue three held the answer, with its reference to "approaching from far to the south." Heading north to the plaque from this area, there should then be a view to the west (sunset), confirmed by the Northeastern Catskill Trails Map of the New York-New Jersey Trail Conference. If you wander way off to the left (west), you will come to Scribner's Hollow near the town of Hunter, apparently named after the publishing executive's wife. Clearly, the plaque was on the Escarpment Trail well north of the Sleepy Hollow Trail. But which summit held the object of my desire?

Clue one, with its apparent reference to the 3500 Club, intrigued us. By 3500 Club rules, a winter peak is defined as one climbed between the winter and spring solstices. If you don't have to wait for the solstice to climb the summit, we reasoned, maybe it's both a summer and winter peak—in other words, one of the four peaks that aspirants must climb in both summer and winter to earn their patch. Of these four—Slide, Panther, Balsam and Blackhead—only Blackhead lies on the Escarpment Trail. That was the first peak targeted in my quest.

On a bright and cool day in early afternoon in November of 2001, Joan and I arrived at the end of Big Hollow Road alongside Batavia Kill—a pretty but desolate area with two trailheads, one heading to Acra Point and Windham High Peak, the other to the Blackhead Range. We took the red-blazed Black Dome Range Trail, the fastest way up, reaching Blackhead in about two hours. Near the top are beautiful views to the south (aha!) and west toward Black Dome.

I was brimming with anticipation as we summited, earnestly searching for a herd path with a southerly view, a "No Camping" sign and other elements of clue four. It's amazing how the mind shapes reality when you want something badly. I soon discovered a herd path with a questionable cliff and a more questionable southerly view, and even a "No Camping" sign. Feverishly following the clue by compass, I hacked my way through thick brush, and might even have passed an old campfire (the ring of fire). What I found were a thousand cracks in the sedimentary rock that could have hidden the plaque. Soon I was on my hands and knees, gloves off, clawing and scratching though snow and dirt in a few likely crevices. Finally, reality intervened. A promising herd path miraculously appeared on the way out, but by then the sun was setting and Joan had already left. She was never bitten by plaque fever, but did enjoy the hike that lovely day.

After this miss, nearly three years had passed since Rich Moore published his clues. I called him, explaining my progress and cagily playing "hot beans, cold beans." He was encouraging, but didn't give much away. Back to the clues. We must have misread clue one, so we moved on to clue two. Where was this Great Northern Viewpoint, 3.5 miles from the plaque's summit? Studying the maps, we saw that Windham, most northern of the Catskills, does have a northerly view.

Tom Farre finding hidden plaque near Layman's Monument. Photograph courtesy of Tom Farre.

By chance—or was it an Internet search?—I came across this statement on the 3500 Club's Web site, www.catskill-3500-club.org: "Windham High Peak is the northernmost peak along the Escarpment Trail. It is also known as the 'great northern viewpoint' for the spectacular view at the eastern end of the summit. From this vantage, on a clear day you can see the Adirondacks, Green Mountains, the Berkshires and the Taconics." So, the plaque must be on a summit 3.5 miles from Windham. Back to the map. Measuring 3.5 miles on the map's scale with a divider, I put one point on Windham and turned the other in a circle to see what it would encompass. No summit; no closer to the plaque.

By then it was spring. Just to keep the quest going, Joan and I hiked from Route 23 to Windham, on the lookout for herd paths leading to southerly views and rings of fire. We enjoyed the Escarpment Trail for its sense of primeval wilderness, saw a couple of herd paths with views and the awesome viewpoint from the top, but didn't find anything. Our search was blind, because we didn't understand the first two clues.

Looking again at the map, I convinced myself that if I twisted the divider and fudged a bit, Black Dome was close to 3.5 miles from Windham, and a southerly view was marked by a star. That must be it. Warm sunny day, great hike and views, a herd path with a small cliff as described in clue four, and even a "No Camping" sign. I diligently followed the bearing and came to a heart-shaped ring of pebbles, about four inches in diameter. A ring of fire! Not a campfire, but a burning ring as in the Johnny Cash song. (Tricky guy, that Rich Moore.) After a lot of digging and clawing and reaching into holes, nothing. It's amazing, by the way, how many plaque-worthy crevices there are in the Catskills.

Discouraged by the hours of fruitless study and three dry peaks, I called Rich again. He seemed perturbed that I had hiked to Black Dome, suggesting that I revisit the clues. He also mentioned that Jim Sabiston, another ADK LI member, was on the quest in the same general area. I e-mailed Jim and we discussed our progress. Equally baffled, he was systematically hiking to every spot the plaque could be. Small world—he had also seen the heart-shaped ring on Black Dome and thought it meant something. Jim's approach would probably pay off, but I was tired of hiking blindly. I wanted to find the plaque by deciphering the clues. If not, I quit.

Somewhat relieved that it was over, I lay down on the couch to watch TV. Then, something came to me. A voice seemed to whisper: *maybe you're measuring the wrong way. Maybe there's another way to measure 3.5 miles from the Great Northern Viewpoint that will pinpoint the plaque.* Heart pounding, I got out my trail map and, instead of measuring with the divider, as the crow flies, I referred to the mile-by-mile "trail notes" on the back of the map, measured as the hiker hikes. There must be something 3.5 miles south of Windham on the Escarpment Trail. Sure enough, I found the exact spot.

Jim was planning a hike to this place the following weekend. Next day, a Tuesday in September of 2002, I drove to the Catskills and hiked right to the plaque. Elated, I wrote "I FOUND IT" in big letters in the trail register, and showed it enthusiastically to some hikers who must have questioned my sanity. Jim said that on seeing my register entry a few days later, he was a little disappointed. He also said that he had planned an earlier hike to what turned out to be the hiding place, but at the last minute joined Arlene Scholer's hike to Blackhead instead.

I later realized that, in clue one, you didn't have to wait for the solstice because the "summit" was not a 3500 Club peak. And Rich explained that "John Paul would know" referred to the Latin root of cerulean. Since then, the plaque has been hidden and lost under a huge root on Big Indian, remade from an aluminum slab, hidden and re-hidden at North Point, and found by Dave Koehler. At this writing it lies stashed again with a new form of clues befitting the digital age (see www.adkli.org).

Where did I find the plaque? If you've been following closely, you probably know. But I won't ruin it if you want to search for yourself—I've hidden a modest prize in the same place, for anyone to find. If you think you know, you can e-mail me at tom@tomfarre.com. Happy hunting! 🏃

100

GHOSTS IN THE CATSKILLS?

THE STOPPEL POINT PLANE WRECK

Chris Maget

On Memorial Day weekend 1999, I planned a twenty-three-mile hike of the Escarpment Trail with Spencer, a friend from San Diego. This trail was described in *Backpacker* magazine as having "lush, thick, green forest with beautiful views and scenery." Leaving Spencer's rental car at the finish point on Route 23, we hopped in my car and drove to the entrance of North-South Lake State Park. The views were incredible as we hiked around South Mountain four and a half miles to the campground, where we filled our water bottles.

The views from Artist's Rock and Newman's Ledge were spectacular, like sitting in the cockpit of an airplane. My friend, who is used to alpine vistas out west, commented on how beautiful these mountains are. After a long break at North Point, we went 1.7 more miles to 3,450-foot Stoppel Point. Noting signs saying, "No camping within 150 feet of the trail," I bushwhacked to find a spot flat enough for our tent. I noticed something big and white ahead of me. "Doggonit! Someone left their trash up here!" was my first suspicion. I can't stand it when someone is too lazy to haul their own trash back out of the woods.

Walking closer, I could tell that it was quite large. *Who the heck would bring something this big all the way up here?* I said to myself. Then, I couldn't believe my eyes—in front of me was the tip of a wing of an airplane! It was about three feet by three feet. I used to fly in single-engine planes, and to me this looked like it was from a relatively small plane. I called Spencer over. While preparing dinner of Lipton pasta and cheese, I couldn't stop thinking about that wing tip: Did the pilot die? Was it a snowy night? What went wrong? Where was the rest of the plane?

After dinner I set out to search for the wreckage. Maybe, just maybe, I'd get lucky. After fifteen minutes of bushwhacking, I came to my senses. Finding anything more would be like finding a needle in a haystack. The forest went on for miles and miles; the brush was thick. The next morning I awoke to the sound of a porcupine chewing on my flip-flop outside my tent. When I tried to shoo him away, he started dragging it into the woods. Now, every time I put on my flip-flops and see those teeth marks, I think of that trip.

On the trail by 8:30 on day two of this wonderful trek on the Escarpment Trail, I was in the lead. Ten minutes into the hike I saw something ahead on the trail. As I got closer, there, to my amazement, was the entire fuselage of the airplane! It was a four-seater single-engine Piper Cherokee. The wings were all ripped apart from the impact of the crash. The engine, propeller and instrument panel were all missing. I assumed the FAA airlifted them out so they could determine the cause of the crash. I looked into that cockpit and wondered what was going through the pilot's head in the seconds before the crash. I'd say the wreckage had been sitting there for at least ten years.

Because of the extra pack weight required to take along everything needed for an overnight hike, I hadn't packed a camera, and now I was kicking myself. We spent twenty minutes examining the wreckage. Spencer made a mental note of the tail numbers: N1316T. For the remainder of the hike, I couldn't get the image of that plane out of my mind. A week later Spencer faxed pages from the National Transportation Safety Board, which keep records of every plane crash for the last twenty years in their database. The pilot had taken off from Poughkeepsie, New York, on May 26, 1983, after a warning that the weather was bad: six miles visibility with fog, the ceiling only 1,000 feet (the mountains exceed 4,000 feet!) The report says: "The aircraft collided with trees near the top of mountainous terrain at an elevation of about 3,400 feet. No evidence of a pre-impact, mechanical failure was found." The pilot, the only person on board, died.

Later, Spencer and I started reminiscing about the hike. "Isn't it amazing that this plane crashed May 26 and we were there May 27? Wouldn't it be some-thing if this guy's ghost comes back to the mountain?" Then it hit me. When we were chowing down dinner, I'd said I heard somebody over on the rock lookout near our campsite. We couldn't see the lookout because of trees, and I remember feeling bummed out that our solitude was broken. I'd said to Spencer, "We've got company." As soon as whoever it was stepped off the rock and back onto the trail, they would have been in full view. We were talking pretty loudly, and I was sure that whoever was there would look over in our direction to see where we were. After a few minutes of not seeing anyone, however, I just assumed it was my imagination.

Minutes later I stopped mid-bite because I heard people talking again. I couldn't hear what was being said, and Spencer didn't hear anything, but finally his curiosity was piqued and he walked over to the rock. I wasn't too keen on him striking up a conversation; I just wanted peace and quiet. It might be an authority who would tell us to move, even though we were camped legally.

"There's nobody over there," he said when he returned. But there was no ques-tion in my mind that about five times I had heard people talking. Someone could have hiked to that overlook, turned around and hiked back to North Point, but that was unlikely for a couple of reasons. We were three miles from the campground, and it was six o'clock; retracing the trail back to the campground that late in the day would have been unlikely. Plus, the terrain is quite rugged. Second, Spencer and I were talking loudly enough that anyone would have been curious to see who was nearby.

We had not yet found the wreckage of the plane at that point, and we didn't know we were there on the anniversary of the crash and the pilot's death. Could the Catskills be haunted? ⚉

Stoppel Point plane wreck. Photograph by Larry Gambon.

101

MY LATE MOTHER AS A RUFFED GROUSE

A POEM

Will Nixon, #1070, #420W
Originally published in *Vanguard Voices of the Valley,* Vol. 1, Issue 2
(2004), and to be included in a forthcoming collection of poems
by the author published by FootHills Publishing.

Ashokan High Point, Catskills

Never before had a grouse failed to explode
from the underbrush with a wing-beating panic:
a feathered cannonball fanning a leaf-ripping tail.
But this bird didn't budge. It kept pecking
at leaf litter as methodically as a maid
checking under cushions for coins.
For several minutes, I focused my binoculars
on its lady-bug eyes, its black-banded tail,
but didn't want to spoil the magic by staying too long.

Bushwhacking through acres of mountain laurel,
I navigated tangled stalks like woody barbed wire.
Finally, a boulder ramp led me down to a clearing.
But which direction to the reservoir lookout,
rumored to lie east of the blueberry bald,
I couldn't sense any better than from above.
Yet behind me, I spotted the grouse half-sliding,
half-hopping on clownish chicken feet to catch up.
It stopped on the rock, cocked its head sideways,
then eyeballed me with an orange intensity.
Oh, yes, I remembered that look,
unblinking, undeterred, unashamed
of being in charge, yet being in love.

Could this bird really be my late mother?
At her burial last winter I scattered grouse feathers
to honor her passion as an Audubon birder.
Did I unwittingly plant the seed for her return?
Crippled by strokes, she lived so long in a nursing home
she had no idea I lived in a cabin, not Hoboken
or Manhattan. To her, I was always 23 and married,
for some unfathomable reason, to my cousin, Muggsie.

Yet this grouse clearly knew what she wanted.
Softly she cooed and finally winked.
I murmured my best grouse impersonation,
eager to talk no matter what we happened to say.
I sat on the grass, an invitation she accepted
to prance close to my boots, cocky as a city pigeon.
For her country outing, she'd dressed
in subdued browns and whites, but make no mistake:
her feathered crest sharpened her head.
When her blinking turned almost flirtatious,
I lowered my eyes, apparently a fresh invitation,
for she paraded alongside my leg, pausing
every few steps to nip at a blueberry flower.
With my hands I could have cradled her like a dove:
cooing, content. Was that what she wanted?
Behind my back, she pecked at my daypack zipper.

How could I explain my bachelor's cabin:
the dirty socks from last week's hike still hanging
on the upstairs railing, the dirty dishes forever
crowding the sink? Did she think
she'd be satisfied eating seeds from a bowl
made of plastic and sharing my cold wooden floor
with the mice? Didn't she know
I could be arrested for bringing a grouse home
under the Wildlife Protection Act?
Did she know how rarely I swept?

No, I needed to end this strange encounter.
I stood and shouldered my pack, nodded good-bye.
But giant steps up the rock didn't do any good.
She hopped up her own crooked ladder
of laurel stalks, then paused at the next dirt patch
for me to catch up. How could I shake her?
Whenever I plunged in a new direction,
climbing and tripping through bushes,
she scampered nearby, easily low-hurdling
trunk tangles and roots. I barged like an oaf,
but she didn't act disappointed in me as a grouse.
She waited and cooed with encouragement.
Not until I broke loose on the blueberry bald
did she stop at the edge of her laurel protectorate.
Yet no matter how long I rested on the only boulder,
pretending to admire the quixotic flight
of black butterflies sampling blueberry nectar,
I knew she waited with unbending love and devotion
in the bushes I couldn't avoid to hike home. 🏃

Ladyslipper. Photograph by David White.

ABOUT THE EDITOR

Carol Stone White lives in upstate New York with her husband David. They hike extensively in the Catskill, Adirondack, White Mountain, and Finger Lakes regions, and are regular and winter members of the Catskill 3500 Club. Dave is Membership Chairman of the club, and Carol, Conservation Chair. They participate in trail maintenance projects and lead hikes.

They are authors of *Catskill Day Hikes for All Seasons*, published by ADK in 2002, and are editors of ADK's comprehensive guidebook, *Catskill Trails*, 3rd Edition, volume 8 of ADK's *Forest Preserve Series*. They measured 345 miles of Catskill trails by surveying wheel to update the guidebook. Carol is editor of *Women with Altitude: Challenging the Adirondack High Peaks in Winter*, a book about thirty-three women Winter 46ers, published by North Country Books in 2005. Her next book, *Adirondack Peak Experiences*, will be published by Black Dome Press.

Carol received the sixth Susan B. Anthony Legacy Award in 2007 when she appeared with polar explorer Ann Bancroft and long-distance cold-water swimmer Lynne Cox on a panel entitled "Daring the Impossible: Strong Women Take on the World."

The Whites are members of the Adirondack Mountain Club, Dave serving as a director from the Iroquois Chapter. They are members of the Adirondack Forty-Sixers Club, having summited the 46 Adirondack high peaks, and became Winter 46ers in 1997. Carol served from 2003–2007 on the Executive Board of the Forty-Sixers Club. They completed climbs of New Hampshire's 48 peaks over 4,000 feet in summer 1999, and in winter 2006. They are 111ers of Northeastern USA, climbers of the New York-New England 4,000-footers, and they have climbed eight of the 14,000 footers in Colorado.

Carol's work was in public policy and political positions. As a congressional coordinator for Common Cause and president of a League of Women Voters chapter, Carol concentrated on campaign finance reform, congressional reform, and defense policy, writing weekly newspaper columns. She was chairman of a village planning board for six years and was elected to the village board of trustees, serving as water commissioner. Carol was president of a Housing and Urban Development project to work with Boards of Realtors to ensure the fair marketing of housing. She was president of a city Food Bank, edited an inner-city periodical, and fund-raised for the A Better Chance program to benefit inner-city youth. She was president of a regional committee of Elect Hillary for U.S. Senate. Carol is a tour guide for the Oneida Community Mansion House, and markets fair trade handcrafts to benefit low-income artisans in developing countries.